• • • • • • • •

The Censored War

The Censored War

American

Visual

Experience

During

World War Two

George H. Roeder, Jr.

Yale University Press

New Haven and London

Published with assistance from the Louis Stern
Memorial Fund.

Designed by James J. Johnson.
Set in Times Roman & Futura types by Keystone
Typesetting, Inc., Orwigsburg, Pennsylvania.
Printed in the United States of America.

Library of Congress Cataloging-in-Publication Data

Roeder, George H., Jr.
   The censored war : American visual experience
during World War II / George H. Roeder Jr.
      p.   cm.
   Includes bibliographical references and index.
   ISBN 0-300-05723-7 (cloth)
         0-300-06291-5 (pbk.)

   1. World War, 1939–1945—Propaganda.
2. Propaganda, American—History—20th
century.   3. World War, 1939–1945—
Censorship—United States.   4. World War,
1939–1945—Pictorial works.   I. Title.
II. Title: American visual experience during World
War II.
D810.P7U47   1993
940.54'88973—dc20   92-31859

A catalogue record for this book is available from the
British Library.

The paper in this book meets the guidelines for
permanence and durability of the Committee on
Production Guidelines for Book Longevity of the
Council on Library Resources.

To Gabrielle, Becky, Tres, and Ethan

CONTENTS

• • • • • • • •

ACKNOWLEDGMENTS

SO MANY COMPETENT people have put such effort into making this a truthful and readable book that the reader may safely blame inaccuracies, unintelligible prose, lapses in judgment, and other shortcomings on my inability to recognize good advice when I get it. For reading the manuscript in its entirety and offering detailed critical comments I thank Paul Ashley, Paul Boyer, Peter L. Brown, Phil Brown, Paul K. Conkin, David H. Culbert, Clayton R. Koppes, Jim McManus, Gabrielle Basso Roeder, Richard Roeder, W. Fletcher Thompson, and Jana Wright. Michael S. Sherry read the manuscript twice and was a constant source of useful research leads and good advice.

This book is built on a foundation of evidence mined largely from the unsurpassed resources of the National Archives. For my project, among the most valuable of these resources was the expert knowledge of the staff, including archivists Wilbert Mahoney in the Modern Military Section and, in the Still Picture Branch, Dale Connelly, Rutha Dicks, Jonathan Heller, Nicholas Nathanson, and Fred Pernell, assistant bureau chief for reference.

As I wrote this book I could not have had a better academic home than the School of the Art Institute of Chicago, where my students and colleagues did all they could to keep me intellectually and visually alert. Those who helped with specific problems in my research and writing or provided administrative support include Paul Ashley, Carol Becker, Lisa Brock, Peter L. Brown, Nadene Byrne, Roger Gilmore, Roland C. Hansen, Anthony Jones, Lynn Koons, Jim McManus, George Moroz, Michael Nagelbach, Joyce Neimanas, Richard Peña, Benjamin G. Seaman, John Stopford, Sandi Wisenberg, Beth Wright, and Jana Wright. Thanks also to Jack Brown, David Travis, and Colin Westerbeck, and to my students and colleagues at Northwestern University, including University College.

ix

I also wish to acknowledge the help of the staff at the following institutions: the Library of Congress; the Hoover Institution on War, Revolution and Peace in Stanford, California; the Special Collections Division of the UCLA Research Library; the Wisconsin Center for Film and Theater Research, Madison, especially Maxine Fleckner; the California Museum of Photography at the University of California, Riverside; the Imperial War Museum, London, especially Kay Gladstone; the archives and manuscript division of the State Historical Society of Wisconsin; the Film Study Center of the Museum of Modern Art; the United States Army Military Institute, Carlisle Barracks, Pennsylvania; and the American Film Institute in Washington, D.C., especially Susan Dalton.

Among the many people who generously shared their memories of World War II with me, I particularly wish to thank Barrett Gallagher, Timmie Gallagher, Cavalliere Ketchum, Ted Koop, Donal McLaughlin, Ralph Morse, Carl Mydans, and Dempsey Travis.

For helping keep me well housed and physically and mentally nourished as I did my research in various locales, my thanks go to Ted and Arleen Ankeney, Phil and Jennie Brown, Tony and Trish Doogan, George and Helene Fredrickson, David Hornung and Abby Newton, Doug and Linda Nelson, and Kent Peterson.

For aiding me with specific sections of the book, for research leads, and other assistance I wish to thank Robert H. Abzug, Alfred Appel, Jr., Howard Becker, Gregory D. Black, Tom Cripps, Tom Crouch, Janet Cyrwus, Doris Dana, Nguyen Huyen Dat, John Dower, Perry Duis, Lewis Erenberg, Scott Fincher, Andrew T. Gerstmyer, Paul Glad, Robert Heinecken, Larry Heinemann, David Joravsky, Michael Lesy, Russell Lewis, Lawrence Lichty, Tom Longfellow, Garnett McCoy, Stanley Mallach, Karen Becker Ohrn, David Peeler, William Reeder, Sam Sax, Carl S. Smith, Joel Snyder, Mort Sosna, Maren Stange, Leo Steinberg, George Talbot, Jack Thompson, and Russell C. Tornabene.

Being an ideal editor, Richard Miller at Yale University Press devoted equal attention to clear articulation of the book's main themes and to correcting whiches that should have been thats. The executive editor of the Press, Charles Grench, gave my project essential guidance and support.

I gratefully acknowledge the financial assistance of the School of the Art Institute of Chicago, which in addition to many other forms of support provided me with three Faculty Enrichment Grants, and of the National Endowment for the Humanities, which by selecting me for a one-year Fellowship for College Teachers and Independent Scholars supplied the large block of time needed to write the book.

My families also provided indispensable material, intellectual, and psychological support. Loving thanks to Dorothy E. Ensor, the Cross and Basso families, Richard Roeder, Iris Benjamin, Virginia Ormsby Roeder, Becky, Tres, and Ethan, and to my partner in all undertakings, Gabrielle Basso Roeder.

ABBREVIATIONS

• • • • • • • •

AG   Army Adjutant General

BPR   War Department Bureau of Public Relations

BSS   Bureau of Special Surveys

CPI   Committee on Public Information
       (World War I)

IWM   Imperial War Museum, London

LC   Library of Congress, Washington, D.C.

NA   National Archives, Washington, D.C.

OFF   Office of Facts and Figures

OWI   Office of War Information

PR   Public Relations

RG   Record Group, National Archives

SHSW   State Historical Society of Wisconsin,
       Madison

SPB   Still Picture Branch, National Archives

USIS   United States Information Service

WD   War Department

W&C   *War and Conflict: Selected Images from the
       National Archives, 1765–1990,* ed. Jonathan
       Heller (Washington, D.C., 1990)

· · · · · · · ·

The Censored War

• • • • • • • •

Join the Navy and see the world—through a bombsight.
　　　　—Naval aviator in the movie *Flight Command*, 1940

P R O L O G U E

IN THE SPRING OF 1945, amid celebrations marking the end of World War II in Europe, the blood of an American soldier was first shed on the pages of *Life* magazine. Editors preserved the anonymity of the dead G.I. by blocking out his face in the series of photographs by Robert Capa that documented his final minutes, but in a few a pool of blood next to the body remained conspicuously in view. Earlier in the war these photographs would have been concealed in a file, known to its keepers as the "Chamber of Horrors," maintained in the newly constructed Pentagon. By September 1943 concerns about public complacency led officials to release from this grim archive photographs that showed death, but not yet bloody death. During the next two years, as military successes magnified those concerns, government officials and media editors confronted Americans with increasingly vivid depictions of war's impact. Images of death joined ranks alongside flag-lined main streets, star-spangled advertisements, and poster-saturated public spaces as components of a visual environment mobilized to make a distant war seem real to those who were expected to supply the resources, human effort, and political support needed for victory.[1]

1

This book tells the story of that mobilization. It is about what Americans saw during World War II, why they saw it, and how it affected the way they perceived the world then and later. Censorship and propaganda are central to the story. During the war the U.S. government, with extensive support from other public and private organizations, made the most systematic and far-reaching effort in its history to shape the visual experience of the citizenry.

The target of all these efforts knew what was going on. Especially because many remembered the excesses of World War I, Americans were wary of attempts to control what they saw and what they thought. Officials recognized and often shared the skepticism of their audience. One result of this recognition was the "strategy of truth." As explained by Elmer Davis, head of the government's primary wartime propaganda agency, the Office of War Information, this strategy meant that the government would keep secret only information that could jeopardize military operations or diplomatic negotiations. The government would tell the truth because it had nothing to hide, because citizens in a democracy deserved full and accurate explanations of the actions of those who governed by their consent, and because the strategy produced results. Telling the truth, not deceiving and manipulating, would build the strongest public support for the war effort.

More easily said than done. Those who sought to live up to Davis's ideal found that defining and communicating the "truth" about a war fought from the Arctic to the tropics, with sharpened bamboo stakes and atomic bombs, under circumstances that bred extremes of boredom and horror, required more than a disposition toward honesty. Many did not even try, assuming that they need only give the appearance of truth to satisfy the public. Davis's own actions often emphasized appearances, and he encountered obstacles when he did seek to reveal harsh realities of the war. Many American propaganda practices not only resembled those in other countries but were directly influenced by, for example, British posters from World War I and German newsreels and films from the late 1930s.

Yet the government was right to claim that the United States did more than any other major combatant to maintain a free press during the war. The remark by the German propaganda minister, Joseph Goebbels, that the task of government publicists was "to wage war and not to give out information" accurately described the policy of his country. Authorities in the Soviet Union, Japan, Italy, and China manipulated news as thoroughly as the reach of their various bureaucracies made possible. And although sharply contested elections in Britain, including one that put Prime Minister Winston Churchill out of office at war's end, indicated that its democratic institutions remained vigorous, British officials asserted the need and right to regulate information on their besieged island more rigorously than American counterparts did in their vast and diverse country.

Despite this comparative openness of American information policy, the story told in this book is mainly one of control. Because of growing public immunity to overt propaganda, civilian and military leaders realized that often they could have their greatest impact on public attitudes by withholding information. Intent on providing a sharply focused view of the war, they restricted publication not only of photographs of those maimed in combat but also of pictures of racial conflicts on military bases, violent confrontations between G.I.s and their foreign allies, and other evidence of disunity within their own camp. They suppressed photographs of shell-shocked G.I.s, of those killed in jeep accidents, and of victims of Allied bombing raids and U.S. chemical warfare experiments. Most of their efforts went into presenting the war in simple terms of good versus evil. But a clear understanding of how Americans experienced World War II requires attention to choices and circumstances that introduced complexity into wartime imagery, as well as to those that put limits on this complexity.

Assumptions about the nature of that war continue to influence American life. The war claims a disproportionate share of late-night television movie slots, bookstore shelf space, and museum display cases. In the 1988 presidential campaign, candidates called on no other event as often, or as confidently, to confirm their stature. In their campaign advertisements, Robert Dole and George Bush featured visual reminders of the hazards they faced during the war. As Lloyd Bentsen walked onto the podium at the Democratic National Convention in Atlanta to accept the vice-presidential nomination, the band played the Army Air Corps song ("Off we go into the wild blue yonder") in honor of his wartime service. A float in President Bush's inaugural parade displayed the type of plane he had flown during the war. When Bentsen began his nationally televised remarks in response to the newly inaugurated president's first address to Congress, he invoked their war experiences as a bond that joined them, whatever political differences they might have.

How could the most destructive event in human history hold such a revered place in our national consciousness? Why continue to dwell, often nostalgically, on a war that killed more than 50 million people—the majority of them noncombatants who were burned, crushed, gassed, or starved to death—and left several times that number with missing limbs, shattered faces, diminished mental capacity, and other permanent physical and emotional disabilities? Because it fills a need. On the individual level Americans orient their lives around religious and political beliefs, community practices, and experientially based personal truths which they may share with many but which separate them from many others. In this century of change and of exposure to diversity we have few widely agreed-upon moral reference points. World War II is one. Most Americans believe that it affirmed that the United States can serve the cause of protecting human dignity, that it can get a job done, and that it is possible at least sometimes to see clearly the difference between good and evil in the amoral domain of international relations.

The war infused private lives with a sense of public purpose. In 1988, during a discussion of urban crime and decay, the Chicago journalist John Callaway commented:

I remember during World War II, as a child, going out and collecting newspapers and milkweed pods, which were used for parachutes, and tin cans, and other things that were used for weaponry. And we were asked to contribute to the war effort with our little victory gardens."

Today I am an anonymous part of a big city and I am looking for leadership that will ask—I don't care what it is—to watch out on my block from midnight to eight a.m., please do that. Or we need you on Saturday for four hours to help clean up Lincoln Park. Or we need you to tutor in the jail. Can we say that we are in a different kind of war, and that we can't just ask the government and the police to do it all?[2]

World War II sets a standard against which Americans evaluate other collective endeavors primarily because of what it was. For although is was a grisly, hateful nightmare of a war, the cause was just, the outcome encouraging as well as sobering. We were attacked, some of our opponents were monstrously evil, we won, and at war's end the United States was richer and more powerful than any other nation in the world. The war was long enough to define a major period in the lives of those who experienced it, but not so long as to foster mass discontent. It helped remedy an economic depression that had shaken the faith of many in the country. In 1940 the army found almost half of the young men who reported for physical examinations to be unfit for military service, many because of debilities related to inadequate nutrition and health care. Wartime prosperity and the food and medical services available to members of the armed forces caused American life expectancy, which had remained nearly constant during the 1930s, to leap upward by three years between 1939 and 1945, even with more than four hundred thousand military deaths included in the statistics.[3]

The way Americans saw the war increased its psychic impact. World War II came at a favorable time for building unity by visual means. Hollywood had been the dominant force in world film production for two decades, and especially after the addition of sound in the 1920s it had an unmatched capacity to produce films that propagandized while they entertained. By the 1940s on average each American went to the movies three times a month, and the moviegoing audience cut across class, regional, and ethnic lines. Inside the darkened theaters Americans participated in a communal viewing experience unlike any during World War I, when the proportion of population that regularly attended movies was somewhat smaller and less comprehensive, and unlike any in later wars, when television made inroads on the moviegoing audience. Americans also viewed images of World War II at home, especially through *Life* magazine, in a way that reinforced rather than supplanted the shared experience of the movies.

War multiplied *Life*'s circulation, as Henry R. Luce anticipated it would when he founded the weekly magazine in 1936. By late 1942 *Life* was claiming that tens of millions of civilians and two out of every three Americans in the military read the magazine. Technological changes brought magazine readers and newsreel viewers images that had the power of immediacy: "single photographs could be transmitted across oceans by radio and across continents by wire," and with somewhat less urgency "long-range airplanes could rapidly deliver rolls of films and thousands of prints."[4]

A media-savvy administration made full use of these tools for mobilizing public involvement. The world's dominant entertainment industry, and an aggressive and experienced advertising establishment which the earlier world war had helped call into being, joined in the effort. To write of the power of wartime visual imagery is not to assume that it had a precisely measurable or predictable effect. The scant evidence indicates that viewers often ignored even the most carefully contrived images, or responded to them in ways radically different from those intended by their creators. But the evidence also suggests that the outcome of battles fought to determine the form and content of wartime imagery did have consequences. What Americans saw between 1941 and 1945 helped determine what type of society they shaped during and after the war.[5]

In chapter 1, I explain why authorities first suppressed, then disseminated, visual evidence of the human meaning of statistics counting the American dead and wounded. Chapter 2 explores visual strategies used by government officials and others to give all Americans a sense of equal participation in the war effort without alarming those who feared loosening of distinctions based on race, gender, class, and other factors. In chapter 3, I argue that the most pervasive feature of wartime visual imagery was its polarized depiction of the world, and then describe institutional and individual efforts to overcome the limitations of that imagery. The fourth and final chapter examines the consequences of perceptual habits nurtured during the war, including their influence on attitudes toward American involvement in Vietnam. Four visual essays extend as well as illustrate ideas presented in the text, contrasting published with censored materials and documenting how those categories changed over time.

This book serves as a reminder that context helps determine the meaning of all images, even powerful ones such as those of dead youths. The high degree of public approval for the war in the Persian Gulf, with its tightly controlled news coverage, reinforced one of the supposed lessons of the Vietnam War: the more Americans see of a war, the less likely they are to support it. Working from the assumption that the "sights of war . . . promote national flinching," the political commentator George Will asserted in *Newsweek* magazine that "if there had been television cameras at Gettysburg, there would be two countries: the carnage would have caused the North to let the South go." Images of war do sometimes lead viewers to favor withdrawal from a war without achieving its goals, but not as inevitably as Will suggests. American policymakers withheld pictures of American dead at the outset of

World War II because they feared such a consequence, then later in the war effectively made use of the pictures to intensify public commitment to the war effort. It is impossible fully to understand twentieth-century events like World War II without careful attention to the role played by visual images in stirring and shaping public attitudes. It is equally impossible to understand the roles played by particular visual images without careful attention to the historical circumstances that provided their frame.[6]

I have seen war. . . . I have seen blood running from the
wounded. I have seen men coughing out their gassed lungs. I
have seen the dead in the mud. . . . I have seen children
starving. I have seen the agony of mothers and wives. I hate
war.
　　　　—Franklin Delano Roosevelt, Chautauqua speech, 1936

CHAPTER 1

Rationing Death

MODERN WARFARE PRODUCES corpses in lavish abundance. Nonetheless, during World War II the United
States government rationed photographs of the American dead more stingily than scarce commodities such
as sugar, leather shoes, and rubber tires. Officials used
images of pain and death to respond to what they
perceived to be the public-relations needs of each
phase of the war. "Public relations" often meant manipulation of opinion in ways that served narrowly
conceived military, political, or business purposes.
But sometimes it included serious efforts to inform
citizens about such significant matters as the battlefield
experiences of American soldiers who soon would
return to civilian life.

Precedent and caution ruled at the outset of the
war. Propagandists, like generals, are guided by lessons learned in past wars when fighting a new one.
World War I taught them to avoid transparently upbeat
depictions of the wartime experiences of American
soldiers. Official releases during the Second World
War seldom distorted these experiences as blatantly as
materials circulated during the earlier war by the Com-

7

mittee on Public Information (CPI). A typical CPI silent-film caption read, "Along the roads the heroes wounded in the fight move back—their only sorrow that they can fight no longer." Other lessons learned from the earlier war suggested that the public would accept strict government control over information from combat areas, and that withheld images were less likely to rouse skepticism than prettified ones. During the entire nineteen months of American involvement in World War I, the government prohibited publication of any photographs of the American dead. A similar prohibition lasted for the first twenty-one months of American involvement in World War II.[1]

Military circumstances encouraged this visual silence. The war started for the United States with a series of defeats and stalemates, which led government officials to fear that the public might become demoralized or impatient for peace. As *Time* magazine observed, in the first six months after the Japanese attack on Pearl Harbor the United States had "not taken a single inch of enemy territory, not yet beaten the enemy in a major battle of land, not yet opened an offensive campaign." Officials were especially worried that a significant portion of the population would press for a compromise settlement with Germany. A mid-1942 survey indicated that "three out of every ten Americans would view favorably a negotiated peace with German army leaders." When nearly a third of the citizenry held views so sharply divergent from official policy, the public commitment necessary to meet the war's massive demands on life and property seemed threatened.[2]

Censorship provided one answer to the threat. The government not only prohibited release of secret information about weapons or troop deployments, but also established guidelines warning against the publication of material that could be "distorted" and "used as propaganda against the war effort." Under a broad definition and strict enforcement of these guidelines the government could have censored almost anything. President Franklin D. Roosevelt's desire to maintain the appearance—and whenever it seemed safe, the substance—of candor prevented this from happening. Early in 1941 the Joint Army and Navy Public Relations Committee had proposed, at an initial cost of $50 million, a system for "complete censorship of publications, radio, and motion pictures within the U.S.A." Finding the proposal "fishy," Roosevelt emphatically rejected this "wild scheme," noting that the Joint Board "obviously . . . knows nothing about what the American public—let alone the American press, would say to a thing like this."[3]

Roosevelt, serving an unprecedented third term, did know something about the public and the press. When he set up an Office of Censorship shortly after Pearl Harbor he gave it authority much less sweeping than that envisioned in the joint committee's plans. The office had power of mandatory censorship over all international communications not covered by military censorship and over domestic information originating from military installations and certain industrial facilities with military contracts. Its censorship of most other domestic information, however, relied on voluntary compliance by the press and the public with its guidelines.[4]

Nothing was voluntary about censorship in American combat zones. There the military allowed only accredited photographers pledged to abide by its rules, which varied over time and among services. Typically photographers submitted exposed film to field censors, who after classifying photographs in accordance with policies set by military and civilian leaders would send them back to the United States for further review and for distribution. *Life* photographer Margaret Bourke-White described a variation of this procedure used when she was covering the 1943 Italian campaign. She sent her negatives by army mail pouch directly to the Pentagon, where they were developed "either by the Signal Corps or by *Life* technicians under Army supervision." Then "pictures which passed censorship were sent on to *Life*. . . . Certain technical subjects had to pass British as well as American censors." Captions for the pictures passed through two American military censors, "then the complete layout was censored once more in Washington, so the text and pictures could be reviewed as a whole before publication." Officials put few restrictions on what pictures photographers took, assuming correctly that censors would keep objectionable material out of sight. Because they were far more likely to get in trouble for letting through a photograph they should have blocked than for restricting one they might have released, in doubtful cases censors were more likely to stop an image than let it pass.[5]

Elmer Davis wished to change this emphasis. Davis, appointed director of the Office of War Information (OWI), formed in June 1942, to coordinate the flow of war-related words and images from government to public, was a respected radio commentator and a Rhodes scholar with no previous government experience. Although he never forgot that he was the head of the chief wartime propaganda agency, he took seriously his promises "to tell nothing but the truth" and "to see that the American people get just as much of it as genuine considerations of military security will permit." Thus even as Davis acknowledged that "security" required something short of full disclosure of all war news, his use of the adjective *genuine* announced his intention to avoid excessive recourse to this excuse for keeping information from the public.[6]

Others were less reluctant. Two months after Davis took office he received a prescient letter from George Creel, the former head of the CPI, which during World War I had combined functions now divided between Davis's office and the Office of Censorship. Creel noted that rather than having the freedom to build his own organization "from the ground up," Davis had to piece OWI together out of existing agencies that had been "running wild due to divided authority." Because Roosevelt hated to fire anyone, especially those loyal to him, OWI inherited much "dead wood." Nelson Rockefeller's maneuvering would allow him as Coordinator of Inter-American Affairs to compete with OWI for control of information flowing to and from Latin America. Most serious of all, warned Creel, "your control over Army, Navy and State is not real in any sense of the word." Supposedly those departments were to establish information policy in consultation with OWI, but " 'coordination by conference' never worked and never will work." When a conflict arose, the habitually restrictive military would use their pivotal role in the transmission of information to control access to it. "He was about right on all points," Davis later noted on the bottom of Creel's letter. Despite Davis's conviction that Americans wanted their war news to be "brutally frank," for nearly two years the photographs that best fit this definition accumulated in a "Chamber of Horrors" whose very existence remained secret.[7]

Some of the pictures finally did appear because of the intervention of the one man who could give Davis the leverage to pry images out of the chamber: President Roosevelt. Creel said in his letter to Davis that during World War I he had been able to resist constant attempts by the army and navy to "sit in arbitrary judgment" over what reached the public because every time they questioned his authority "[President] Woodrow Wilson hammered them down." Roosevelt had a different style. He was more inclined to give those to whom he had deputed authority leeway to define their responsibilities by hammering on each other. In the contest between Davis and the military, the military had most of the hammers.[8]

Fortunately for Davis, some military leaders shared his preference for a policy of openness. As early as June 1942 the army adjutant general advised all commanding generals that current visual reporting was inadequate to keep political and military leaders accurately informed on the war, and that better coverage would also help produce "an enlightened people." Others tried to follow the procedure Davis attributed to the chief of naval operations, Admiral Ernest J. King: withhold all information until the end of the war, then announce who won. The ultimate mediator among these voices was in no hurry to present the American public with a clear view of battlefield horrors. Roosevelt's visits to European combat zones as assistant secretary of the navy during World War I made him sensitive to the potential impact of visual encounters with war. During America's first year in the war only a few published photographs had acknowledged the costs of American involvement, such as one of a Marine in agony from wounds suffered at Guadalcanal. In early 1943 advisers warned Roosevelt that the government's inability and unwillingness to provide more forceful pictorial coverage of the war might lead to public perceptions inconsistent with war aims. An OWI memo warned that the public was getting the impression that "soldiers fight, that some of them get hurt and ride smiling in aerial ambulances, but that none of them get badly shot or spill any blood." It advised that the government release harsher pictures to prepare the public for the greater casualties to come and to reduce grumbling over minor inconveniences at home. Such pictures "would have a powerful impact on the source of strikes and absenteeism" and would rouse the public as had, during World War I, a picture that had showed an American soldier who remained "fighting mad" after his eye was shot out.[9]

Proponents of candor offered grim photographs as an antidote to the problems of success. If in 1942 officials feared that American military setbacks would demoralize the public, in 1943 they feared that victories would lead to overconfidence. The first few months brought news of Soviet victory over the German armies at Stalingrad, continued advances in North Africa, the recovery of Guadalcanal, and damaging air attacks on Germany. In May *Newsweek* ran photographs of Americans badly injured in the Pacific campaign, and announced that "to harden home-front morale, the military services have adopted a new policy of letting civilians see photographically what warfare does to men who fight." In August, however, OWI's news bureau complained in internal memos that the Army Signal Corps was again growing more restrictive in giving OWI access to material, that the Marine Corps had closed its files to OWI after the agency released for publication a photograph showing a Marine's grave with the inscription "Here Lies a Devil Dog," and that the navy's picture files had been "absolutely closed to our Photographic Section for a long time."[10]

The military denied these allegations of noncooperation. Davis considered the situation sufficiently serious to tell Roosevelt in late August that he would resign if the president did not instruct the War and Navy departments to cooperate with OWI in its attempts to give the American public a realistic depiction of the war. His decision resulted, Davis explained, more from "an accumulation of minor disagreements with the army and navy public relations bureaus" and the need for greater credibility with the press than from a dispute over any one issue. Davis was motivated not only by his personal beliefs but also by OWI's mandate to guard against use of security requirements to "unduly restrict the flow of information." He asked the president to "either confirm OWI in its authority and establish adequate machinery for OWI to carry out its responsibilities or . . . liquidate the present agency and establish a new organization with a new Director."[11]

Davis's timing was good. Recent events had heightened administration fears of public overconfidence. The Allies had gained control of all North Africa in May 1943. By about the same time they had countered the U-boat threat effectively enough to assure Allied dominance in the Atlantic. Negotiations were under way that led to Italian surrender in September, and American forces were on the verge of dramatic advances in the Pacific. An OWI survey of public opinion completed one week before Davis threatened to resign indicated that although dissatisfaction with official information was not as great as it had been the previous winter, it seemed to be on the increase again. On the day Davis gave his ultimatum, OWI's regional observers reported that heightened optimism about the war might lead to complacency and thus "lagging production," but also noted growing resentment that "the war news is incomplete and sugar coated." The proportion of Americans who believed that government news releases made the situation look better than it was went from 28 percent in July 1942 to 39 percent in June 1943. Officials hoped that increased candor about the realities of war might reduce public skepticism.[12]

Roosevelt confirmed Davis's authority. In the future the burden would be on the military to demonstrate that material should not be released rather than on OWI to make the case that it should. Davis's triumph can be attributed to the changing circumstances of war, because by this time congressional budget cuts that sharply reduced OWI's size had diminished further the agency's always limited power. Even after Roosevelt's support of Davis the military continued to exert great influence through its physical control of all material from combat zones. But Roosevelt and Secretary of War Henry L. Stimson made clear their judgment that the time for loosening restrictions had arrived. The War Department's Bureau of Public Relations (BPR) reexamined more than two hundred photographs from the Chamber of Horrors and cleared dozens for release. Most showed intact bodies and revealed little of the agonies of death. Some, however, did have the power to shock. One showed the bodies of American paratroopers sprawled like discarded rag dolls on a Sicilian field; another featured a close-up view of the leg of a soldier whose foot had been shot away.[13]

This was just the beginning. As part of the more open policy a radiogram went out under Chief of Staff George C. Marshall's signature to commanding generals of all theaters of operations informing them that Roosevelt and Stimson remained unhappy with visual coverage of the war. Material produced to this point was "entirely unsatisfactory," as proven by comparisons to British depictions of the desert war or Soviet images of Stalingrad, "the city that stopped Hitler." Marshall urged generals to give effective and enthusiastic support to their photographic units and send Washington material that would "vividly portray the dangers, horrors, and grimness of War."[14]

Growing press restlessness had encouraged this new policy. Although the military complained that news organizations maneuvered to get around their regulations, the nation's newspapers and magazines loyally followed directives important to the war effort. The government had informed the press, for example, that it wished to keep secret the visit to Washington of Soviet foreign minister Vyachislav Molotov in the late spring of 1942; when Molotov walked past a crowd of photographers as he entered the White House, "not a camera clicked." British prime minister Winston Churchill wrote that after the White House sent word to the press that they should keep silent about his 1942 Washington visit with the president, reporters guarded details of his movements as carefully as those of an American battleship, and "no word ever appeared." Reporters and photographers in combat areas developed an especially strong sense of being part of the U.S. team. Supreme Allied Commander General Dwight David Eisenhower wrote to his brother in 1944 that "almost without exception, the 500 newspaper and radio men accredited [to my command] are my friends."[15]

War was one thing, politics another. In the 1940 election, as previously, many of the nation's newspapers opposed Roosevelt (although not nearly enough to justify his claim that 85 percent were against him), and most defined continued protection of the populace from administrative excesses as part of their wartime patriotic duty. Three months after

Pearl Harbor the *New York Journal American* complained that the government refused to "hand out unpleasant 'facts and figures.' . . . Their 'information' is treacle for children." According to the *Journal American*'s outraged count, the official information apparatus had swollen to three thousand full-time employees and used part of the time of more than thirty thousand other government workers. This apparatus threatened to evolve into the sort of "bureaucratic propaganda centers of 'enlightenment' " set up by Nazi propaganda minister Joseph Goebbels. In sum, the paper charged, "The fat cats in Washington fiddle with 'figures' while the people PAY, WORK AND DIE." Plausible rumors that the White House tapped some journalists' phones and planted informants in newsrooms increased the strains. Most editors agreed with the charge by the trade journal *Iron Age* that too much war news was "dry-cleaned."[16]

On the last issue critics directed complaints more against the military than against civilian agencies. Journalists respected former Associated Press executive Byron Price, director of the Office of Censorship and a twenty-year veteran of AP's Washington office. The activities of OWI were more controversial, but Elmer Davis also was widely trusted and the press considered him their ally in the attempt to get the military and other government agencies to open up. In 1941 the columnist Drew Pearson, never known to understate a conflict, described the navy as "beyond doubt . . . the most high-handed agency in Washington in its attitude toward the press." He reported "definite evidence that Navy Intelligence has been tapping telephone wires and shadowing newsmen who have unearthed news which the Navy does not like." Traumatized by the humiliating losses at Pearl Harbor and bearing most of the combat action during the early part of the war, the navy became the first symbol of war news obstructionism. The newspaper experience of Navy secretary Franklin Knox helped ease the tensions slightly, and as the burden of military effort shifted toward the army, so did the locus of press-military conflict. Whichever service they had to deal with, many journalists shared the view of the *Christian Science Monitor* editor Erwin D. Canham that military censors often made "petty and absurd decisions."[17]

Such complaints masked similarities between press policies and those of the government. Few news organizations had challenged visual censorship during World War I. As the historian James L. Baughman has noted, the national news magazines that came into prominence in the two decades after that war represented "a journalism of reassurance, not information." The few especially shocking pictures among those released in September 1943 may have been included because military authorities wished to show that neither the press nor the public wanted too much candor. If so, they proved their point: almost all newspapers and magazines declined to run them. The photo editor of the *New York Daily News* explained that he decided not to use the picture of the soldier whose foot had been blown off because "I personally try to select pictures that will go down well when I have my coffee in the morning." Although *Life* came closer than any other wartime magazine to fulfilling its stated intention to show "the truth . . . the good and the bad," and not to show only pictures that would "please the eye and soothe the nerves," even its editors carefully avoided images deemed too disturbing. *Life* accompanied its first photograph of Americans killed in the war, George Strock's powerful, elegantly composed picture of three American soldiers lying dead on Buna Beach in New Guinea, with a full-page editorial. The editors drew on familiar sports imagery to assure that the new visual message inspire viewers rather than discourage them: "We are still aware of the relaxed self-confidence with which the leading boy ran into the sudden burst of fire—almost like a halfback carrying the ball down a football field."[18]

Despite this institutionalized caution, during the final two years of the war a consensus emerged for increasingly explicit portrayal of what American soldiers experienced on the battlefield. Initial response to the September release of pictures of the dead encouraged more of the same. Some readers expressed distress over the pictures, which, they charged, "made a mockery of sacrifice" or would undermine support for the war, but a larger number approved. Editorial writers almost uniformly supported the new policy. The *Washington Post* said it was time that the government treated Americans as adults, and the photographs "can help us to understand something of what has been sacrificed for the victories we have won." The paper advised, however, that "an overdose of such photographs would be unhealthy," and strongly warned that it was "intolerable" to use these photographs to "manipulate" the public. The editors called on owi to disabuse the army and the even more suspect navy of "the notion that they can alternately dose the public with stimulants and depressants in accordance with the mood they desire to create." Some involved in bond drives welcomed the possibility of having new stimulants at their disposal. One wired immediately from New Orleans with this request: "please rush airmail gruesome photos of dead American soldiers for plant promotion Third War Loan."[19]

The released photographs had had the desired effect. An owi analysis indicated that news of the Italian surrender had led to the feeling (dispelled somewhat by stiff German resistance in Italy) that the "war was next to being all over," but "publication of photos showing some of our boys killed in action had a sobering effect on people and brought the realities of war closer home." A month after the release of the pictures an owi survey of workers in five war plants in the New York area found that 75 percent believed the photograph of dead American paratroopers in Italy would make an effective poster and increase war bond sales. The survey also revealed that "few think its subject matter too gruesome." In the same month another owi report noted that because the public had been overexposed to all sorts of propaganda the only messages that still had the power to reach them were appeals from wounded servicemen and "those 'hate' pictures that showed American war dead. Everyone seems to agree that the latter are the strongest appeal and make the people so mad they dig down deep."[20]

The longer the war went on, the more futile it seemed to suppress harsh pictures. Casualties within families or communities confronted more and more people with evidence of war's capacity to kill and maim. The invasion of occupied France on D-Day (June 6, 1944), the push into Germany that followed, and island battles in the Pacific yielded a rapidly growing stock of death pictures to choose from, as over two-thirds of all Americans killed in World War II died in 1944 and 1945. Strategic plans also favored more emotionally forceful images. In January 1944 Elmer Davis told the War Information Board, which advised OWI, that one reason for the recent decision to release stories and pictures of Japanese atrocities was the belief that such releases would "nullify any voices that might be raised here if we should undertake bombing of Japanese cities." Important as these factors were, the primary reason for the more open policy remained fear that public complacency was damaging the war effort, as indicated by worker absenteeism, job switching, strikes, and decreases in voluntary enlistments. An OWI analysis from December 1943 referred to this as the "Over-the-Hump Psychology" and identified as its features a growing "selfishness," the reluctance of civilians to make sacrifices proportionate to those made by soldiers, and a concern on the part of individuals, businesses, the farm bloc, and unions to divert much energy into the scramble for postwar advantages.[21]

Marshall spelled out these concerns in a cable sent to commanding generals in January 1944. He asked them to rush to Washington pictorial material showing the war "as it is actually being fought, without the usual effort to eliminate the tragic aspects of battle," including "scenes showing casualties during and immediately after action." He specifically requested motion picture footage for use in films intended to discourage absenteeism and strikes among industrial workers. This trend toward more explicit portrayal of American war dead continued right up to the end of the war. It was slightly moderated by, among other factors, the desire to prepare the public for peace settlements that would leave Germany and Japan with enough economic strength and political stability to serve as buffers against expansion of Soviet influence.[22]

Respect for the feelings of soldiers' families also counted. Elmer Davis did not know in advance the exact date of the long-awaited Allied assault on German positions in France. But as this massive cross-Channel attack became imminent, he reminded planners of the upcoming bond drive that whenever the great invasion took place it would be a time of severe emotional strain for millions of Americans with loved ones in the service. Davis insisted that organizers must handle bond promotions with "good taste." Similarly, John Huston claimed that because of the "emotional effect it would have on the families" he eliminated from his documentary *San Pietro* a scene in which the taped voices of servicemen interviewed one day before they were killed in battle could be heard as their pictures appeared on the screen.[23]

Because of such legitimate considerations, as well as for the more questionable purpose of manipulating public attitudes, some images remained forbidden from the beginning to the end of the war. The original draft of Marshall's January 1944 cable had asked commanding generals to send pictures with "no effort to eliminate the horrible or tragic," but Marshall or one of his subordinates deleted the word "horrible" from the version actually sent. Censorship guidelines issued by SHAEF (Supreme Headquarters, Allied Expeditionary Force) in June 1944 prohibited release of "photographs of a 'horrific' nature, or of mental cases." The following February, when BPR surveyed generals to find out how they interpreted censorship policies as they applied to hospitalized American soldiers, Eisenhower replied that in his command the practice, like that of the British, was to allow photographs where the casualties were "walking wounded or are obviously cheerful," but that "photographs of a horrific nature are always stopped." A rule maintained throughout the war forbade publication of any photograph revealing identifiable features of the American dead. Different criteria governed depictions of the dead and wounded from other countries, especially non-Western ones.[24]

Censors kept emotionally wounded Americans out of sight throughout the war and after. The policy of BPR concerning pictorial or other publicity on "psychoneurotic" casualties remained one of "complete silence" until May 1944. It loosened only slightly after that, although a secret study carried out by the Office of the Surgeon General concluded that "psychiatric casualties are as inevitable as gunshot and shrapnel wounds." Contrary to the assumption embedded in the phrase "battle-hardened veteran," the longer a soldier fought, the greater the probability of emotional breakdown. The study found that on average an infantryman could "last" about two hundred days before breaking down.[25]

No army had ever made a greater effort to recruit only the mentally healthy. Through pre-induction examinations the U.S. military rejected because of "neuropsychiatric disorders and emotional problems" 970,000 men, or approximately one of every eighteen tested. Even with this extensive screening, such are the stresses of modern war that over a million American soldiers, more than three times the number who died in combat, "suffered psychiatric symptoms serious enough to debilitate them for some period." The overwhelmingly negative public response to General George S. Patton's behavior when he slapped a soldier hospitalized for battle fatigue suggested that despite censorship many Americans on the home front knew that the soldier's breakdown was neither abnormal nor proof of unwillingness to serve.[26]

News organizations expressed no desire to run photographs of physicians sedating battle-crazed soldiers. But the government decision to release images from the Chamber of Horrors did not end all controversy. In early 1944 the revelation of several instances where officials withheld information merely because it was embarrassing to authorities led to editorials describing some aspects of military censorship as "stupid, repugnant and intolerable." The *Houston Post* complained that censors assumed "that the American people lack the intestinal stamina to hear the bad news." Mimicking the language of the government's own "strategy of truth," the *Pittsburgh Press* concluded that "the only way to get full public cooperation is to tell the people the truth." Those government officials who favored more openness used such editorials in support of their arguments against providing the public with what Palmer Hoyt, director of OWI's Domestic Branch, described in a January 1944 speech as "spoon-fed" information.[27]

Hoyt referred mainly to censorship of words. Pictures too were spoon-fed to the public; but perhaps because of the multisensory nature of war, as well as the technical limitations of early twentieth-century photography, the most striking images to come out of World War I were written ones. This remained true even when the lifting of censorship after the war allowed the release of gruesome photographs of mutilated and rotting corpses. None of these pictures had the power of, for instance, British officer Stuart Cloete's description, published years after the incident, of his experience serving on a burial party after the 1916 battle of the Somme: "As you lifted a body by its arms and legs, they detached themselves from the torso, and this was not the worst thing. Each body was covered inches deep with a black fur of flies, which flew up into your face, into your mouth, eyes and nostrils as you approached. The bodies crawled with maggots. . . . We stopped every now and then to vomit . . . the bodies had the consistency of Camembert cheese. I once fell and put my hand through the belly of a man. It was days before I got the smell out of my hands."[28]

During World War II newspaper and magazine editors and government censors kept tighter restrictions on pictures than on words despite this ability of words to disturb. No photograph released during the fall 1943 War Loan campaign depicted a scene like that described in a passage by the writer John Steinbeck used in an advertisement for the campaign: "I have seen children hauled out of a blasted building; lumps of rubbish, dirty meat in pinafores." The reason was partly a practical one. Military authorities could easily screen all physical materials leaving combat zones, including photographs, but could not control what writers took home in their memories. But this was not the whole reason, since the government chose to make use of Steinbeck's words. Officials perhaps assumed that visual images were likely to be comprehended and remembered by a much larger audience than written material and therefore had to be handled with greater care. Such had been the assumption of the New York courts two decades earlier when they upheld a law requiring that newsreels be approved by the state film censor. The judges considered censorship necessary because "the audience for film, often including the 'child and illiterate adult,' was more susceptible to influence than newspaper readers."[29]

Words were not invariably harsher than visual images. At the outset of the war the National Broadcasting Company advised its reporters that their combat radio broadcasts should not be "unduly harrowing." Indeed, words could serve, as in the *Life* editorial accompanying the Buna Beach photograph, to cushion the impact of visual images. Similarly, the country's five major newsreel companies used narrations designed to make the visuals they presented seem both dramatic and encouraging. Their twice-weekly offerings, included as part of the regular show at movie theaters, reached tens of millions of viewers.[30]

What the newsreel war often looked like in 1942 and 1943, according to one OWI analyst, was a "travelogue." Because they required government permits and other assistance, newsreel companies cultivated the good will of whoever was in power in Washington. In 1932, for instance, they complied when President Herbert Hoover asked them to downplay the politically embarrassing "Bonus March" on Washington and the government's use of force to dislodge the marchers. Although wary of war coverage during the 1930s because "it is expensive, it is dangerous for the cameramen, and it seldom if ever produces pictures worth looking at," as soon as World War II began newsreel companies recognized that it created a hunger for news that would grow proportionately with American involvement, as would the companies' need for government cooperation. To make such cooperation more likely, they gave highly favorable coverage to events such as Roosevelt's signing of the Lend-Lease Act in March 1941 and assured the president that they would not allow critics of the act equal time. After Pearl Harbor the companies devoted roughly three-quarters of their screen time to coverage of the war, making them more dependent than ever on the government for opportunities for their camera crews (who required the same accreditation as still photographers), clearance of film they shot, and access to the huge volume of footage generated by military film units.[31]

The companies differed significantly. An OWI analysis described MGM News of the Day as "the most politically and socially liberal . . . in promoting Russia, negroes, and war," Fox Movietone as "steady middle-of-the-road," Paramount as "truly outstanding for the calibre and amount of its documentation," Pathé as extreme in its "indifference to government suggested or inspired stories," and Universal as "almost hysterical" in its attempts to get humor into everything, as when one of the company's newsreels says of American pursuit ships, "When these babies get on a Jap's tail it's good-bye Mister Zippo-Nippo." Whatever their bias, each had no choice but to acquiesce to official censorship policies.[32]

Not everyone in government had the same idea as to what these policies should be. The Office of War Information carefully monitored newsreels and had considerable influence on what stories they featured. The agency's Newsreel Division reported early in 1943 that for the first time in five months the week's newsreels did not include "a story set up or arranged by this Division." Here as elsewhere, however, OWI efforts to encourage openness ran into resistance. A 1941 memo had stated army policy on the matter: commanders should cooperate with newsreel companies only if cooperation did not create any extra expense or work and if the companies agreed to submit all material for review and never exhibit "any reel or any part thereof which has been disapproved by the War Department." In May 1942 the newsreel coordinator for the motion picture industry complained that because of such obstacles the industry "had no pictures from any war area that might be called outstanding" and had "exhausted our last hope of obtaining any cooperation from the Army or the Navy." When OWI was established one month later, it had no effective means of loosening military control over combat film. The civilian agency had to request invitations for its representatives to attend screenings of footage that the navy made available to the newsreel companies.[33]

By October OWI reported that the newsreels had made some progress in being able to "bring the cost of this war in human lives directly to the people." The navy had released to the newsreels, from Guadalcanal, strong footage of Japanese dead and pictures of American Marines with "torn and dirty uniforms and their generally disheveled appearance." But a year later, just one month after the first still photographs of dead appeared in magazines and newspapers, the newsreels were still working under severe restrictions: "The war is certainly beautiful through the eyes of the motion picture camera for this week's showings," wrote an OWI analyst. "No more peaceful a scene was ever made by a travelogue as that our war correspondents recorded through their lens of that palm-dotted atoll. . . . There is something lacking. . . . I have a suspicion it might be in the film pool at the Pentagon." But the policy of greater revelation affected newsreels as well as still photography. Footage of the fighting at Tarawa Atoll and elsewhere showed American dead. Newsreel analysts in OWI reported in December "by far the best American war action pictures to date, equaling if not surpassing the Russian war shots in depicting actual combat scenes." Such coverage became more common during the last twenty-one months of the war.[34]

No one seriously challenged the government's authority to exert some control over footage originating in combat areas. Movies made in Hollywood were a different matter. In previous decades government relations with the motion picture studios had left a legacy of cooperation and distrust, both of which persisted throughout the war years. Cooperation reached new levels as war threatened and then broke out in Europe. Early and sustained administration involvement assured that Warner Brothers' *Juárez* (1939), the first film ever to receive its premier showing in Mexico's presidential palace, would be a paean to U.S.-Mexican friendship. It depicted Benito Juárez as he led the fight for Mexican independence, drawing inspiration from the American wartime president whose treasured picture kept watch over his headquarters, Abraham Lincoln. Even before Pearl Harbor the film industry created the Motion Picture Committee Cooperating for National Defense (renamed the War Activities Committee soon after the bombing of Pearl Harbor), which among other things distributed without charge current films to American troops (43,000 prints shipped by war's end).[35]

Moviemakers shared President Roosevelt's estimate of their industry's potential. Like him they believed it could become the most powerful force for building public support for the war. They also believed they knew better than bureaucrats how to achieve this while turning a profit. Many studio heads were especially concerned that the government might use claims of wartime need to break the power of the major studios, long threatened by an ongoing antitrust case which sought to weaken the oligopolistic control that the production companies maintained over the distribution of their product through extensive ownership of theaters and coercive film-booking practices. Deferral of this case to the postwar years helped pave the way for a wary wartime partnership between image makers in Hollywood and Washington.

In a letter to Lowell Mellett appointing him coordinator of government films, written ten days after the Pearl Harbor attack, Roosevelt defined the ambiguous terms of the relationship. He advised that "the motion picture must remain free insofar as national security will permit." Mellett, a newspaper editor before he became an aide to the president in 1939, headed the Bureau of Motion Pictures in OWI when legislation established that agency in June 1942. In addition to producing some films of its own and coordinating distribution of those produced by other government agencies, the bureau had the task of assuring that all films coming out of Hollywood served, or at least did not undermine, war aims. Its efforts were hampered by internal disputes, by industry executives' determination to protect their established prerogatives, and by the desire of the studios to maintain mutually beneficial relations with the military services, whose views were not always congruent with OWI's. As in other areas, the military had a considerable head start over the newly created wartime agency. Six months before Pearl Harbor the director of BPR reported that "the continuous and equitable contact of this branch with the picture industry assures their confidence and cooperation to a remarkable degree." During the war the studios found this cooperation more indispensable then ever owing to their increased need to use military facilities, equipment, and footage in film production. Military noncooperation could doom a film more rapidly than OWI objections. When the War Department refused to aid Paramount with the proposed 1943 film *Advance Agent to Africa,* despite assurances that the film would be "made strictly to glorify the United States Army, as WAKE ISLAND glorified the Marine Corps," the company killed the project.[36]

Making the most of its limited power, OWI sometimes helped bring a movie into being, discourage its production, or effect a major shift in its emphasis. More frequently, OWI actions brought about minor changes in the film scripts it reviewed, which totaled 1,652 by war's end. Because OWI staffers ranked earnestness as the highest virtue, one of their most frequent complaints was that filmmakers did not treat crucial issues with sufficient gravity. If Dagwood Bumstead carried out his airplane spotting and blackout enforcement duties with bumbling incompetence, perhaps viewers would lose faith in the civil defense program. Although budget cuts forced OWI to reduce its operations in 1943, the agency maintained its influence over film content through its strengthened working relationship with the Office of Censorship, which could deny filmmakers the export licenses essential for acceptable profit margins.

These power struggles made little difference in Hollywood depictions of gore because well-established industry practices were roughly consistent with government recommendations. Early in the 1930s independent producer Jesse Lasky warned moviemakers to avoid "excessive brutality and intimate details of killing and murder" because they could lead to costly confrontations with local and state censorship boards. Such concerns caused the industry to tighten and strengthen its self-censoring Production Code in 1934. In its hesitation to portray the horrors of war, particularly as they affected Americans, Hollywood merely conducted business as usual. To be sure, Americans saw fictional counterparts of their country's soldiers die on the nation's seventeen thousand movie screens soon after Pearl Harbor, nearly two years before the release of photographs and newsreels of actual death. But in these early films American deaths, always portrayed as heroic and meaningful, never hinted at the capacity of the machinery of modern warfare to mutilate the human body. They also were rare: by OWI's count, between May and November 1942 only five of sixty-one feature films with war scenes showed Americans dying in combat. This led OWI analysts to fear that because so many enemy and so few Americans died in Hollywood's war, audiences would conclude that enemy soldiers were more willing to die for their country.[37]

The office of War Information sought to fine-tune the presentation of death and suffering. For instance, in an "Information Manual" prepared for the industry in 1942, OWI suggested this guideline: "In crowds unostentatiously show a few wounded men. Prepare people, but do not alarm them, against the casualties to come." The office also advised that "the blood and thunder type of war story is not desirable at this time" because "a deluge of pictures of this type might have an unfortunate effect upon public morale." As Hollywood depicted violence more graphically as the war wore on, the government called more often for restraint. In 1943 OWI asked the producers to "minimize the bloody aspects" in *Corregidor,* and the War Department successfully persuaded Metro-Goldwyn-Mayer to "tone down" its depiction in *Thirty Seconds over Tokyo* (1944) of the ordeal one airman went through when his shattered leg required an operation. Contradictory as the messages Hollywood received from Washington seemed to be, most could be accommodated through interpreting with different emphases this OWI guideline: "The mortal realities of war must be impressed vividly on every citizen. This does not mean dwelling at length on pain, anguish, and bloodshed. Nor does it mean sugar-coating the truth."[38]

The movement toward more vivid portrayal of war's "mortal realities" makes it easy to date films from the period. The first post–Pearl Harbor productions, such as *Shores of Tripoli,* Twentieth-Century Fox's biggest money maker in 1942, promoted a jaunty view of war as adventure reminiscent of World War I propaganda films. *Shores* perpetuated the fatuous story that when asked what they needed, besieged Marines at Wake Island had replied, "Send us more Japs." Later in the year Paramount released *Wake Island,* which provided a more somber view of that battle and ended with the principal characters, after a brave defense, about to be overrun by the Japanese. Fox's immensely popular *Guadalcanal Diary,* because of its November 1943 release date, was able to incorporate documentary footage of tides washing over the bodies of dead Americans on a beach. These scenes were of short duration, however. A reassuring, often lighthearted narrative voice, stirring music including the Marine's Hymn, and editing that created an equivalent visual rhythm set the film's dominant tone. Quotations from Richard Tregaskis's book, on which the film was based, sometimes added a sterner note. The narrator described American troops returning from battle as "weary, silent, stunned; men with glazed eyes holding their sides limping along . . . boys with a memory of death in their eyes." But nothing in the film's narration or visual imagery came close to the specificity about death found in the book: "here [a dead body] with a backbone visible from the front, and the rest of the flesh peeled over the man's head like the leaf of an artichoke; there a charred head hairless but still equipped with blackened eyeballs." At the end of the film the heavy bandages over the eyes of one hospitalized soldier suggested the cost of the battle, but the smile that formed on the wounded soldier's lips as an officer read a commendation of valor to those who fought at Guadalcanal assured that the price was worth paying.[39]

Happy Land, released the following month, presented a briefly painful imaginary account of the impact of a war death on an American family. A few minutes into the film a small-town pharmacist, Lou Marsh, and his wife learned by telegram of the death of their only child, Rusty. For a few minutes the film showed Marsh becoming bitter and withdrawing from the life of his community. Then the ghost of Rusty's great-grandfather, a Civil War veteran, appeared and rekindled Marsh's interest in both personal and civic life. The remainder of the film celebrated, through looking back on Rusty's life, the joys of growing up in the American midlands (the fictitious setting was Heartfield, Iowa, played by Santa Rosa, California). Every scene helped give meaning to Rusty's death. He entered the navy before Pearl Harbor because he was well informed on world affairs and considered protection of American interests an unquestioned duty. He died heroically, putting his own life at risk to help a shipmate. The end of the film left no doubt that sadness over Rusty's loss would be a powerful daily presence for the rest of Marsh's life. But he had found peace through his understanding that the death was necessary, that Rusty "couldn't have been any happier if he lived to be 100." A visit from one of Rusty's combat mates, who assumed the role of surrogate son, provided emotionally restorative continuity.

The Fighting Sullivans also placed intense emotional pain into a context designed to reassure and inspire. Based on the true story of five brothers who died together when the Japanese sank the cruiser *Juneau,* this 1944 Twentieth-Century Fox film (initially released under the title *The Sullivans*) continued the process of revealing the war's domestic cost. The scene in which an officer informed the Sullivans of the death of their five sons must have been excruciating for millions of viewers full of anxiety for the safety of spouses, parents, children, and other friends and relatives in the service. Perhaps this anxiety also made viewers especially receptive to the meaning given these deaths by the film's account of the unpretentious commitment to democratic ideals that the boys developed as they grew up, also in Iowa (Waterloo), and by the way their upbringing, experiences, and values naturally led to their participation in the war. In the film's closing scene, after the bereft parents dedicated a new ship named in honor of their sons, the camera faded to heaven, where the five young men cheerfully signaled their approval of the proceedings below.

If *Happy Land* and *The Fighting Sullivans* depicted emotional suffering, other films from the final two years of the war gave unsettling indications of its physical impact. Even the toned-down version of a leg amputation in *Thirty Seconds over Tokyo* was far harsher than anything that appeared early in the war. In Warner Brothers' 1945 film *Objective Burma* the director, Raoul Walsh, perhaps expressed his own goals through one of the movie's characters, a journalist who ran risks out of his desire to help those on the home front know "a little better what war is about." If Walsh did wish to clarify the war, he had only mixed success. The film included unrealistic shots, such as one showing Errol Flynn removing the pin from a hand grenade with his teeth, an oft-repeated Hollywood fantasy that drew responses of disgust from many combat veterans. It presented such a "travesty of what actually happened in Burma" that, especially because it exaggerated the American role there in disregard of British predominance, it set off intense controversy in England and "was withdrawn after only one week in London's West End." Its visual depictions of Allied death were decorous ones created in Hollywood studios.[40]

Earlier movies had similar limitations, but other features of *Objective Burma* could have appeared only near the war's close. In a variation of the principle that verbal descriptions of death could go further than visual ones, dialogue transformed innocuous visual material into disturbing imagery. In a scene set in a Burmese village where Japanese had massacred American soldiers, the camera showed only the lower part of an apparently intact body. It could not have shown more. The administrator of the movie industry's own censorship code wrote to Jack Warner during the production of *Objective Burma* reminding him that because of code injunctions against "brutality and possible gruesomeness" he should make "no attempt to photograph" mutilated bodies. In the film, however, a soldier's anguished remark that the dead were so badly mutilated that he could not bear to look at them suggested what horrors would be in view if the camera had focused on the body's upper part. The power of this dialogue was diminished by trite anti-Japanese invective: "They're degenerate, moral idiots. Stinking little savages. Wipe them out, I say. Wipe them off the face of the earth." Nonetheless, viewers were not likely to leave the theater feeling as comfortable about the nature of modern war as viewers whose knowledge of this topic depended entirely on 1942 films. No Hollywood film of 1942 or 1945 showed fly-covered corpses, but in *Objective Burma* an unrevealing aerial reconnaissance photograph of three dead soldiers was made vivid by one of the character's comments that soon the bodies would "play host to every fly in Burma."[41]

Occasionally Hollywood films depicted visually, as well as through words, war costs unrecorded in published photographs and newsreels. Officials censored actual pictures that revealed the mental distress of American soldiers, but Hollywood's greater latitude led to the inclusion of scenes of emotional breakdown in films such as *Love Letters* (1943), *Destination Tokyo* (1943), and *I'll Be Seeing You* (1944). In *Objective Burma* one American soldier cracked up and began to yell and sob when a rescue plane failed to spot his group. But even at their most revealing, wartime movies excluded many aspects of combat. As the combat veteran Paul Fussell has pointed out, detached body parts were not only a battlefield hazard (many soldiers were injured and some killed when struck by a decapitated head, booted foot, or other bodily debris) but were such a common wartime sight that German submarines carried a supply of animal entrails that they could release to make attackers believe they had been destroyed. No film, newsreel, or photograph released during the war documented this U-boat practice. In the war as presented to the public, intestines stayed where they belonged, and with very few exceptions heads and limbs did as well. The files of material censored during the war also included photographs of American soldiers who died in training accidents, who shot themselves, and who were killed or wounded by "friendly fire."[42]

A few advertisements included images not permitted in censored material. Normally the values expressed through wartime corporate advertisements were consistent with those manifest in government-produced material. What differences there were diminished during the war, as the historian Barry Karl observed: "business managers and government officials entered . . . World War II as adversaries and ended as partners." But throughout the war corporate graphic artists sometimes dipped into the pool of forbidden images to give extra power to the advertisements they designed. A New Haven Railroad ad, one of the best known of the era, showing a young soldier on his way to war, suggested in the text that possibly there was a tear in his eye, although official images never showed soldiers crying. To promote a petroleum-derived tranquilizer developed in its laboratories, the Shell Oil Company ran an ad with a drawing of an American airman on the verge of being driven crazy by the sounds of surrounding anti-aircraft fire. Paintings also sometimes presented scenes not permissible in photographs. Those by Tom Lea reproduced in *Life* included one extremely bloody view of a fatally wounded American soldier, and a portrait of an infantryman whose eyes were glazed over into the "1,000-yard stare" characteristic of soldiers exposed to extended combat.[43]

As always, timing mattered. In 1942 almost all advertisements avoided images of American suffering. Such images became more frequent the next year, perhaps in part because of an OWI request to the Advertising Council in the summer of 1943 that in order to combat public complacency the council might help introduce "a grim note in future advertisements." The government took its own advice by using the just-released photographs of dead Americans in its ads for the Third War Loan drive in the fall of 1943. In September an official war bond advertisement that ran in various newspapers used the photograph of dead American paratroopers from the Sicilian campaign, accompanied by this text: "Buy more war bonds, lessen our casualties. . . . This is not a pretty picture, but war itself is gruesome." Shortly thereafter another bond ad featured a photograph of a soldier whose leg had been amputated below the knee sitting up in bed with a faint smile on his face. The caption told viewers, "They don't want your tears," but they did want you to buy bonds. By the final year of the war government posters included even harsher photographs, such as one showing the crumpled, torn, dirt-splattered body of a dead American soldier.[44]

What Americans saw by 1945 was more revealing, and sustained a more complex understanding of the war, than what they had seen in December 1941. Americans eventually saw more not because the government loosened control, but because it used its power to encourage a different emphasis in the visual presentation of the war. Officials made these changes in response to evolving wartime needs and circumstances, including diminished public tolerance for sanitized images of war. These officials perceived pictures of the American dead as extremely hazardous material during the war's early years. Before it ended they considered them the most powerful weapons in their motivational arsenal.

Playing the Death Card

The captions make clear which images were censored and which published during wartime. Most of the censored images in the visual essays came from files at the National Archives designated CE. To the best of my knowledge, all images in this essay with a CE identification number (see Credits for identification numbers) remained in the file of censored material for years, and in most cases for decades. They are now accessible to researchers in the Still Picture Branch of the National Archives. If I did not find an image in the CE files but have other evidence that officials restricted its publication, I indicate the nature of the restrictions and of the evidence in the captions or main text.

Partly to protect the inspirational value of other images of death, authorities withheld photographs that suggested that American soldiers might treat the dead with irreverence or contempt. This censored picture, taken by Army Signal Corps photographers in the Volksberg area of France on 6 December 1944, shows a dead German soldier whose body American soldiers had embellished with playing cards.

From the Civil War through Vietnam, imagery available to a large public during the later stages of each American war has been harsher than that released during the early stages. At the top is a sketch made in the field by the artist Alfred Waud at the battle of Antietam in August 1862. When engravers and editors in New York, remote from the battle, prepared an image based on Waud's drawing for publication in *Harper's Weekly,* they toned it down (bottom). For instance, they rotated the man in the left foreground 180 degrees so that *Harper's* readers would not have to view the stump of his amputated leg. The longer the war continued, the more insistently artists in the field put its horrors into their visual reports, some of which made their way into *Harper's*. Photographs showing the carnage of battle were immediately available to those able to visit the galleries where the photographers displayed them, but they did not reach a mass audience because newspapers and magazines did not have the technical means to print photographs until more than two decades later.

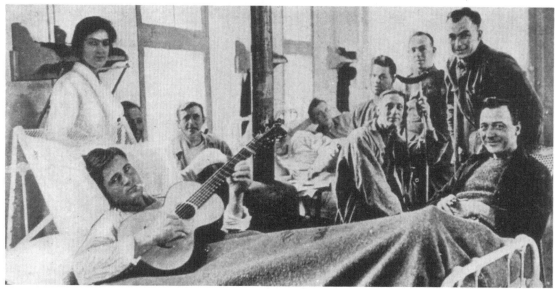

THE AMERICAN WOUNDED IN FRANCE

Most images published during the twenty months of American involvement in World War I were selected and presented in a way that offered a reassuring view of the wartime experiences of American soldiers. In March 1918 the *Independent* printed what it called "the first photo of our soldiers convalescent at base hospital, France." The caption explained that the soldier playing a guitar was leading the others in singing "Pack Up Your Troubles." The war ended seven months later without any relaxation of government censorship of photographs of the American dead, but by the late summer of 1918 magazine readers encountered more sobering pictures of the wounded than any that had appeared previously. Perhaps the most extreme was an Army Signal Corps photograph of a seriously wounded American soldier being placed on a stretcher, which appeared in *Colliers* on 27 July 1918.

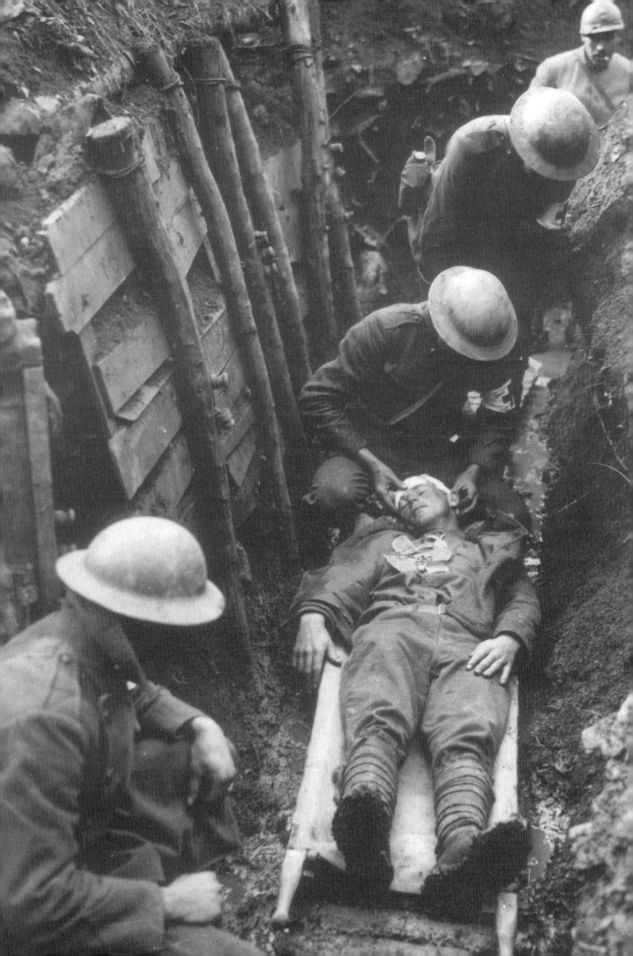

IT is not pleasant to have your peaceful life upset by wartime needs and

restrictions and activities. . . . It is not pleasant to die, either. . . . Between you who live at

home and the men who die at the front there is a direct connection. . . By your actions,

definitely, a certain number of these men will die or they will come through alive.

If you do everything you can to hasten victory and do every bit of it as fast as you

can . . . then, sure as fate you will save the lives of some men who will otherwise die because

you let the war last too long. . . . Think it over. Till the war is won you cannot,

in fairness to them, complain or waste or shirk. Instead, you will apply every last ounce of

your effort to getting this thing done. . . . In the name of God and your fellow man, that is your job.

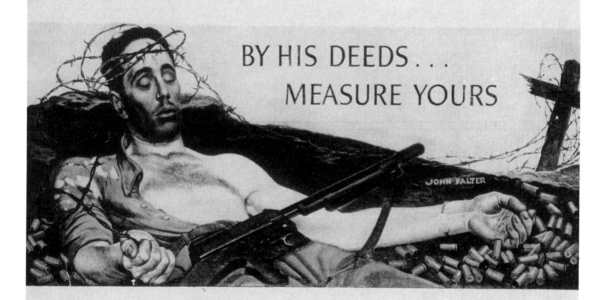

BY HIS DEEDS . . .
MEASURE YOURS

JOHN FALTER

The civilian war organization needs your help. The Government
has formed Citizens Service Corps as part of local Defense Councils.
If such a group is at work in your community, cooperate with
it to the limit of your ability. If none exists, help to organize one.
A free booklet telling you what to do and how to do it will be
sent to you at no charge if you will write to this magazine.
This is your war. Help win it. Choose what you will do — now!

EVERY CIVILIAN A FIGHTER

CONTRIBUTED BY THE MAGAZINE PUBLISHERS OF AMERICA

During the first twenty-one months of World War II, when censors withheld all photographs of the American dead, those images of the dead that did appear were comforting ones. An example is the Christ-like depiction by John Falter that appeared in a March 1943 announcement run by the Magazine Publishers of America (left). Later in the war Allied victories made guarding against complacency seem a more urgent task than providing reassurance. One result was posters such as "Stay on the Job," which the government used to remind workers involved in the production of war materiel that diligence in the workplace would speed an end to the killing of Americans on the battlefield. The dirty mangled garment, maggots, and solitary death depicted in this poster from the final year of the war are the visual antithesis of qualities in earlier imagery which created an aura of cleanliness, order, and brotherhood.

Life magazine used an accompanying editorial (see p. 14) to guide responses to its first photograph of American dead, George Strock's picture from Buna Beach, New Guinea, which appeared in September 1943 (above). Earlier in the war *Life* editors had responded to readers' complaints about its display of gory photographs of non-American dead by asserting, "The love of peace has no meaning or stamina unless it is based on a knowledge of war's terror. . . . Dead men have indeed died in vain if live men refuse to look at them." But *Life* did not discuss how far the photographs published were from fully revealing the horrors of warfare. For example, the magazine did not choose to counteract the sensory limitations of photography by mentioning that in his letters back to New York Strock reported that he rarely bathed in New Guinea because "the damn water smells like dead Japanese bodies." The poster at right is an example of how the government, as well as Hollywood (see pp. 22–23), sought visually to present the Sullivan family's tragic loss of five sons in a way that would inspire rather than depress other Americans.

the five Sullivan brothers
"missing in action" off the Solomons

THEY DID THEIR PART

OWI Poster No. 45   Additional copies may be obtained upon request from the Division of Public Inquiries, Office of War Information, Washington D.C.

These images are examples of material kept out of public view for most of the war. The one showing the body of an American soldier with severed arm nearby is a still from a film that took its title, *Two and One-Half Minutes,* from the statistic of how often an American soldier was killed. The Treasury Department made the film in 1944 for use in industrial plants engaged in war production, especially those threatened by labor problems. It was released for more general viewing only in the war's final months as part of a special effort to counteract public war weariness and overexposure to propagandistic calls to action. Officials censored all photographs showing American soldiers losing control of themselves, but on rare occasions they did release photographs suggesting something of the psychological impact of war. The picture of weary Marines who had fought two days and two nights at Eniwetok Atoll was passed by censors and was widely seen in 1944.

Captions as well as images grew harsher by war's end. *Life* accompanied Robert Capa's series of photographs of a soldier killed in Leipzig on 18 April 1945, with a quote from "The Day of Battle" in A. E. Housman's *A Shropshire Lad,* ending with the lines, "Stand and fight and see your slain / And take the bullet in your brain." Despite this increased candor, many photographs remained in the censor's files, like the one of an American soldier who accidentally fell to his death in Australia in 1944 (top). The apparently unheroic circumstances of his death and the absence of a uniform would have hindered caption writers seeking to put the blood spilled in this photograph into a meaningful context. The American soldier in the bottom photograph is in uniform and died in battle, but the photograph was not released, probably because of the distorted configuration of his right leg.

Although both of these similar images are from late in the war, the army released the one at the top and withheld the one below it. Censors blocked out the face of the injured G.I. in a 1944 photograph of a jeep that hit a German land mine near Metz, Belgium (top), but the soldier's agony is obvious. Officials' disinclination to allow publication of photographs of casualties sustained in accidents rather than in combat probably explained why they did not release the picture (bottom) of a medic treating a member of the 82nd Airborne Division, who was injured when a C-47 transport plane crashed during a training flight in France. Officials wished to present the American effort as consistently purposeful. Visual images of accidents served this end less well than pictures of damage done by enemy action. Another reason for withholding the bottom picture might have been the disturbing evidence provided by the debris in the left rear of the picture of the visual similarities of mangled men and mangled equipment.

On 17 December 1944 German soldiers killed more than seventy Americans captured at Malmedy during the final German offensive of the war, the Battle of the Bulge. In its 5 February 1945 issue *Life* ran some of the photographs taken after Americans regained the position in January and found the frozen bodies of the victims. These photographs, such as Johnny Florea's picture of a medical corpsman (left), were among the most disturbing to appear during the war. The caption noted that as he died the corpsman "clutched at his throat," and explained that Florea's photograph had been "retouched to obscure the dead man's face." Army censors withheld many other photographs of the incident, including those which exposed internal organs and brain tissue, revealed that the Germans had driven wooden stakes through some of the victims (right), depicted the dead in bizarre positions, and showed the dead abstracted into trial exhibits by having had numbers placed on them to aid in the army's war crimes investigation.

Censors stopped all photographs showing the American dead being handled like inanimate material objects, such as one showing G.I.s piling the bodies of the American dead from the 3rd Army front into a truck in 1945 (left). They also had no desire to circulate evidence that officers often assigned African-American soldiers to such unpleasant tasks as burial details. For less obvious reasons officials also withheld a photograph of wounded American soldiers in North Africa awaiting evacuation (right), perhaps because the men in front seemed inadequately distressed over their departure from the battlefield.

This photograph, among the last of those censored during the combat phase of World War II, shows two G.I.s removing the remains of an American flier from a temporary grave in the jungle in Burma, where he had died in a plane crash earlier in the year. The photograph was taken on 14 August 1945, the day when Allied leaders announced the Japanese surrender. Had it been released at the time, the V shapes discernible throughout the picture (as formed, for instance, by the corpse's legs and by the arms of the G.I.s) might have provided Americans with a poignant reminder that victory would carry different meanings to different American families.

Every single man, woman and child is a partner in the most tremendous undertaking in our American history.
—Franklin D. Roosevelt, radio talk, December 9, 1941

CHAPTER 2

A Cast of Millions

WORLD WAR II was the first movie every American could be in. As portrayed by the government and the news and entertainment media the war had a compelling story line, a huge assemblage of costumed performers, easily identifiable good and bad guys, and an outcome that viewers could anticipate but not take for granted. With the spectacle of the Japanese surrender aboard the USS *Missouri,* including the convergence of nearly two thousand American military aircraft over Tokyo Bay, coming shortly after the atomic bombings of Hiroshima and Nagasaki, it even had an ending as dramatic as the beginning at Pearl Harbor. But more effectively than any film, World War II offered each citizen the dual role of spectator and participant.[1]

A fierce struggle engaging tens of millions of people around the globe could not fail to attract spectators. The demands of the war, and the way it was presented, assured that most spectators would see themselves also as participants. The theme propagandists promoted most insistently was that everyone had a part to play. Yet this theme presented them with a major problem: How could they encourage those excluded from equal participation in American society to become fully engaged in the war effort without frightening a large

43

portion of the population who agreed with practices that linked opportunity to race, gender, class, religion, and ethnicity. As an OWI analyst remarked concerning one aspect of the problem, that agency sought to find ways "to improve Negro morale without incurring too much criticism from whites."[2]

Balancing needs to correct and protect customary social arrangements, a persistent challenge to Americans, was given new urgency by the war. President Roosevelt, in addition to his role as commander-in-chief of the armed forces, served as both corrector- and protector-in-chief of American society. But as recognized by the OWI analyst, one person's needs of social change were another's fears. The conditions that some sought to correct, others wished to protect. The agonies of the Depression had tipped the balance in favor of correction during the 1930s. The majority that reelected Roosevelt in 1936 felt the crisis called for significant change. They disagreed with accusations from the right and the left that his policies undermined basic American values of individual initiative and freedom of choice, or merely propped up an unfair system that assured a few great wealth but kept many in poverty. Even before Pearl Harbor, the outbreak of war in Asia and Europe and the threat to the United States posed by German and Japanese aggression shifted the emphasis back to protection. As Roosevelt later put it, "Dr. Win the War" replaced "Dr. New Deal."[3]

Visual imagery played a key role in efforts to encourage widespread participation in the war effort while minimizing concern over disruptions to the social order. Imagery often served as a substitute for, or one barrier to, more substantive changes in the distribution of opportunity within the United States. Few images sharply criticized existing discriminatory practices. Yet wartime photographs, movies, newsreels, posters, and advertisements provided positive images of a wide array of racial, class, religious, and ethnic groups. Virtually all images, whether questioning or affirming existing social relations, shared one thing in common: they suggested that the point of view to which they gave visual support served the needs of the war effort.

Race was the most explosive issue. Millions of Americans judged every government action largely by its impact on race relations. Most wished to maintain distinctions, often enforced by law as well as custom, that banned blacks from neighborhoods, jobs, schools and universities, churches, railroad cars, museums, beauty pageants, professional sports teams, scout troops, tornado shelters, restaurants, and hotels. On the basis of four thousand interviews conducted in five cities, OWI found that 96 percent of the whites surveyed favored residential segregation, and 76 percent approved of segregation of buses and streetcars. Nine out of ten whites believed white and black soldiers should not train together; three out of four blacks believed they should. In 1940 almost all black sailors did menial labor in ship galleys. Blacks in the army served in strictly segregated units. The War Department advertised that "applications from colored persons for flying cadet appointments or enlistments in the Air Corps are not being accepted," and the Marine Corps continued its tradition of not enlisting blacks. These racial barriers became burdensome to leaders in the private and public spheres trying to satisfy wartime needs for workers and soldiers, but personal belief and political pressures made them reluctant to challenge them.[4]

Even cautious moves met strong resistance. In 1943 Liberian president Edwin Barclay visited Washington and appeared briefly in the Senate to receive recognition for his country's loyal wartime support. All but two Southern senators walked out. The protesters also denounced President Roosevelt for allowing Barclay to become the first black, except servants, to stay overnight at the White House. After OWI brought out a pamphlet praising black achievements, Alabama congressman A. Leonard Allen attacked the agency. He claimed that white southerners were the "best friends" of "that race." The OWI pamphlet's implied criticism of segregation could lead only to disunity, which in turn might make more difficult the task of soldiers like his son. One OWI staff member wrote to another in response to Allen's speech: "Apparently his son is fighting a war to maintain the caste system in the South." The South Carolina legislature had given some support to this interpretation by passing a resolution asserting that American soldiers were "fighting for white supremacy."[5]

In the private sector small actions could lead to large reactions. If responses published in *Life*'s "Letters to the Editor" column are representative, during the war years racial issues drew the most heated responses. After the magazine ran an article commending black contributions to the American war effort, some readers praised the article for "building up confidence, morale and patriotism in our country," while others found it odious. A reader from Kentucky asked, "How in the name of God do you expect to contribute to the promotion of unity in this country when you display pictures of white women working under the supervision of Negro men, while in the same article you excuse the degraded actions of Lincoln in sending Negro troops against the homes of those people who had raised them. Why remind the Southern people of an injustice as foul as any Hitler ever conceived? Your Negro war article is inflammatory to the point of treason."[6]

Wartime visual images reflected the hatred and hope generated by the interaction of racial antagonisms and democratic aspirations. Despite such critics as Congressman Allen, during the war years the federal government probably distributed more respectful visual images of blacks than it had in its previous century and a half of existence. Nongovernmental organizations also produced an unprecedented number of favorable images. Encouraged in part by OWI's suggestion that movies "show colored soldiers in crowd scenes" and "occasionally colored officers," Hollywood sometimes went beyond demeaning stereotypes. Hitler's venomous diatribes against blacks as well as other groups became a foil for counterimages. In the 1943 Columbia film *Sahara* a black (Libyan) soldier (the character was inserted by the screenwriter John Howard Lawson) displayed much more dignity than a captured German who complained, as the soldier secured him, that he did not want to be touched by a member of an inferior race. The MGM production chief Dore Schary had a black included in the group of soldiers featured in another film made in that year, *Bataan*, even though this led to the depiction of something that did not then exist in the real army, an integrated combat unit. It seems unlikely that before the new conditions created by the war Emerson Radio and Phonograph Company would have run an advertisement featuring one black and three white babies (names: Lincoln, Lee, Leary, Levy) playing together. Emerson explained in the caption to their 1943 ad that "Babies Are Not Born to Hate" and that this scene of racial harmony would make Hitler mad. In sum, during the war years Americans encountered a more extensive visual dialogue on the present state and future possibilities of racial relations in the United States than they had at any other time since the Civil War.[7]

This dialogue took place within strictly defined limits. Images of racial reconciliation such as that in the Emerson ad avoided the most emotionally charged issues related to race. Few showed blacks exercising authority over whites (as in the *Life* photograph that so offended the Kentucky reader), challenging white privileges such as exclusive access to certain jobs, or mixing socially with whites. Unwritten rules of the time made it unthinkable that the Emerson ad would have shown blacks and whites dancing together at a high school prom. There were exceptions, however. An unusually tough-minded ad run by Morton's Clothing Store in Washington, D.C., in 1944 under the title "Saboteur—Who Me" depicted a distinguished-looking lady in a fine room with two blue stars on her window (signifying two family members in the armed forces). The ad explained that even if they had loved ones in the service, Americans who spoke disparagingly of those of a different race or religion undermined the war effort by arousing "hatred or mistrust among groups of Americans."[8]

Most images were less confrontational. Material intended for white audiences seldom depicted blacks in aggressive poses. A poster showing Joe Louis wielding a bayonet was a rare exception. Louis's well-publicized efforts to use his immense prestige as the world heavyweight boxing champion to bring the black community fully behind the war effort made this image acceptable. Although millions of blacks took special satisfaction in Louis's victories over white boxing opponents, his 1938 victory over the German champion Max Schmeling helped make Louis a symbol of national as well as racial pride. One month after Pearl Harbor Louis, whose fights attracted a radio audience outnumbered only by the audience for Roosevelt's most listened-to broadcasts, "knocked out Buddy Baer in exactly two minutes and fifty-six seconds, then turned his purse over to the New York Auxiliary of the Navy Relief Society and went into the Army." The bayonet poster quoted Louis's statement that God was on America's side. *The Negro Soldier* (1944), a government-produced film, showed blacks and whites together for large-scale activities where integration might be efficient, as when black and white soldiers did calisthenics together. In its depictions of living quarters and other intimate social situations the film kept blacks segregated, as they in fact were in all the military branches.[9]

Above all, visual images pertaining to race relations always asserted the compatibility of the racial attitudes they championed and the goal of winning the war. The clearest example was the double-V symbol introduced early in 1942 in the widely read black newspaper the *Pittsburgh Courier* in response to a letter from a reader. A single V had by 1940 become the preeminent symbol of the Allied war effort. Widely evoked in the United States before Pearl Harbor, after December 7 it became the most commonly used emblem of commitment to the war other than the American flag, appearing at the beginning and end of films, in advertisements and posters, and in innumerable public displays. Louisiana State University used flashing red, white, and blue bulbs to inscribe a huge V on its memorial tower. The double V adopted by the *Courier* gave equal status to the war for Allied victory and the war for equal rights at home. Black newspapers widely displayed this image, believing that the end of discriminatory practices was essential to a unified war effort. The *Courier*'s rendition of the symbol showed two large V's with an eagle in between; it carried the caption, "Democracy. Double VV Victory—At home—and abroad."[10]

The government never adopted the double V as one of its symbols. If it had it might have given new meaning to the phrase "home front" by sparking a second civil war. Yet whenever federal agencies supported controversial social policies they too bolstered their position by leaning on the claim of war needs. In 1942 OWI released a poster showing a white and a black industrial worker bending together over a task. The largest print on the poster proclaimed "UNITED WE WIN," and to reaffirm the compatibility of racial cooperation and national interest the dominant visual image was an American flag which covered one-third of the poster's area. Pictures that perpetuated conventional images of blacks also suggested visually that the social relations depicted contributed to a united war effort. As in earlier years, blacks in advertisements were often performing some service for whites. But during the war those they served usually were soldiers.[11]

After race the touchiest issue was class. The contradictory message conveyed by wartime visual images was that social classes did not exist in the United States, and besides, the members of the upper class were just like everybody else. The Committee on Public Information offered a similar message during World War I. One photograph distributed by that agency showed the son of "millionaire packer" Louis Swift being treated like other trainees in military camp. World War II equivalents included photographs of movie stars, athletes, and the sons of political leaders going off to war and Woodbury soap advertisements showing socially prominent women doing volunteer work.

Hollywood took the lead in downplaying class differences. In October 1942 President Roosevelt issued an executive order mandating "insofar as practicable" a cap setting maximum salaries for civilians (all military salaries were far below the caps). Although Congress eliminated this salary cap five months later, it called attention to movieland affluence, normally a source of pride but potentially embarrassing amid talk of the need for wartime sacrifices. Because the cap applied neither to investment earnings nor to most other forms of income other than salary, highly paid stars and studio executives were disproportionately represented among the less than three thousand Americans whose incomes were affected. In response Hollywood made a special effort to convey the sense that its luminaries were just plain folk who also happened to have wealth and fame. In the 1944 Warner Brothers film *Hollywood Canteen,* which celebrated the club of that name where movie stars served sandwiches to and danced with visiting servicemen and servicewomen, one soldier confessed that he used to resent the status of stars but now realized that in American society everybody really is equal. At the canteen he could experience for himself "all them big shots listening to little shots like me." [12]

Wartime imagery minimized class differences by elevating workers as well as by humanizing big shots. It reflected growing recognition of the industrial base of modern warfare and the influence of the Depression-dominated 1930s, when many paintings, murals, and films, some inspired by Soviet social realism, gave prominence to the virtues and hardships of manual workers. Wartime images, however, depicted workers contributing individually or in harmonious groups to the war effort rather than taking collective action to redress some grievance against the government or employers. Mildly class-conscious as they were, Betty Grable's lines in MGM's 1944 film *Pin-Up Girl* were unusual in their explicit attention to class: "I am a truck driver's daughter—I have to be an enlisted man's girl." When advertisers paired a military man and an attractive woman during wartime, the man almost always was an officer, but the ads never made specific reference to the strong though far from invariable connection between social class and military rank. Like blacks, workers were portrayed more often and more respectfully during the war than in most earlier periods, but the range of acceptable images remained narrow, more narrow than during the class-conscious previous decade. [13]

Many of the workers depicted were women. A 1942 government survey revealed that only 33 percent of childless wives, and 19 percent of those with children, expressed willingness to take a job outside the home. Less than one in three men accepted the idea of their wives working. Yet by the final months of the war the number of women in the work force was 50 percent higher than it had been in 1940: women constituted 57 percent of all employed persons outside the military, and 80 percent of all women in the work force wished to continue working after the war ended. The government and other employers achieved these figures in part through dissemination, especially during the peak production years of 1943 and 1944, of visual imagery that showed women contributing to the war effort as industrial and service-sector workers.[14]

Most images emphasized the superficial nature of wartime social changes. The Office of War Information distributed paired photographs that showed women applying house-wifely habits to industrial tasks. In one pair a woman hung bedsheets in her backyard and hoisted sheets of metal from a factory vat. The movie star Veronica Lake lost much of her popularity when she cut off her alluring peekaboo bang because female workers who imitated her put themselves at risk. The photograph *Life* concocted to warn against this hazard, which showed the unshorn Veronica with her hair supposedly caught in a drill press, reinforced the notion that women in heavy industrial jobs were fundamentally out of place. The message was made explicit by a badge that women driving buses in Washington, D.C., wore on their uniforms: "I am taking the place of a man who went to war."[15]

Despite such precautions, wartime circumstances inevitably raised fundamental questions about gender roles. One of the greatest films about World War I, the French director Jean Renoir's *The Grand Illusion* (1937), had showed Allied prisoners of war donning women's clothing for a theatrical performance at their prison camp. Several American films from World War II had similar scenes, although their creators made conspicuous efforts to assure that they did not cause any confusion about sexual identity. When a black man performed a convincing drag routine in *This Is the Army,* a shot of his bare chest as he changed costumes reminded viewers of his masculinity. Military authorities remained alert for sexually ambivalent images. Censors at the War Department's Bureau of Public Relations in Washington withheld from publication a photograph, cleared by a field censor, showing enlisted men wearing Women's Army Corps uniforms. Perhaps what seemed entertaining to those in distant military encampments where men outnumbered women by more than fifty to one seemed not only undignified but even subversive to those living in the very different circumstances of wartime Washington.[16]

Another war-stimulated conflict of identities that official wartime visual imagery sought to defuse or deny was that between American citizenship and other ethnic commitments. European-rooted ethnic divisions caused less official apprehension in World War II than they had in World War I, when one-third of the nation was foreign-born or had at least one foreign-born parent. In both wars the government produced images celebrating the American melting pot. One poster listed under the caption "Americans All" names of U.S. soldiers who had died in combat: DuBois, Smith, O'Brien, Cejka, Haucke, Pappandrikopolous, Andrassi, Villotto, Levy, Turovich, Kowalski, Chriczanevicz, Knutson, Gonzales. The government produced and showed to troops *Twenty-Seven Soldiers* (1944) to demonstrate that Allied soldiers of many different nationalities could work together in harmony.

Closely related to ethnic issues were religious ones. Most public officials were not equipped intellectually or practically to pay much attention to American religious diversity.

As one analyst wrote in 1943, "nowhere in the government is the religious press read systematically from the standpoint of their policies and attitudes." Nonetheless, all knew that religious differences were potentially divisive. The Office of War Information urged Hollywood to create images of unity to counteract the attempts of Axis agents to exacerbate such divisions among Americans: "Negroes are told they are fighting a white man's war; whites are told that the negroes are disloyal. Jews are alarmed by lies about discrimination; Gentiles are told that this war was engineered by the Jews. Protestants and Jews are told that Catholics take orders from Fascist Italy."[17]

Although ethnic and religious tensions played a divisive role in behind-the-scenes Hollywood, almost all wartime films treated American diversity as a source of strength. No one believed more fervently than Sicilian-born Frank Capra that *e pluribus unum* represented the American reality as well as the national motto. A highly successful Hollywood director before he joined the army as an officer soon after Pearl Harbor, Capra supervised the production of numerous army films, most notably the seven-part *Why We Fight* series. The series, required viewing for soldiers, contrasted American tolerance to the repressive uniformity of the country's authoritarian enemies. *Prelude to War,* the first film in the series, conspicuously quoted from Jewish, Moslem, and Christian holy books, as well as from the sayings of Confucius. Filmmakers who remained in Hollywood delivered similar messages. In *Guadalcanal Diary* a Roman Catholic priest led G.I.s on their way to to Pacific combat zones in singing "Rock of Ages" during shipboard ecumenical religious services. One soldier, whom another complimented for his enthusiastic, full-voiced singing, explained that his teacher had been his father, a cantor at a synagogue.[18]

Celebrations of the American melting pot did not lead to equal visual representation. As Paul Fussell observes, notably absent from depictions of military personnel in wartime advertisements in mainstream magazines were "any features which might be interpreted as Jewish, or Central European, or in any remote way 'Colored.'" Hollywood did not proscribe, but did severely circumscribe, Jewish roles in the cinematic version of the war. The screenwriter Alvah Bessie recalled the studio head Jack Warner's instructions regarding the one Jewish soldier in *Objective Burma*: "'I like the idea of having a Jewish officer—what's his name, Jacobs—in Burma. See that you get a good clean-cut American type for Jacobs.'" At the end of that film, when Errol Flynn finds Jacobs and his fellow soldiers dead, "the camera shows their name tags in close-up. Jacobs' tag lacks any religious denomination, where the others' are all stamped with 'P' or 'C.'"[19]

Propagandists often created different images for different groups. Segmentation, a tactic familiar to politicians skilled at delivering customized messages, became particularly useful during wartime to officials struggling with the task of creating a sense of national unity among a population with beliefs and goals grounded in extremely varied personal, familial, and communal experiences. The largest number of wartime visual messages intended for a specific audience were the thousands of different films, publications, and posters the government prepared for soldiers and sailors. Most were training materials that taught military personnel necessary skills and procedures, but films meant to boost morale or to dissuade viewers from behavior inimical to their military responsibilities received the largest production budgets. The government released a few of these, such as some films from Capra's *Why We Fight* series, to the general public.

These practices give an additional twist to a generalization made by Gerald Linderman on the basis of his study of the American Civil War: "Every war begins as one war and becomes two, that watched by civilians and that fought by soldiers." During World War II government-produced visual imagery helped enlarge this difference. Of course, Americans fought and watched not two but many different wars under the deceptively unifying name of World War II. Race, gender, class, choice, and chance, as well as civilian or military status, shaped individual visual experience. Estimates of the percentage of soldiers who experienced combat vary according to the definition of combat used, but all agree that the majority of G.I.s never saw an armed enemy soldier. Assignment to a Texas training post or a Pacific supply base was far more common than participation in an amphibious landing at Iwo Jima or in any other operation involving exchange of fire. Most soldiers could not learn through observation how to estimate the date of death of corpses from their color, which "changed from yellow to grey to red and to black until they subsided and dripped beneath the soil." Nor did most have to endure the sights that led popular journalist (and "civilian") Ernie Pyle to write the column found on his body when he himself was killed while covering the Pacific campaign in April 1945. Pyle wrote of

> the unnatural sight of cold dead men scattered over the hillsides and in the ditches along the high rows of hedge throughout the world.
> Dead men by mass production—in one country after another—month after month and year after year.
> Dead men in winter and dead men in summer.
> Dead men in such familiar promiscuity that they become monotonous.
> Dead men in such monstrous infinity that you come almost to hate them.[20]

Official messages to soldiers emphasized the experiences that united them with one another. Even as the government flattered civilians with images comparing home front and combat activities, it told soldiers that what they were going through was different from anything stay-at-homes could imagine. As one compensation for the hardships they endured they could take pride in the special knowledge derived from their experience. Soldiers in training saw grim views of battle in *Combat Bulletin* and *Army-Navy Screen Magazine* before similar material was released to the public. The army showed soldiers such material not only for instructional purposes but also to keep their attention. The instructors' manual for the War Department training film *Combat in Towns* notes that "even men with combat experience can be expected to pay close attention to this film, since it is made up of actual combat photography and so will not be regarded as 'mere training stuff for rookies.'" Although films made for soldiers included pictures of American dead, posters made for them showed instead gruesome pictures of dead Germans and, especially, Japanese. The images produced for soldiers that differed most sharply from those for civilians were in training materials urging the soldiers to adopt tactics that propaganda aimed at civilians associated only with the enemy. One large poster with the heading "Surprise—A Powerful Weapon," prepared for the Army Orientation Course by the Army Service Forces, showed a man sneaking up behind a German soldier on guard duty, then plunging the blade of an axe into his back.[21]

Other visual materials aimed at soldiers alluded to their insiders' knowledge that war made people talk dirty as well as fight dirty. In this respect war resembled other forms of sometimes risky and often tedious work done primarily by groups of men. While the Production Code assured that characters in Hollywood movies would have to express the horrors and banalities of war in a vocabulary where "darn" and "shucks" were at the outer limits of propriety, some films produced exclusively for soldiers made eye-winking acknowledgement of their actual language habits. Thus when *Army-Navy Screen Magazine* (first issued in the spring of 1943) presented the cartoon character Private Snafu, the narrator explained that "snafu" stood for "Situation normal, all fuh-, fuh-, fuh-, fuh-, fuh-," before finally concluding the phrase in the version presented to civilians, "all fouled up." Glimpses inside soldiers' living quarters in Snafu cartoons also revealed that servicemen kept pictures of women featuring full frontal nudity, which also are evident in some censored photographs of World War II barracks. Material publicly released during the war left the impression that barracks pinups never went beyond scantily clad females.

Official imagery contributed to experiential difference among soldiers as well as between soldiers and civilians. As a set for *Easy to Get,* a film made exclusively for black male soldiers, the Signal Corps constructed "a whole street duplicating a section of a Negro quarter in a southern town." In the opening sequence of this misogynic film, young corporal Baker, on leave in his hometown, romanced a sweet-looking young lady who seemed "well educated," only to discover when he got back to his base that he had gonorrhea. He admitted to the white military physician that the woman had told him she was scared of "rubbers" but that he had not worried because she "looked clean." The physician authoritatively informed the corporal that she was just a "filthy and diseased" pickup. Later during a clip of Joe Louis pummeling Max Schmeling in a heavyweight title bout the narrator proclaimed that "this massacre could not have taken place if Joe hadn't of kept himself clean."[22]

White male soldiers received a somewhat less stern and condescending message.

Throughout the war separate materials for whites and blacks followed the practice described in a meeting on government information policy early in the war: "a pamphlet for the whites and a much simpler pictorial one for the Negroes." The "VD" films for white soldiers were no more encouraging in their view of women, invariably portrayed as the disease-spreading gender, since men usually were shown catching a venereal disease rather than passing it on. It is no surprise that after viewing one such film George Baker's cartoon character Sad Sack put on a rubber glove before shaking the hand of a buddy's girlfriend.[23]

Rank also influenced the visual experience of military personnel. The weekly *Staff Film Report,* prepared for high-ranking officers, not only included strategically significant material excluded for reasons of secrecy from films prepared for those in the lower ranks, but also gave a more candid view of American death and suffering. For instance, an edition of the *Report* produced soon after the liberation of American prisoners in the Philippines included vivid and moving descriptions of their sufferings. The army deleted these accounts from newsreels prepared for lower-ranking soldiers.[24]

Status counted on the home front as well. The government and many employers tried to make industrial workers feel that they had a special mission in the war, one that united them with soldiers and set them apart from other civilians. A 1944 Army Pictorial Service film, *Men of Fire,* "made exclusively for men and women of American industry," contrasted the tough life of a soldier with the easy life of store clerks, but suggested parallels between the noise, heat, and hard work of combat and that of the factory. Other films directed at workers sought to inspire feelings of guilt as well as pride. In 1944 the Treasury Department made an especially graphic series of brief films for use in plants troubled by labor problems. One of these films, *Two and One-Half Minutes,* showed the body of an American soldier with his severed arm lying nearby and surgical probing of the tattered stump of the arm of another American soldier. The title reminded viewers of the rate at which G.I.s died. Policymakers assumed that after viewing such material during a coffee break workers would be less likely to strike or to show up late to work on Monday mornings. By the time of the Seventh War Loan campaign (May 14–June 30, 1945), when the government wished to counteract any letdown caused by German surrender and to narrow the experiential gap between soldiers and civilians, officials released even these harsh Treasury Department films for public viewing.[25]

Presentations in factories acknowledged a fundamental management-labor split. The Philadelphia stock broker Thomas A. Scott told of going to manufacturing plants with a union organizer to sell war bonds. The organizer would say, "Now, he's a stockbroker. We don't like each other, but doggone it, he's got a message for you." Then Scott would say, "I don't like him either, but doggone it, we're in this together and both sides are fighting: capital is fighting, labor is fighting, we're all fighting on the same team." In fact, Scott and the union organizer did come to like each other during their bond promotion tour, but for effect they kept up the pretense of animosity. A promotional skit based on the idea that capital and labor were separate entities with generally antagonistic interests temporarily harmonized by war could be presented to factory workers to whom the concept would come as no surprise, but not to a wider audience.[26]

Officials also acknowledged the importance of class in their internal deliberations. A survey done to evaluate the effectiveness of the early 1944 Fourth War Loan drive concluded that to people in lower income groups "the war is a great struggle in which the boys they know are taking part"; they will buy bonds because they want to bring the boys home as soon as possible. Those in "upper income groups . . . take a more sophisticated view." They were more aware of personal financial consequences and of the need for bond sales to keep inflation down. The survey's authors advised that because it was impossible to reach everyone, special attention should go to mobilizing the upper classes. They had the most money and organized and promoted the bond drives. The government did not fully adopt the proposed strategy; top officials such as Treasury Secretary Henry Morgenthau, Jr., believed in mass involvement in funding the war and structured bond drives accordingly. He argued against locating a bond sales booth at Rockefeller Plaza in Manhattan because "that's the place where they sell the most precious jewelry and . . . high price furs. . . . Those aren't the kind of people I want to reach." The major bond drives did seek to involve the largest possible percentage of the population, but in designing these drives officials acted on the assumption that class mattered, even as they distributed visual materials meant to suggest that it did not.[27]

No one denied that race mattered in 1940s America. The government aimed many images at a black audience, an effort facilitated by the existence of a widely read black press. The Office of War Information, for example, sent to black newspapers and magazines a series of story-like cartoons illustrating the careers of distinguished blacks. One featured C. C. Spaulding, who was raised on a farm, then worked as a dishwasher in Durham, North Carolina, and with few assets except "character" and "efficiency" started an insurance company, North Carolina Mutual. Spaulding, whose company had written policies worth $60 million and was "serving Negroes all over the country," was described as a major buyer of war bonds and a philosopher, and was shown sitting at his desk, in dark jacket with tie, signing an important-looking document. Some black publishers objected to this journalistic segregation, but most used the material prepared specifically for their constituencies.[28]

Other material appeared in black and in white. For the Second War Loan drive OWI distributed an advertisement showing a white soldier throwing a grenade. The agency distributed to black publications a version identical in every respect except that the soldier was a (light-skinned) black. In addition to producing some separate films for black and white soldiers, the military produced racially targeted material for civilian audiences. The

Bureau of Public Relations worked with the Signal Corps on production of "a short on Negro WAACs, to be shown in Negro theaters only, to aid colored WAAC recruitment."[29]

Government action helped create segmentation in an area where it had not existed previously. Staffers at OWI who monitored newsreels complained that the five production companies ignored black America. In November 1942, for instance, only one newsreel, produced by MGM, included a story that featured blacks. When a group of black entrepreneurs proposed founding the All-American Newsreel Company to make newsreels intended for movie theaters with predominantly black audiences, OWI encouraged them. The agency provided technical support. At a time when the government did not allow black journalists to attend most key press briefings, OWI helped the new company gain access to government facilities, film footage, and spokespersons. After OWI officials viewed the news company's first effort, "all agreed that it was a surprisingly good job." The Office of War Information continued to support the effort throughout the company's two-year life.[30]

Numerous OWI internal memos made suggestions as to how to shape the behavior of housewives, the major population group that agency analysts considered least engaged with the war. As one response to the problem, Bendix produced a patriotically ornamented laundry-room victory chart, distributed to 325,000 owners of the company's washing machines, which told women how they could serve the war effort by altering their method of washing clothes. Analysts at OWI suspected that even the federal government might have been the recipient of audience-specific visual material. They reported rumors that the movie industry furnished government reviewers with films which included material that Hollywood knew the reviewers would find to their liking, and then cut this material before distributing the films nationally.[31]

Although the war elevated nationally shared cultural values and practices over local ones, some propaganda reflected regional preferences. The Office of War Information knew from its appointed correspondents who reported on conditions around the country that local circumstances produced differing concerns and attitudes. In March 1943, for example, one correspondent reported that, in part owing to a large immigrant population from Eastern and Central Europe, "fear of Bolshevism" ran high in Chicago; whereas in Manchester, New Hampshire, the limited amount of war-related activities lead another correspondent to conclude that there "the war is remote and people feel complacent." Much of the responsibility for carrying out war bond campaigns and scrap metal drives devolved on local committees. Although they depended mainly on standardized materials prepared at the national level, they slanted their efforts in ways appropriate to their communities. With such practices in mind, for the first 1944 War Loan campaign the Treasury Department helped promote an exhibition visually honoring "the unconquerables," the inhabitants of Greece, Czechoslovakia, Poland, and other countries under German control. Although the exhibition as a whole reached general audiences, the preparation of separate posters for each of the nationalities allowed promotional campaigns especially directed at particular ethnic communities.[32]

Private companies, like the government, had neither the knowledge nor the inclination systematically to take into account ethnic and local preferences as they went about their business. But they too sometimes responded to those preferences as they devised strategies for selling their products. Newsreel companies reported that some southern theater owners deleted all footage on blacks, and in Memphis and elsewhere theater owners altered feature films "to eliminate Negroes who do not portray menial characters." Some studios allegedly produced films that could accommodate such do-it-yourself editing. According to the film historian Alan Woll, MGM so constructed *Thousands Cheer* and *Ziegfeld Follies* that exhibitors could delete performances by Lena Horne without disrupting the story.[33]

Hollywood designed few films specifically for the convenience of southern frame snippers. But movie companies regularly kept out of sight topics more controversial than a Lena Horne performance. In *Hollywood Canteen,* to emphasize the ethnic diversity of the American fighting forces, the dialogue contained the names of different soldiers who visited the canteen. The narrator mentioned that in addition to many whose families had arrived from Europe in the past one or two generations, visitors included "our own colored boys." In the film the black Golden Gate Quartet sang a lighthearted song about the war, announced plans for a barbecue in Berlin, and defined democracy as a system where all work together: black and white, tall and short, people from many different religious and national backgrounds. Working together might have been acceptable, but not dancing together. Although in actuality some white actresses whose experiences in theater had accustomed them to interacting with people of many different backgrounds defied custom and danced with black servicemen at the canteens, neither *Hollywood Canteen* nor the similar *Stagedoor Canteen* nor any other film showed racially mixed dancing at these social centers.[34]

Public officials as well as moviemakers sometimes suppressed visual materials they feared might threaten domestic unity. They turned to suppression when a topic did not lend itself to creation either of images that successfully reconciled the differing needs of a general audience or of images that safely could be directed at a particular audience. The government prevented publication of controversial material originating from sites in the United States over which it had censorship control. Thus the Office of Censorship banned publication of all photographs of the race riots that occurred on military bases in Louisiana, New Jersey, and elsewhere. The federal government also asserted its right to review all material seeking entrance from outside the country. The Office of Censorship instructed postal censors that among the imported images that should be kept out were films or photographs that put emphasis on "labor, class, or other disturbances."[35]

Military as well as postal officials used their censorship authority to obscure changes taking place in the experiences of black American soldiers. Competition over women, often a source of conflict among soldiers, became especially vicious when involving race. As a young infantry private at the end of the war, the historian David Brion Davis was shocked to find fellow American soldiers "ready to declare war on 'the God-damned black sonsabitches' who dated German girls." In 1943, when several American publications printed photographs of black G.I.s dancing with white women in England, BPR hastily ordered military censors to stop all photographs showing blacks mixing socially with white women. Early in 1945 "vigorous protest" by black troops led General Eisenhower to call for a slight modification of the restrictive policy. He agreed that publication of such photographs would "unduly flame racial prejudice in the United States," but suggested that BPR allow blacks to mail home their own photographs after censors stamped them "For personal use only—not for publication." The army refused to release pictures showing wounded members of the black 92nd Division or burials of soldiers from that unit because of "tendency on part of negro press to unduly emphasize" its achievements. It also guarded against the accreditation of black journalists "of known radical character."[36]

Attempts to present racial issues fairly were less thoroughgoing than attempts to suppress images that might disturb whites. They also met with less success. Staffers at OWI criticized Detroit newspapers for their coverage of that city's violent 1943 race riot. The papers showed by far the greatest concern for injuries sustained by whites and published photographs of only a "few Negroes injured," although more blacks had been killed and injured. When OWI representatives asked one Detroit newspaper to hand over photographs that allegedly provided evidence of "police brutality and general Nazi-storm-trooper methods," the photo editor said he could not because "the police have just subpoenaed all riot pictures." At about that time OWI's inclination to get involved in such confrontations lessened as staff members with backgrounds in corporate advertising and related fields who did not want the agency to play an activist role in race relations gained ascendancy over a liberal contingent that did.[37]

Most public and private image makers agreed that they should not call attention to profound conflicts within the country. Feature films and government shorts depicted humorous scrambles for the few available hotel rooms or apartments in the nation's crowded capital, but not bitter disputes between recently arrived workers in war industry towns and established residents who considered the newcomers trash bent on destroying their community. Before he began work with the famed Steichen photographic unit, Barrett Gallagher, an officer in the U.S. Navy, headed one of the military units that provided protection to merchant ships. Sources of tension during months-long journeys were numerous because the merchant marines who worked on these ships received ten times more pay than their military defenders. They saw no reason to forgo, at a time when shipowners were making record profits, the high wages they had won through hard bargaining.

Although not officially part of the military, merchant marines were highly vulnerable to enemy attack; during the war only the regular Marines had a higher death rate. Gallagher recalled that after the sinking of one ship, members of his unit saved themselves by remaining together and clinging to debris after civilian sailors exercised their contractual right to first claim on available rafts.[38]

This competition for life rafts was too irresolvable an example of conflict among Americans to fit into the acceptable category of all-in-fun, boys-will-be-boys rivalry. Although rich in dramatic possibilities, it was not portrayed by Hollywood or Washington during the war. Also kept out of public view was the intense rivalry among the services for press attention, as reflected in General Marshall's comment after one splendid army action that received little coverage: "Had it been a Marine Division every phase of a rather dramatic incident would have been spread throughout the United States." Hollywood films were not any more likely than government documentaries to include lines such as those spoken by General Eisenhower at a time when he was frustrated by Admiral King's resistance to coordinating army and navy operations: "One thing that might help win this war is to get someone to shoot King."[39]

The activities of Milton Stark show how intertwined government and private efforts could become. Stark, a white who owned several movie theaters with a largely black clientele and a photographic supply store in Baltimore, also worked as a "racial liaison" for the Office of Emergency Management. During the 1943 Detroit riots he reported to OWI that he was concerned because All-American News had sent cameramen to Detroit. He hoped the company would not use footage shot there in its newsreels because that "would serve only to spread further disunity and racial prejudice throughout the entire country." Stark claimed he should not have any trouble persuading the company to withhold scenes of the riot. He had talked to the company head, Edward Gluckman, who assured him "that all material in the reels will be *favorable* rather than inflammatory." Stark added, "I feel I can control this to a large degree, since contracts for the newsreel service to theaters which I control personally will represent a large percentage of the total income possibilities of the project." He exaggerated his own economic power, but Stark's position was consistent with that of others in government and business on whose support All-American was dependent. The company never ran a story on the Detroit riots.[40]

Authorities kept out of view more than images. The War Production Board used high fences to hide piles of rusting scrap metal, patriotically donated but never used, which might have cast doubt on the urgency of government collection campaigns. Officials placed detainment centers for conscientious objectors in remote sites where the prisoners could not give public witness to their objections. In the winter of 1943–44 the War Department moved convalescent soldiers from Palm Beach to central Indiana because of complaints from property owners that the sight of badly wounded soldiers prevented the resort area from performing as well as it might the task of providing civilians with needed relaxation from the stress of their wartime duties. Such actions weakened the government's credibility at the end of the war when it tried to squelch false rumors that it was keeping out of view large numbers of "basket cases," soldiers who had lost all four of their limbs. In fact, only two quadruple amputees survived their horrendous injuries. The government did successfully minimize attention to one uninspiring by-product of modern, motorized warfare: the frequency of car, truck, and other military vehicular accidents, which killed 12,000 G.I.s and left 230,000 injured.[41]

Keeping disturbing sights out of view was one way to avoid arousing fears about war's personal and social consequences. Another way was to create reassuring visual comparisons of military and home front activities. This home front analogy became the most frequently played motif in the campaign to encourage full participation in the war effort. Early in the war BPR decided to undertake a publicity campaign "to stress to the individual war worker and his family, his importance as a *soldier* of production. Definitely *identify* labor as part of America's big Army. Play up fellow soldier chum." The comparison was the easiest to achieve visually when propagandists compared riveters to machine gunners or pictured farmers on tractors next to soldiers driving mine-flail tanks, but they also used images of civilians in military dress and poses to suggest that service station attendants, bus drivers, secretaries, and housewives had a role in the fight.[42]

The home front analogy served multiple purposes. In a 1943 Kimberly Clark advertisement a soldier throws a grenade while in the dream-like background a newspaper boy, perhaps the soldier's brother or younger self, tosses a paper porchward. Association with combat duties affirmed the value of delivering newspapers and other home front tasks. The comparison of grenade-throwing to familiar activities, emphasized by the ad text, which mentioned that wood pulp was used in both grenades and newspapers, let those at home know that the "boys" in battle were not doing or experiencing things beyond their civilian imaginations. As shown by *Life*'s comparison of a dead soldier to a football player, the home front analogy also served to nudge interpretation of images in a reassuring direction. During World War I publicists had frequently used sports comparisons and other variations of the analogy. In 1918 *Stars and Stripes* described a soldier's first battle experience: "Remember how it used to be in football games?—Once you mixed into a scrimmage and got roughed up a bit your dander was up and all stage fright was forgotten. And so it is in the game of war." Images in World War II, although less egregious, served similar functions.[43]

One function was to break down perceptual habits that distanced the public from combat forces. The playwright and government information official Robert Sherwood noted when a German submarine attacked the USS *Kearney* two months before formal American involvement in the war that "this incident was taken pretty much as a matter of course by the American people who always have considered the men in their regular armed forces—Navy, Army, and, most of all, Marine Corps—as rugged mercenaries who signed up voluntarily, as do policemen and firemen, for hazardous service; it was, of course, tough luck when any of them were killed in the line of duty. . . . There was little or no self-identification of the normal American civilian with the professional American soldier or sailor." Frances Veeder, like many others who have left accounts of wartime experiences, reported that some Americans treated soldiers with contempt. She remembers one landlady who made her and her sister find new lodgings after they invited a soldier to dinner: "A lot of people looked upon the G.I.'s as dirt."[44]

Such attitudes were neither typical nor rare in 1941. They became less common over time as more and more Americans had close relatives or friends in the services. Modifications of military dress also helped civilians identify with soldiers. As late as 1939 U.S. Army troops "wore the high-collared tunic and stiff forage cap that had devolved from the formal uniforms of the nineteenth century. Then during World War II came the 'Eisenhower' jacket—a variation on standard golfing apparel—and battle dress that was a modification of the lumberjack's heavy woolen shirt. At the same time aircrew personnel began wearing baseball caps and coveralls."[45]

Blurring of visual distinctions between civilian and military also occurred on the home front. Millions of civil defense volunteers wore helmets or other visible designations of their status, and membership swelled in organizations such as the Boy Scouts which attired participants in uniforms. Some clothing manufacturers, like BVD, designed civilian clothing that bore resemblance to prestigious military attire. Campbell's Soup Company and Coca-Cola ran advertisements that emphasized the similarity between the "uniforms" worn by brand-name products and those worn by soldiers. Lucky Strike "went to war" by replacing its traditional green package (green dye was needed for military use) with one that bore a closer resemblance to the colors of the American flag. The government encouraged visual uniformity by such actions as Executive Order M-217, which to assure efficient use of resources limited colors of shoes manufactured during wartime to "black, white, navy blue, and three shades of brown."[46]

In wartime imagery, uniformity did not conflict with individuality. To emphasize the compatibility of public and individual needs, publicists tried to nurture in each citizen "a sense of *personal involvement* in the war." As part of war bond drives schools, businesses, civic organizations, and entire communities could "buy" needed military equipment by selling a sufficient number of bonds. If a school sold $15,000 in bonds, the military inscribed the name of the school on two commemorative plates. They presented one to the school and installed the other in a PT-19 Fairchild "Cornell" Primary Trainer bought by the Army Air Forces for that amount of money. On the upper extreme, organizations that sold $450,000 in bonds could personally "buy" a B-17 Flying Fortress. Individuals who wished a yet more direct sense of involvement could go to Woodward and Lothrop's Department

Store in Washington, D.C., buy a twenty-five-dollar bond, and autograph a label which would then, through arrangement with Textron Fabrics and the War Department, be put on a bomb. As a store advertisement explained, the bomb signer had a "choice of two flavors: Tokio or Berlin." The 1944 film *Justice,* prepared by the Treasury Department for the Sixth War Loan campaign, repeatedly asked viewers, "Have you killed a jap soldier today?" They could answer yes if they had bought bonds and been productive workers.[47]

Civilians often initiated opportunities to identify with the war effort. Employees of war plants proudly wore their identification badges around town and many workers of all sorts requested adoption of uniforms at their workplaces. The socially and politically prominent, some of whom held military rank although their duties were in the civilian sector, also took pride in being seen in uniform. As David Brinkley reported, among Washington's elite "of fighting age" the preferred attire "was a military uniform, preferably one deftly and artfully made by Lewis and Thomas Saltz in their men's store on G Street. Women owning neither a Red Cross uniform nor a USO Hostess button simply had to bear up." Throughout the country neighborhood groups installed public displays with lists of all those from their community in the services, and placed in their front windows "service flags" which indicated by the number of stars how many people from that home were in the military.[48]

Even Donald Duck and Mickey Mouse made the transition from entertainment figures to national symbols as they took on military and civil defense tasks. Pictorial magazines and newsreels showed prison inmates marching in military formation in support of the war effort. Unknown to the public, OWI had worked vigorously to get prisoners involved in war projects and then to secure press coverage of this evidence that war-mindedness had spread even among some of the society's most alienated members. But displays of prison patriotism were not merely government and media contrivances. Even some prisoners serving life sentences showed great enthusiasm for the chance to identify with a vital larger cause.[49]

War united generations. Many welcomed this message at a time when the age segregation produced by extended schooling and the emergence of such institutions as nursing homes marginalized the social contributions of young and old. Retirees returned to work, and youth organizations found a new sense of purpose. The Office of War Information asked the motion picture industry, because of its "incalculable influence on school-age youngsters," to help bring "every boy and girl" into the "Children's Army" made up of youngsters who pledged to advance war goals. Opportunities for intense involvement offered by the war helped lead Cavalier Ketchum to his profession of photography, although he was only eleven when the war ended. Seven members of his extended family served in the military. At his father's request, as soon as each week's *Life* arrived he examined war-related photographs in search of a familiar face (in four years he never found one). He remembers the day in September 1943 when the first photograph of American dead appeared in the magazine: he looked through the back of the page in an effort to identify the soldiers, who died lying face down on a beach.[50]

Many children without as detailed a mission shared in the heightened engagement adults felt during the war years. On the basis of hundreds of interviews that he conducted for an oral history of the period, Archie Satterfield reported that "children of the war years remember that period as the most exciting years of their lives. They remember collecting shoulder patches; watching war movies in which the Allies always won; learning hundreds of new types of planes that instantly flew overhead; reading about new tanks, half-tracks, landing crafts, and seeing these, plus planes, jeeps and artillery, going past on trains."[51]

The war also brought new opportunities to the physically disabled. A film sponsored by the Firestone Tire and Rubber Company and distributed by owi, *All Out for Victory,* showed the contributions made by "the blind, deaf, aged, crippled and other disabled workers" in war production. Civil Defense administrators made use of the special skills of blind volunteers, who served as messengers during blackouts. They advertised for deaf volunteers, whose lip-reading abilities could be called upon to aid communication in the midst of the cacophony of an enemy attack. In the 1942 Warner Brothers film *Wings of the Eagle,* as in actual practice, aircraft manufacturers employed midgets to climb into the air intake section of newly constructed planes and carry out inspections of parts inaccessible to full-sized workers.[52]

Thus many millions of Americans, young and old, in war zones and on the home front, shared the combat veteran Red Predergast's conviction that "in spite of the really bad times, it was certainly the most exciting experience of my life." In 1976, after the *Milwaukee Journal* ran a series of memoirs of World War II, Roger Detert, who had been seven years old when the war ended, wrote that even though he realized that the war itself was horrible, "I am convinced that there was such a total love, togetherness, faith in God, and feeling toward our fellow countryman, that we never again will feel in our United States." Millions of others considered the war years the most dreadful of their lives. But in either case, the war was the most intense collective visual experience in the nation's history.[53]

Vivid experiences often forced themselves on those in combat areas. The novelist and war veteran Irwin Shaw had a fictional correspondent explain that when in dangerous combat situations "I see everything much more clearly and in more detail than when I am not afraid." Shaw's correspondent recalled every shading of the tattoo on the shoulder of a sailor standing next to him when a Japanese ship made an attack on their vessel near Guadalcanal. Drawing on his service in the Pacific war, William Manchester wrote that when soldiers were stationed in battlefield areas they "learned to know the landscape down to the last hollow and stone as thoroughly as a child knows his backyard or a pet a small park." One World War I veteran reported "a fierce desire to rivet impressions even of commonplace things like the curve of a roof, the turn of a road, or a mere milestone. What a strange emotion all objects stir when we look upon them wondering whether we do so for the last time in this life."[54]

Life on the home front seldom forced such an awareness of human mortality, but it did foster habits of looking at the world in search of symbols that viewers could retain in their memories as reminders of their commitment to the war effort. The *Washington Evening-Star* described a twenty-four-window war-promotion display at the Hecht Company Department Store as worthy of being "photographed mentally." Even before Pearl Harbor, *U.S. Camera* and the British-American Ambulance Corps sponsored a contest in which they asked for photographs documenting that wherever the engaged eye looked it could find the "V" form used to predict Allied victory. The entries, which captured V's in the way a book opened and a tree branched, in the ornamentation of a cast-iron fence, and in many other familiar objects, encouraged viewers to seek out this symbol in their own daily visual experience. Even those in combat areas sometimes viewed the world through frames constructed by war imagery. The correspondent A. J. Liebling wrote that on D-Day, as he approached the Normandy beaches in a landing craft, "we could see a tableau that was like a recruiting poster: an earnest 3-man crew of 20mm rapid fire gun looking skyward, with American flag streaming in background."[55]

These ways of seeing developed in a world saturated with images. Such a world predated World War II. But the war, by further activating the visual environment and inviting everyone's participation in a common effort, created a sense that everything mattered. What went on in the kitchen was important because munitions makers could make use of saved grease. "Victory recipes" suggested imaginative ways to cook without using scarce commodities. The Office of Censorship advised amateur photographers not to take pictures that could be of potential use to the enemy, such as of coastlines or industrial facilities; everything had to be viewed for its possible relevance to the war. Even casual conversation carried special import, because "Loose Lips Sink Ships." The scene in *Thirty Seconds Over Tokyo* in which a 3:10 A.M. phone call summoned Van Johnson to report for a mission is one of many from wartime movies that reminded viewers that in this time of crisis every minute, like every word, counted. Far more often than before or after the war, films carried dedications. Metro-Goldwyn-Mayer dedicated *Journey for Margaret* (1942), the story of the flight to safe haven in America of a young girl threatened by German bombing, to the millions of Margarets around the world. In 1944 Paramount rereleased Cecil B. Demille's 1932 epic of Rome under Nero, *The Sign of the Cross,* "with a prologue in which the crew of a B-17 flying over Rome meditates on the eternal city that had managed to survive Nero, and which will certainly survive Hitler."[56]

In intensity of focus, the closest American parallels to the experience of World War II are to be found in the histories of much smaller groups. One such history is William

Bradford's account of his 1620 journey, with other Pilgrims, to New England, and of the next thirty years of life in that community of believers. In *Of Plymouth Plantation* Bradford interpreted every natural and cultural occurrence in terms of his understanding of God's plan for the Pilgrims. In such a world, to the informed eye significance was visible in all things. Bradford's contemporary, the English poet John Donne, found the cross everywhere he looked:

> Swimme, and at every stroake, thou art thy Crosse;
> The Mast and yard make one, where seas do tosse;
> Looke downe, thou spiest out Crosses in small things;
> Looke up thou seest birds rais'd on crossed wings;
> All the Globes frame, and spheares, is nothing else
> But the Meridians crossing Parallels.[57]

The visual habits Donne revealed through this poem are an example of the complete immersion in a cause which the Army's 1943 psychological handbook for officers sought to nurture: "[All] must be imbued with the spirit of the cause . . . believe in it and want it with every atom of their being." Even if most Americans did not become "war-minded" to that degree, the preponderance of evidence indicates that the Roosevelt administration was largely successful in the primary goal described at the beginning of this chapter: "to encourage widespread and enthusiastic participation in the war effort while minimizing concern over disruptions to the existing social order."[58]

This does not mean that throughout four long years of war Americans sustained a constant level of involvement. As a movie, World War II could be boring and repetitious for participants and observers. The popular war correspondent Ernie Pyle wrote to his wife during the 1943 Sicilian campaign that "it seems like I can't think of anything new to say— each time it's like going to the same movie again." A diary entry in which Wellington Wales described his daily routine in the China-Burma-India war zone indicated that not all Signal Corps picture editors worked with a constant sense of urgent mission: "at 10 each morning we'd see the 'dailies'—the films that came in from the units. The rest of the day was spent in having coffee at ten, 1½–2 hours for lunch, tea at 4, and some editing of still newspictures. And then home at five—Mohamed would be there with a drink ready when we came in the door."[59]

On the home front, propagandists found it hard to maintain the intensity of popular feeling created by the Japanese attack on Pearl Harbor. Numerous observers reported that Americans, protected by two oceans and the country's seemingly endless natural resources, were not really fighting a total war. When early in 1944 a member of the War Advertising Council visited eighteen cities to see how they responded to the Fourth War Loan campaign, he found that only Cleveland and New Orleans had managed truly striking displays of civic support. Other places, he reported, did not come up to the standards set by their annual Christmas decorations. An early report from the Office of Facts and Figures (OFF) on a town meeting in support of the war in Ontario, California, revealed mixed feelings about public displays of patriotism. The "ballyhoo" over the meeting, held in a stadium and having many of the features of a sports rally, concerned some townspeople because it reminded them of the excesses of World War I. During this earlier war, zealots painted yellow stripes on the houses of citizens they accused of not buying enough Liberty Bonds or, in at least one case, paraded them around town in a cage. Some residents of Ontario objected to the way meeting organizers used ostentatious patriotism as a weapon against internal as well as foreign adversaries. When the main speaker at the town meeting used the occasion to attack organized labor, the OFF analyst reported that he seemed to please one-half of the audience, but offended many others.[60]

Neither the speakers' use of the war for domestic political purposes nor its divisive effect were unusual. Resentments over domestic issues stirred up by the war often created feelings more intense than those produced by patriotic displays. As most Americans well understood, their views on internal issues involving ethnicity, race, class, and gender would remain central to their sense of self and perceived interests long after the Axis powers no longer posed a threat to the country. In his biting novel written soon after the war, *The Young Lions,* Irwin Shaw suggested that cynicism about the war's domestic impact was widespread: "Civilians saw too much of the cheapness of war for faith," including the "chicanery and treachery of the . . . farm bloc and the business bloc and the labor bloc." In restaurants they could see "the great boom of heavy eaters, the electric excitement and pleasure of the men and women who were making good money and spending it."[61]

Observers less critical than Shaw agreed that prejudice, greed, trivial concerns, and conflicting loyalties thrived during the war. The government chose not to publicize the fact that 70 percent of its wartime contracts went to one hundred of the nation's largest corporations. Had they done so they could have argued that these giant companies responded quickly and efficiently to massive wartime demands and spread the wealth through giving subcontracts to smaller firms. The poorest half of the population received a considerably higher percentage of family income in 1945 than in 1941. But the war made many of the rich and powerful even more so. One woman from an impoverished Texas farm family who went into war work as a teenager remembered, "you saw these people making a lot of money," and thought, "here are these special, privileged types of people and here I am working and sweating and eating our hearts out for the casualty lists that are coming in. . . . This other side had the Cadillacs and the 'I can get it for you wholesale.' They suddenly owned all the mom-and-pop stores and suddenly owned all the shoe factories." Antagonisms within the military were such that when Richard Nixon ran successfully for Congress immediately after the war his advisers told him not to wear his naval officer's uniform, as he had at his first campaign appearance, because "there were a great many more enlisted men than officers among the district's veterans, and . . . to a man the enlisted disliked the officers." Nixon took their advice.[62]

Few participants could have believed that Americans carried out their war effort with the totally unselfish, harmonious team spirit depicted in wartime ads and posters. But Americans in the 1940s were accustomed to committing themselves wholeheartedly to flawed marriages, sports teams, political parties, and religious organizations. As OWI concluded early in the war: "The public is behind the war effort. People are impatient with many details in the war's administration, alleging that *favoritism* is shown certain groups, *politics* is placed before war, *our allies* aren't all they might be. Yet fundamentally, Americans want this war won, and soon." Polls, anecdotal evidence from the time, and the memories of those involved suggest that this was the case throughout the war. Despite the contradictory messages they received and the great differences in the way their individual viewpoints led them to interpret these messages, most Americans on the home front continued to combine the roles of engrossed spectator and committed participant.[63]

Moving
Pictures

COUNT *THIS* ARMY IN !

THERE'S a trained army more than a million strong working to back up the men in uniform.

It's the army of railroad men, on duty day and night in every state in the Union.

For more than twenty years—ever since the last war ended—this army has been supplied with better and better equipment. And railroads, military authorities and shippers have worked out plans to get more service out of each piece of equipment—to get the most use out of every facility of the world's greatest transportation system.

That's why this railroad army is meeting emergency demands—why, for every minute of the day and night, it is moving *a million tons of freight a mile*—an all-time record for this or any other transportation system in the world.

All this veteran army needs, to meet future challenges, is a flow of new equipment great enough to match the rising tide of America's war production.

UNITED FOR VICTORY

ASSOCIATION OF
AMERICAN RAILROADS
WASHINGTON, D. C.

This advertisement, run in the spring of 1942 by the American Railroad Association, suggested that there was no conflict between the massive mobilization required by war and the much publicized American emphasis on individualism, and that labor and management were committed equally to the war effort and would work together harmoniously for the duration. It is the visual equivalent of a Roosevelt radio address made two weeks earlier in which he said, "Our soldiers and sailors are members of well-disciplined units. But they are still and forever individuals—free individuals. They are farmers and workers, businessmen, professional men, artists, clerks. They are the United States of America. That is why they fight."

War imagery invited citizens to consolidate their sense of purpose. This imagery linked religious and civic beliefs, love of family, friends, and place, and pride in accomplishment to the cause of winning the war. Urban spaces became huge stage sets intended to remind citizens that responding to war needs should be their preoccupation. The photograph above shows Times Square in New York fully mobilized for the Fifth War Loan campaign in the summer of 1944. In addition to special props, such as a giant cash register, the scene included everyday features of wartime life that focused attention, from men and women in uniform to flags. The theme of unity built on diversity found expression in the design of the American flag, which among the world's national emblems is striking for the large number of distinct elements forged into elegant compositional unity. It was reinforced by the Zion Kosher Meat Products advertisement, which featured a black Uncle Sam. In addition to such public spectacle, the war as presented included many intimate domestic scenes. The photograph of a woman knitting (left) gives visual expression to the wartime interpenetration of private and public experience, calling the viewer's attention both to an outside window bearing a service flag and to the home's warm interior. Cheerfully, patiently waiting there was Mrs. Emma Van Coutren of New York City, who had, as the stars on the service flag indicate, ten children in the services.

U·S·A BONDS

Third
Liberty Loan
Campaign
BOY SCOUTS
OF AMERICA

Be prepared

WEAPONS FOR LIBERTY

OURS...to fight for

Freedom of Speech

Freedom of Worship

Freedom from Want

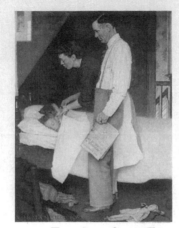

Freedom from Fear

Symbolic figures inspired by earlier traditions of heroic sculpture and representation were common in the American imagery of World War I and rare thereafter. In 1918 the government printed one million copies of a poster (left) by the popular illustrator Joseph Christian Leyendecker commemorating Boy Scout contributions to wartime fund raising. In contrast, World War II imagery usually presented Americans with images of themselves that emphasized their ordinary qualities. One of the later war's most popular images was Norman Rockwell's "OURS . . . to fight for," which appeared as both a *Saturday Evening Post* cover (Leyendecker did covers for the *Post* during the earlier war) and a government poster (above).

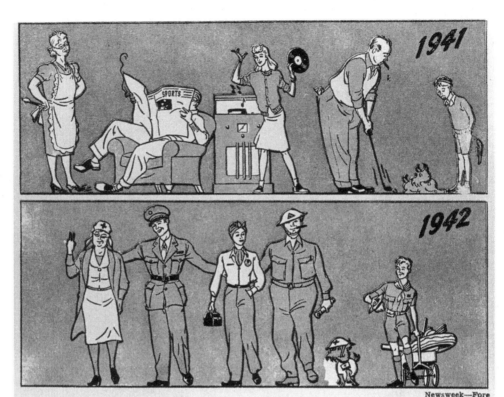

Twelve months of war transformed the American family

Newsweek—Fore

PAPER DELIVERY...1943

Remember the long-legged kid who used to deliver your paper?

He's on a different route now, delivering messages to little seed-eyed sons of heaven. But he's *still* delivering *paper!*

Wood pulp, the raw stuff of paper, is used in producing the hand grenades he hurls. It is used, too, in making plane windshields, explosives, gas tanks, stretchers, camouflage, insulation, packing material, ammunition boxes, parachute rayons, tire fabric, and many other types of matériel.

Wood fiber products are saving thousands of tons of synthetic rubber, steel, aluminum, and phenolic resins, by substituting for these critical materials.

As paper, millions of pounds of pulp are

doing the office work of war . . . 2,000,000 pounds for the first draft registration alone, 4,000,000 pounds for War Bonds sold up to May 1.

Consider the shipping keels laid daily—and think that one battleship's plans alone require 50,000 pounds of blueprint paper!

Wood pulp is indeed a vital raw material of war. And preparing it for the various requirements of our armed forces is the American paper industry's contribution to our victory.

We are proud that the production facilities of Kimberly-Clark Corporation are taking their part in this great effort . . . glad we are contributing our share toward delivering some real "smash extras" to the Axis.

KIMBERLY-CLARK CORPORATION
Neenah, Wisconsin · EST. 1872

NEW YORK: 122 E. 42ND ST. · CHICAGO: 8 S. MICHIGAN AVE. · LOS ANGELES: 510 W. 6TH ST.

In a *Newsweek* cartoon (above) uniforms helped the unfocused family of 1941 become the purposeful family of 1942, its members united in a common cause but each assigned a role deemed appropriate to his or her sex, age, and species. Putting civilians in uniform drew on one of the motifs most used by propagandists in both world wars, the home front analogy, which visually related the activities of ordinary life to those in combat zones. This technique encouraged full participation in the war effort and eased concerns about the war's personal and social impact. If throwing grenades resembled delivering newspapers, perhaps parents need not be unduly worried about sons at war (left). The Kimberly-Clark advertisement also illustrated another common feature of most wartime imagery: hoping to benefit from the unifying narrative provided by public understanding of the war, graphic artists often designed their images to resemble movie stills. Simulated motion gave images a freeze-frame quality, thus linking their message to the larger story of the war.

Wartime photographs, movies, and advertisements presented women engaged in a wider range of occupations than prewar imagery had. Viewers, however, encountered frequent reminders that the new opportunities were only for the duration of the war. The photograph of "brawny U.S. women war workers" carrying 90 mm shells which they helped test at the Aberdeen Proving Grounds was distributed by the Office of War Information with the caption "How women do men's war jobs," and female bus drivers in Washington, D.C., wore patches that stated, "I am taking the place of a man who went to war."

The series of photographs released by OWI suggesting the similarity of work performed by women in the home and factory, such as one showing Mrs. Luella Tyler washing aluminum sheets in a war plant and hanging up cotton sheets at home, could be read as an affirmation of women's industrial roles during and after the war or as a suggestion that women were suited only for those tasks which resembled domestic activities. The Eveready Battery Company ran an advertisement that showed uniformed female soldiers besieged by a mouse in their barracks. Had Eveready depicted male American soldiers frightened by rodents, the company would have become one of the war's casualties.

Carefully selected images of blacks and whites working together and of black achievements became a more familiar part of the American visual landscape during the war years. The Office of War Information distributed photographs and posters showing racial unity at the workplace (top), but the army censored photographs showing soldiers participating in integrated social activities, such as a photograph (bottom) showing the winners of a dance contest at the Red Cross Colored Club in Italy.

UNITED WE WIN

WAR MANPOWER COMMISSION · WASHINGTON, D. C.

A 1942 OWI poster (left) linked Allied victory to racial harmony, but many in government and business considered emphasis on African-American achievements a threat to national unity. In 1944 Maryland newspapers refused to run a photograph showing a black man, Dempsey Travis, as a prize-winning PX manager (above) out of fear that it would offend their readers.

Pvt. Joe Louis says_

"We're going to do our part ...and we'll win because we're on God's side"

TWICE A PATRIOT!

EX-PRIVATE OBIE BARTLETT LOST LEFT ARM—PEARL HARBOR—
RELEASED: DEC., 1941—NOW AT WORK WELDING
IN A WEST COAST SHIPYARD . . .

"Sometimes I feel my job here is as important as the one I had to leave."

The poster of Joe Louis (above) may have been the first visual image favorably depicting a black man in an aggressive position ever distributed by the U.S. government. Even the more common nonaggressive poses, as in the poster featuring Obie Barlett, had few precedents in the history of officially produced images.

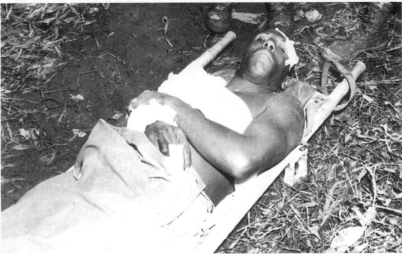

Also unprecedented and controversial were the presentation of a black head of state, Edwin Barclay, the president of the Republic of Liberia, to Congress in May 1943, his overnight stay at the White House, and the distribution of photographs documenting these events. The Roosevelts and Secretary of State Cordell Hull received Barclay (between Franklin and Eleanor Roosevelt) and Liberia's president-elect, William V. S. Tubman, upon their arrival at the White House. Photographs of wounded soldiers from African-American units, however, ended up in the files of censored material because of army resentment of an alleged "tendency on part of negro press to unduly emphasize" the achievements of those units.

The most famous American World War II photograph
draws on all the motifs that made wartime images meaningful. Like the American Railroad Association advertisement, Joe Rosenthal's photograph of a flag raising on Iwo
Jima, 23 February 1945, presents the war as a collective
effort that nonetheless allows recognition of individual
achievement. Through its exclusion of disturbing reminders
of war's destructiveness and its similarity to familiar images
of communal barn raisings, the photograph linked the
work of war with activities on a mobilized home front,
where construction of new production facilities and hous-
ing was a common sight. It achieves the mythological tran-
scendence sought in the imagery of earlier wars in the
more down-to-earth visual language of World War II.
More than any other wartime photograph, it has the appearance of a still from a motion picture.

• • • • • • • •

CHAPTER 3

War

as a

Way

of

Seeing

"THE FIRST CASUALTY when war comes," said Senator Hiram Johnson in 1917, "is truth." Senator Johnson was only half right. Governments at war use the truth whenever it serves their purposes; it is ambiguity which they find intolerable. As Jean Bethke Elshtain concluded after studying war imagery from different places and times, to think in terms of this imagery "means seeing everything as existing in a state of extreme, Manichaean reduction, which erases all intermediate hues . . . and limits everything to . . . the primordial struggle of two forces—good and evil." The political scientist Harold Lasswell, along with other influential analysts of propaganda from the first world war, argued at the outset of the second that such reductionism was especially necessary in twentieth-century conflicts involving entire populations: "So great are the psychological resistances to war in modern nations that every war must appear to be a war of defense against a menacing, murderous aggressor. There must be no ambiguity about whom the public is to hate. . . . Guilt and guilelessness must be assessed geographically, and all the guilt must be on the other side of the frontier." Numerous individuals, institutions, and circumstances counterbalanced this tendency to oversimplification. But the most widely shared feature of the innumerable visual images created in the United States during the war years was their

81

intention to present the conflict between the Allies and the Axis, and other war-related issues, in legible, unambiguous terms.[1]

To say that most of the images were intended to be unambiguous is not to say that they all communicated the same messages. They reflected the diverse viewpoints and interests of their many creators. In 1941 the government's "informational, promotional, and publicity activities" engaged the equivalent of 8,433 full-time workers, and their numbers swelled during the war, supplemented by many in the private sector engaged in similar efforts. The War Activities Committee of the motion picture industry encouraged production of visual material that publicized war needs and goals. The Graphic Arts Victory Committee, representing the manufacturers of printing materials, typographers, lithographers, and others involved in the graphic arts, insisted that their industry must "gear itself 100% to the war effort." The committee prepared a guide detailing why advertising and other printed material was "absolutely essential to the war effort" and explaining how companies could serve both their own and the country's needs through war-oriented promotional material.[2]

This diversity did not discourage attempts to give coherence to the whole. The poet Archibald MacLeish, who headed the Office of Facts and Figures before the Office of War Information absorbed it, had proposed two weeks after Pearl Harbor that one central authority oversee the output of government posters and other visual images in order to conserve materials, allow emphasis on appropriate themes, and avoid confusing or irritating the public through an excessive outpouring of unconnected messages. First OFF, then OWI, coordinated official propaganda within the limits imposed by their internal disagreements and lack of true authority. Until curtailed by funding cutbacks, every week OWI sent four cartoons on war-related subjects to approximately eight hundred newspapers and offered advice and proposed designs to others involved in production of advertisements, posters, and pictorial publications. The idea of trying to focus public attention on a particular theme remained part of OWI's plan, as when the agency asked every national magazine to run covers in September 1943 showing women doing home front war work.[3]

The Office of War Information suggested but usually depended on others to execute. A pamphlet that the agency prepared for local communities wishing to promote the Fourth War Loan advised making the campaign slogan "Back the Attack" a ubiquitous presence by stenciling it on sidewalks and the sides of buses, painting it in red, white, and blue on fire hydrants, having businesses print it on their stationery, and placing posters on factory walls, delivery trucks, telephone poles, and lampposts. The agency also encouraged towns to erect a large thermometer on which to register the community's progress toward its bond sale goal, construct a "war bond house" where visitors could admire consumer products that would be available once the war was over, and request all families to display an American flag on the first day of the campaign.[4]

Even if OWI had enjoyed enforceable authority, its staff of a few hundred could not have monitored the vast outpouring of war-related visual images. The Army Signals Corps alone produced three thousand motion pictures and distributed four hundred thousand prints of them; eventually corps films reached 8.5 million viewers each month. During the Third War Loan drive public and private sponsors and the outdoor advertising industry put fifty thousand 24-sheet poster panels on display in the "most expensive outdoor showing of all time." Continuing the theme of superlatives, the Treasury Department's director of war finance, Ted R. Gamble, told Congress in December 1943 that the war loan campaigns constituted "the greatest advertising operation in the history of the world." Treasury organized seven of these campaigns during the war and a "Victory Loan" drive after its conclusion. The Office of War Information distributed 1.5 million copies of each "normal major poster" and placed one hundred thousand messages in subways, streetcars, els, and buses each month. Fifty million viewers a week saw war information shorts produced by OWI or by the motion picture industry and shown as a public service by fourteen thousand theaters.[5]

A glut of censors further complicated the task of coordination. In addition to the major responsibilities assumed by the Office of Censorship and the military public-relations branches, more than thirty other agencies were involved in censorship of one sort or another. Private organizations also had a say about which images reached the public. The Eastman Kodak Company continued its prewar practice of refusing to process films or photographs that the company deemed to be "criminal, obscene, and subversive matter." Thus diffused authority, conflicting interests, and the sheer volume of images doomed attempts to achieve coherence through centralized authority. An imperfect coherence was achieved, nonetheless, because these images presented the world as seen through the lens of war.[6]

Americans had much to see through this lens. World War II exposed them to more other people and cultures—domestic and foreign—than any previous event of such limited duration. Exposure came through direct experience and through the mediation of words and visual images. As James Covert, who grew up during the war years, observed, "To me World War II was like a gigantic stage production. It was as if I was a character actor on a global stage, watching this huge drama unfold around me." Several million Americans, many of whom had never before been out of the counties were they were born, journeyed across the Pacific or the Atlantic to play their part in the drama. Those at home were so avid to follow their travels that orders for National Geographic maps increased 600 percent. Before one of his first major addresses on the war, President Roosevelt suggested that his radio audience use a world map for reference as he spoke. Among the dozens of wartime films that oriented viewers with maps, usually presented in the opening sequences, were *Across the Pacific, Back to Bataan, Casablanca, The Immortal Sergeant,* and *Wake*

Island. But the circumstances of wartime encounters with other cultures encouraged Americans at home and abroad to see these cultures through the narrowly focused lens of a bombsight, which reduced all things to one of two categories: that to be spared and that to be destroyed.[7]

In wartime imagery the United States destroyed only bad things. Accordingly, wartime films, photographs, posters, and comic strips celebrated the U.S. commitment to precision bombing. At the outset of *Bombardier,* a 1943 film made by RKO with assistance from the Army Air Forces, the proponent of a new bombsight amazed skeptical military officers and congressional leaders when he hit a small target from a plane flying so high that ground observers could not even see it. Viewers were assured that American technology allowed airmen to hit a barrel from an altitude of twenty-four thousand feet and dot an *i* from eighteen thousand feet. When a letter from his mother led one of the bombardier trainees to consider quitting because his activities would lead to the death of women and children, the unit leader assured him that the reverse would happen. By allowing Americans precisely to destroy enemy munitions factories, the new bombsight prevented production of truly murderous weapons.[8]

Initially American officials did strive for precision. From the outset of the war they knew they might need to form postwar alliances with some of the countries they were bombing. In a 1943 memo to "all air force commanders in combat zones" General H. H. "Hap" Arnold, head of the Army Air Forces, borrowing arguments used earlier by proponents of gas warfare, wrote that although war was always horrible, if used with precision the bomber "becomes, in effect, the most humane of all weapons." Whatever the merits of Arnold's reasoning, precision bombsights meant little when bombers were under enemy attack and smoke from earlier bombings obscured targets. Although in many cases American bombardiers hit specific targets, on the average American bombs dropped on visible targets hit only within a 1200-yard range (two-thirds of a mile), a large-enough variation to eliminate distinctions between schools and factories or between private houses and military barracks. When darkness or weather required use of radar for sighting, the range expanded to two miles. Given these limitations, and consistent with the practices of other major belligerents, American policymakers routinely designated large urban areas, rather than specific installations, as primary targets. By war's end the most common method was the use of incendiaries to ignite kindling created by dropping conventional bombs on densely built-up regions.[9]

Visual misrepresentation of the nature of Allied bombing led to misrepresentation of its consequences. American movies often showed the Axis powers using bombs against civilian populations. In *Thirty Seconds over Tokyo* Japanese pilots strafed a crowd of Chinese children, as they did in the 1945 film *God Is My Copilot,* where the children were accompanied by a priest. In another film from that year, RKO's *China Sky,* a hospital became one of the main recipients of Japanese bombs (American filmmakers granted the Japanese a high degree of precision in their bombing efforts when the targets were humanitarian institutions). In contrast were cartoons and animated features depicting American bombing, such as Walt Disney's 1943 *Victory through Air Power*. They gratified viewers with spectacular scenes of bombs destroying enemy munitions plants but excluded human bodies, or parts of bodies, from the debris that soared skyward after the invariable direct hit. The dialogue of some films acknowledged that American bombs killed many civilians. In *Thirty Seconds over Tokyo* bomber pilots expressed concern to one another that this was one of the grim, unavoidable consequences of the job they must do. The film did not show any of these casualties. When, as in *Bombardier,* wartime films did show the victims of American bombs, they always made it clear that they were enemy soldiers or male war workers. In reality the choice to focus the American bombing effort on German and Japanese population centers assured that a large majority of those killed would be women, children, and the elderly.

Many films and magazine features emphasized the care that went into the planning of American bombing missions in order to maximize military damage and minimize nonmilitary casualties. None portrayed activities like those undertaken by the U.S. Army Chemical Warfare Service to develop incendiary bombs designed to cause unstoppable fires. Planning included testing the bombs against mockup German and Japanese towns and urban working-class districts built at proving grounds within the United States, complete with "curtains, children's toys, and clothing hanging in the closets." In some of the tests "teams of firefighters were brought in to quell the blaze with methods the Japanese would use." The tests indicated that when used against actual targets, the " 'fires would sweep an entire community' and cause 'tremendous casualties,' " as indeed they did. Also completely invisible in wartime films were the actions of those crews which, failing to drop their bombs over a planned site and understandably not wishing to land with bombs on board, dropped them on whatever landscape they happened to pass over on the way back to base, even if it was the French countryside. [10]

Especially during the war's final months newspapers, newsreels, and magazines did show aerial views of entire cities that had been devastated by American bombs. Captions often gave them such designations as "urban industrial area." An editorial cartoon in the *Atlanta Constitution* that depicted bodies flying into the air after the bombing of Hiroshima carried the title "Land of the Rising Sons." Such captions helped distance viewers from the human meaning of the bombings, as did showing the cities as they appeared when viewed literally through a bombsight, a technique used in films made for war workers and war loan organizers. Often films would further distance viewers from the violence of battle by depicting it through allegorical graphic animation. *Victory through Air Power* represented the war in the Pacific by an American eagle attacking a malicious octopus that had stretched its tentacles into areas where they did not belong. Such imagery seemed to have had an effect. One American who was in college during the war years said that he "had never thought of the people in bombed cities as individuals" until he read John Hersey's *Hiroshima,* a vivid account, published a year after the event, of the experiences of a half-dozen people who were in the Japanese city on August 6.[11]

Several filmmakers expended special effort to make the American planes that delivered the bombs seem warm and friendly to movie audiences. In *Thirty Seconds over Tokyo,* when a pilot learned while flying his B-25 that his wife was going to have a baby, the crew started singing "rock-a-bye-baby" and the film cut to an external view that showed the plane gently rocking from side to side as it flew. In *Sunday Dinner for a Soldier* (1944) a plane on the way to a bombing mission made a marriage proposal, signified by the tipping of a wing as the aircraft flew over the home of the aviator's beloved. This visual sanitation of American bombing had its verbal equivalent in President Harry S Truman's statement, as he announced the use of the atomic bomb against the populous Japanese city of Hiroshima on August 6, 1945, that the target had been a "military base." And it was—as were Chicago, New York, and London. Only a small fraction of the more than one hundred thousand people who died at Hiroshima were in the Japanese military.[12]

It is hardly surprising that neither government officials nor private citizens who created and selected images wished to call public attention to the indiscriminate destruction that accompanied modern warfare. Those in similar positions made similar decisions during World War I, and the governments of every other major participant in World War II controlled the flow of visual images at least as tightly, although they often made different decisions as to what to show. Early in the war, for purposes of intimidating the populations of other countries, official German films showed some of the dreadful results of resistance to German occupation. Soon after its involvement in the war began, the Soviet government released pictures of some of that country's war dead, a decision reflecting different cultural traditions concerning death and the need to rally a population under a direct German assault that made keeping war death out of sight an impossibility in many parts of the country.

Nor is it surprising that propagandists consistently depicted the enemy as evil. Indeed, polarization reached the extreme of suggestions that the enemy belonged to a separate species. Americans almost always targeted such propaganda at the Japanese, whom movies and other media usually had presented unfavorably in the prewar decades. Wartime imagery compared them to rats, monkeys, snakes, and vermin. Among the thousands of such visual comparisons were the covers of *Time* and *Collier's* depicting Japanese soldiers as apes, and a float in a mammoth New York parade that included the American eagle "leading a flight of bombers down on a herd of yellow rats which were trying to escape in all directions." Military authorities censored photographs showing American soldiers treating wounded Japanese soldiers, perhaps because these images of one human being helping another blurred the visual distinctions considered necessary to a win-the-war attitude. John Dower noted in his study of the imagery and reality of the American-Japanese conflict, *War without Mercy,* that "as late as February 1945 the Pentagon was still blue-penciling scripts on the grounds that the passages in question would evoke 'too much sympathy for the Jap people.' " Such policies, as well as cultural prejudices and the desire to revenge Pearl Harbor, help explain why close to half of all American soldiers agreed with the statement "I would really like to kill a Japanese soldier," but less than one in ten agreed when the soldier to be killed was German.[13]

Axis leaders became better known visually than any American political figure except the president. Caricatured faces of the Japanese emperor Hirohito and general Tojo (prime minister for most of the war), the Italian leader Benito Mussolini, and, most often of all, Adolf Hitler, scowled at Americans from the walls of train stations, from the sides of postal trucks, and from movie screens and comic strip panels. *Variety* reported early in the war that the government believed Americans would be "better haters" if not led by this emphasis (visual and otherwise) on enemy leaders to "the false idea that the enemy is a bunch of poor, misguided people who deserve more pity than bullets and bombs." But government spokespeople disagreed among themselves on the issue. A directive from OWI's Bureau of Motion Pictures to Hollywood filmmakers instructed them that "this country does not regard the German and Japanese people as our enemies, only their leaders."[14]

The Office of War Information warned of the dangers of negative imagery. Assertions of Japanese racial inferiority, in addition to undercutting claims of the high moral standards of the American war effort, would offend Asian allies. They might add to the already significant number of American blacks who in polls expressed some sympathy with the viewpoint that the most fundamental division in the Pacific war was between whites and people of color. United States officials wanted Asians to regard Americans as liberators, not conquerors, and knew that the Japanese were trying to undercut this effort by making propagandistic use of films and other documents that gave evidence of American racial bigotry. For these reasons, in an "urgent note" to all those involved in the Sixth War Loan campaign of late 1944, OWI advised that the Japanese should be described as brutal but not as slimy; cruel rather than bestial; tough and wanton instead of toothy; scheming, fanatical, and ruthless rather than rat-like, yellow, and slant-eyed. Because of such concerns, the Marines disavowed a "license for hunting Japs" distributed by their recruiters in Chicago. Yet for the Seventh War Loan campaign the following spring the War Department produced for public viewing the film *Action at Anguar,* which had the narrator speak this line as viewers saw actual footage of Japanese soldiers burning alive: "By this time we had shot, blasted, or cooked six hundred of the little apes." As this example from one of the government's own films suggests, policymakers had little more success overall in eliminating racially based imagery than advocates of precision bombing did in keeping American aerial attacks restricted to military targets.[15]

This dichotomized way of seeing linked images Americans devised of the enemy with those they devised of themselves. If the enemy was treacherous, cowardly, and heartless, Americans were fair, courageous, and caring. The enemy won only when they had great numerical superiority; when Americans won it always was by overcoming odds against them. The enemy was militaristic; Americans were reluctant to go to war but, like Sergeant York, invincible once aroused. Thus every war movie had at least one Pearl Harbor–type deceitful attack; the most heroic, effective, and unceasing American actions almost always came in response to some enemy outrage.

German Nazism, Italian fascism, and Japanese militarism supplied enough actual outrages to satisfy the needs of any propagandist. Repressive Axis policies invited emphasis on the contrasting diversity and openness of American life. Films in Frank Capra's *Why We Fight* series, for instance, showed authorities conditioning German children and Japanese soldiers to respond like automatons to their dictates, then showed Americans retaining their distinctive ethnic, religious, regional, political, and occupational identities even as they merged into an effective fighting force. A dominant theme of the images America presented to itself during the war years was that these individual differences led to stimulating variety but never to profound conflict.

Enter Brooklyn. No other community, not even the much-depicted nation's capital, so frequently played a supporting role in wartime movies. The role was always the same. William Bendix and other Brooklynites established the fact that Americans were a diverse but compatible group. They sounded different, had different experiences while growing up, and had unique concepts of geography and politics. These differences set up confrontations with fellow soldiers that were often comic but sometimes the source of dramatic tension, and always resolved in mutual understanding and self-sacrificing brotherhood by the end of the film.

The tradition that every war film have at least one soldier from Brooklyn was in fact a realistic touch. Approximately 327,000 from that borough served in World War II, and seven thousand died. It also allowed filmmakers to introduce another favorite symbol of American diversity: spectator sports. Soldiers from Brooklyn who were not fans of baseball's Brooklyn Dodgers were less common in wartime films than Japanese soldiers whose faces expressed a genuine emotion other than hate or fear. Avid as their commitment to the Dodgers was, it did not prevent larger commitments to their region and their country. In *Guadalcanal Diary* Bendix rooted for the New York Yankees to beat the Saint Louis Cardinals in the World Series because the Yankees had a claim on his hometown loyalties once the Dodgers were out of the running. More generally, Bendix's love of baseball, the "national pastime," was one demonstration of his Americanism. His sports enthusiasms were an acceptable way to show the love he had for his country, which he could not express directly without seeming corny.[16]

Service rivalries played a role similar to that of sports rivalries. Whereas censors typically suppressed accounts of actions by Americans in one service that threatened lives of those in another, in the movies soldiers and sailors who got into a fist fight in Act One saved each other's lives in the finale. Although never spelled out in government guidelines, an invariable rule prevailed in all wartime films: if a member of one service insulted another service, before the film ended some action had to take place that specifically disproved the charge made in the insult. In treating civilian life, wartime movies generated dramatic tensions through disputes between store clerks and querulous customers, teachers and students, cops and the public, and romantic rivals. But unless the unfolding of the plot revealed one of the disputants to be a truly bad person, differences among Americans were the surface that when scratched revealed an underlying similarity of values.[17]

The same applied to interactions between Americans and foreign allies: differences in language and behavior could lead to humorous misunderstandings but not to unrelenting hatred or contempt. Neither Hollywood films nor newsreels depicted the type of virulent conflict William Manchester described in his memoir of the Pacific war. Manchester explained that in one encounter between American and Australian troops "imprudent G.I.s mocked the Diggers, promising to lay every Aussie woman, married or not. Shots were exchanged—some men were actually killed." Equally unacceptable were depictions of deaths and injuries of American soldiers caused by self-inflicted wounds, racial conflict, government blunders, misdirected "friendly fire," or the contrivance of fellow soldiers, who sometimes found ways to place intensely disliked members of their units in situations likely to cost them their lives.[18]

The persistence of the happy ending in some of the bleakest Hollywood war stories demonstrated the strength of forces bending wartime imagery into polarized patterns. The convention of a happy ending had reigned for decades before the war, but under different circumstances the war might have presented a severe challenge to it. The unconventional endings of some postwar *film noir* productions might be seen as a delayed response to just such wartime challenges, but more often ways of seeing encouraged by the war helped entrench the tradition of a happy ending, as in the contrived conclusions of *Happy Land* and *The Fighting Sullivans*. Sometimes the widely known facts of contemporary events required a deferred happy ending. In *Wake Island* and *Bataan,* although all American defenders were dead, captured, or about to be killed at the end, no viewer could doubt that their heroic resistance would contribute to the victorious outcome of the war. *Bataan* closed with a vision of the Americans captured there marching out of captivity with worn but determined and thankful looks on their faces. Consistent with the movement toward less evasive imagery as the war progressed, the number of films with somber endings increased, but all suggested that whatever the war's costs, all was for the best. At the end of the 1944 film *Tender Comrade* Ginger Rogers was in grief after having received word of the death of her husband in the war; but with their baby, Chris, as an uncomprehending audience, she explained that his sacrifice was worthwhile because it would make a better world for Chris. A tough film from the war's last year, *Pride of the Marines,* though it conveyed much of the terror, pain, and emotional agony suffered by blinded Marine hero Al Schmid, intimated at the end not only that his life was enriched by a perfect love, but that his sight might be returning. Hollywood did not make up this ending; the real Schmid returned to his prewar sweetheart and did recover some vision in one eye. But that was part of the reason Warner Brothers chose to film his story.[19]

In most cases the government neither encouraged Hollywood to concoct happy endings nor worked them into officially produced material. Indeed, OWI and other agencies guarded against creating within the public the expectation that each of their personal segments of the shared war story would have painless outcomes. Perhaps to avoid stirring false hopes among the hundreds of thousands of other American families who would not enjoy a miraculous reversal of the bad news they had received, BPR did not release a photograph showing the joyous reunion with his family of a coastguardsman erroneously reported killed. Nonetheless the government's wartime messages, like those of Hollywood, suggested that neither the war nor the conditions of American life presented citizens with situations for which the probable outcome was a tense, imperfect, temporary resolution, rather than a satisfying and definitive one.[20]

The sharpest challenge to maintenance of clear distinctions between allies and enemies required by polarized wartime ways of seeing came from the presence in the country of a few hundred thousand Asian-Americans. Henry R. Luce, born of missionary parents in China, was especially concerned lest Americans confuse residents of Japanese and Chinese ancestry. Shortly after Pearl Harbor the magazines he published, *Time* and *Life,* ran detailed, illustrated articles, based on highly dubious assumptions about connections between ethnicity and behavior as well as appearance, on "How to Tell Your Friends from the Japs." Filmmakers found easier ways of identifying the ethnic affiliations of characters so that the audience could sort out good and bad. Among the onlookers at a military parade depicted in *Shores of Tripoli* was a spectator who waved an American flag and wore a sign that said, "Me Chinese." Newsreels featured stories such as "Chinatown Hails Captured Jap Sub" to emphasize the difference.[21]

Not even the Constitution could restrain the imperative to maintain clear distinctions between enemy and ally. The government violated at least half of the ten amendments comprising the Bill of Rights with its decision to remove Americans of Japanese ancestry, the majority of them U.S. citizens, from the communities where they lived and worked, and to place them in guarded camps in sparsely inhabited areas of the West. This move was dictated primarily by political expediency (the action won widespread approval) and fears, later discredited, of espionage. Other reasons for this action included concern over violent attacks on Japanese-Americans by hostile neighbors, and the greed of some of these same neighbors, who because of the relocation were able to buy at greatly reduced prices much of the detainees' property. But a consequence of the relocation was removal of 110,000 living reminders that the bestial Japanese faces that glowered from wartime posters and cartoons did not tell the whole visual truth.[22]

The government acknowledged visual motivations for its actions. An OWI bulletin sent to the motion picture industry emphasized that Japanese-Americans were sent to relocation centers partly because they "*look like* our Japanese enemies." Relocation actually complicated the types of visual distinctions Luce had tried to maintain. Because it placed actors of Japanese ancestry behind barbed wire, it assured that the omnipresent Richard Loo and other Chinese-American actors would be cast in roles such as the interrogating Japanese general in *Purple Heart*. It also meant that when Twentieth-Century Fox filmed *Little Tokyo, U.S.A.*, it used neon signs in Los Angeles's Chinatown as a substitute for those in that city's Japanese business and entertainment district, which had been darkened by the internment. But most moviegoers probably were unaware of these inconsistencies. Because relocation was more about perceived threats and differences than about substantive ones, it helped maintain the wartime illusion of clear distinctions.[23]

Many Americans resisted this compulsive wartime need to suppress ambiguity. If one purpose of the Allied effort was to allow people to make informed choices about their own destinies, then among the war's heroes were journalists, entertainers, artists, and public officials who used visual means to open up an honest dialogue on the war's nature and meaning. For those who sought to give firsthand reports on the conflict, the dangerous undertaking of getting in a position to be able to see and record the war was just the beginning of the process. This often required lugging cumbersome equipment over mountainous or swampy terrain or through jungles that posed a variety of threats, including temperature extremes that wreaked havoc with photographic chemicals. As the British photographer Michael Lewis recalled, "When you're lying on the ground, you only know what's happening immediately around you, maybe a couple of hundred yards." From that position "you have a lot of experience of shellfire, of gunfire, of fighting at a distance—an enemy you hardly ever see. It's mostly sound anyway . . . not like the films one sees everyday . . . where the viewer is in the position of God." Other cameramen noted it was "almost impossible" to film battles effectively when it involved "one man . . . shooting one way and another man shooting the other way" and that "people fighting obviously want to be invisible if possible." When commissioned to film the North African campaign in 1942,

Hollywood producer Darryl Zanuck also took note of the difficulty of capturing the visual manifestations of war, remarking that "I don't suppose our war scenes will look as savage and realistic as those we usually make on the back lot."[24]

Adding to physical and technical difficulties were bureaucratic and political ones. Professional photographers accredited to military units sometimes found themselves treated as outsiders. The *Life* correspondent Robert Landry complained while covering the African campaign that "the Signal Corps men and Yank Mag. photo man are doing all the covering and the pool men get nothing." He reported the "general feeling and usual gossip" was that "they do not welcome us as private photogs and would feel a lot better if we were either not here or in the Army." Official military photographers had their own problems, since especially early in the war they received little training for their demanding task. The official military history of the Signal Corps summarized the photographers' status this way: "Too often through all ranks and grades the photographic mission was an irritating gadfly—sometimes to be slapped down, more frequently to be brushed away, and often merely to be ignored." Whatever their status, most photographers reported that the longer they were with a unit and the more they shared with the men the war's hazards and tedium, the more fully they were accepted and the more cooperation they received.[25]

Even the most respected could not evade omnipresent censors. The artist George Biddle, who spent months in the field making drawings of the war, reported that photographers, knowing that "unpleasant material is censored," did not take such shots because "photographers don't waste their plates on censorable material." But some of the war's most effective photographers, including Carl Mydans, Ralph Morse, and Barrett Gallagher, recalled that they did not let this influence them. Although they received few guidelines from the military, they knew fairly well what was likely to be acceptable and what not. Mydans even learned through the grapevine while in a Japanese prison camp early in the war, before a prisoner exchange allowed him to return to work, that the U.S. government was withholding pictures of American dead. Despite such knowledge, the three took whatever pictures seemed most important to them, and hoped that eventually their best pictures would find viewers. Censors were not the only obstacles. Morse complained that most managing editors were more responsive to the concerns of the business and legal offices next to their own than to photographers in distant lands, and lacked "guts" when it came to pushing for publication of potentially controversial material.[26]

One difficulty surpassed all these others: finding ways to communicate the enormity of the experience of war. Innumerable veterans insisted in memoirs and interviews that those who were not there could not really understand this experience. It encompassed more than the obvious horrors. It included aggressive impulses raised then given no outlet during long stretches of waiting with no clear-cut action. It involved encounters with a wide range of distinctive smells, sounds, and other sensations, some the result of living in inexpressible filth. Communicating truths about the pain and death of war presented Americans with a particularly difficult challenge. Their culture had no common language of visual communication for dealing with these phenomena, which seldom received frank discussion or straightforward portrayal in peacetime society.

For a century before War Department personnel established the Chamber of Horrors, death had been drifting toward the periphery of American visual experience. During the nation's early years almost all Americans died at home, where members of the family prepared them for burial. By 1941 increasing numbers of Americans died in hospitals. The practice of using professional "funeral directors" to prepare a corpse for viewing had spread from the upper middle-class enclaves in the Northeast, where it took root in the mid-nineteenth century, to become common practice in urban areas, where the majority of the population lived. Moreover, this farm-to-city population shift, along with the disappearance of the horse as an urban beast of burden, reduced visual encounters with the death of large animals. The spread of photography in the United States after 1839 at first led to the common practice of making photographic records of loved ones within hours of their demise. Soon, however, this new medium, through its offshoot of the 1890s which set images in motion, was employed more often to bring Americans images of strangers simulating death—albeit strangers whose visual presence became familiar as they attained the status of movie stars. These stylized images of death proved inadequate to convey the sights of modern war.[27]

The incomprehensible scale of the carnage compounded the problem. War linked the histories of mass production and mass destruction. During the American Civil War the concept of a "billion" first entered the language of production, when Secretary of War Edwin M. Stanton estimated Union needs at 1,022,176,474 short-arm cartridges. Even before the development of manufacturing techniques that made possible such ten-digit requisitions, humanity had shown a marked talent for destroying life and property, as in the Thirty Years War (1618–1648), which eliminated half of the population and most of the livestock, towns, and buildings of large regions in Central Europe. Not until World War I, however, did "tens of millions" become a useful unit for measuring obliteration of human lives during a short time period, with 20 million killed during its four years, when all participants applied their most advanced industrial and organizational techniques to the manufacture of one commodity, corpses. With the toll reaching 50 million during the six years of World War II, photographers and other visual artists and reporters had to deal with their version of a problem recognized earlier in the century by the French writer Philippe Berthelot: "When a man dies, I suffer; when a million and a half die, that's statistics."

The ability of combat to redefine the meaning of ordinary experiences created another barrier to communication. One soldier told the photographer Margaret Bourke-White that he had "come to hate moonlight . . . ever since my best friend was killed on a moonlight night." Many World War II combat veterans came to associate lush green fields of grass with maiming land mines. Thus "for years after the war, ex-soldiers seized up when confronted by patches of grass and felt safe only when walking on asphalt or concrete." World War I had elicited many similar responses. Before becoming one of the twenty thousand British soldiers killed on the first day of the 1916 battle of the Somme, Second Lieutenant William Ratcliffe had written to his parents, "Everywhere the work of God is spoiled by the hand of man. One looks at a sunset and for a moment thinks that that at least is unsophisticated, but an aeroplane flies across, and puff! puff! and the whole scene is spoilt by clouds of shrapnel smoke." World War I made such transformations a staple of contemporary literature, but visual records of that war seldom expressed such complexities.[28]

Dead animals were one of those complexities. Repeating Ernest Hemingway's reactions in the earlier war, during World War II the artist George Biddle reported with surprise that one of the things which affected him most was the sight of such innocent victims of the slaughter. An RAF pilot's account of what he saw at Normandy after D-Day suggests the immensity of the task facing Biddle and others who wished to express visually their experiences: "The roads were choked with wreckages and the swollen bodies of men and horses. . . . Strangely enough it was the fate of the horses that upset me most. Harnessed as they were, it had been impossible for them to escape, and they lay dead in tangled heaps, their large eyes crying out to me in anguish." Seven years earlier Picasso had painted *Guernica,* a rare pictorial counterpart to this written description. Artists and visual journalists had few viable guides as they struggled to communicate the overwhelming experiential reality of World War II.[29]

The resources they brought to this challenge varied dramatically. Bourke-White needed first of all persistence and determination to break into the otherwise all-male fraternity of American war photographers. She then needed courage to venture onto the streets to record the sights of Moscow under bombardment despite hazards posed by enemy artillery and Soviet war ministry orders to shoot on sight anyone outside after curfew. She had developed the courage in part through her habit of seeking out the highest and most precarious vantage points for making her striking photographs of New York and other cities. Through a lifelong interest, nurtured by her father, in industrial processes, she also had developed the ability to capture in the same image both the beauty and the potential brutality of modern technology, an ability that served her well as she captured the visual contradictions of contemporary warfare.[30]

Birthplace, not gender, made Robert Capa an outsider. Using bluff and deceit when necessary, the Hungarian-born photographer overcame the bureaucratic problems that resulted from his lack of American citizenship. Richard Whelan, his biographer, credits

Capa's multitalented Polish colleague David Szymin with teaching Capa that "although a photojournalist has to be aggressive, and even callous, in order to get into position to take the most dramatic photographs, all his efforts will be wasted unless, at the actual moment of taking his picture, he can replace his boldness with sensitivity and tenderness." Drawing on this insight, confirmed by his experiences while covering the Spanish Civil War, and following his own dictate to get as close as possible to the front, Capa created some of World War II's most powerful images.[31]

Carl Mydans' years in a Japanese prison camp, along with his experience documenting Depression hardships as a Farm Security Administration photographer under Roy Stryker's tutelage in the 1930s, no doubt increased his awareness of the impact of war on the individual. His photographs from the war's later years were compelling human documents which reminded viewers that suffering crossed national, class, and racial boundaries. Ralph Morse, twenty-four at the time of Pearl Harbor, showed both stamina and patience when he sought out the most active combat areas. In the last year of the war he produced one of its most moving photographic essays. Almost all pictures of the American wounded showed them receiving care in the field or being transported for further treatment in a hospital, or depicted them convalescing in a hospital. In his essay on George Lot, Morse connected these different images and gave viewers a sense of the prolonged agony the wounded often faced. He was with Lot when he was shot and recorded his initial shocked reaction, then documented the months of painful treatment.[32]

Morse's youthful energy enlivened his photography. Others brought decades of training to the task. Edward Steichen, initially a painter, had helped Alfred Stieglitz introduce modern art to the country in the years before World War I. The two also had done much to advance the cause of serious photography, although Stieglitz later criticized Steichen for using his photographic skills to serve the advertising and public-relations needs of major business corporations. Early in World War II Steichen assembled a small group of skilled, mainly young but promising photographers who received navy commissions and orders to travel freely within the combat zones to record the most important aspects of the naval war. Through their example they helped improve the performance of many of the navy's four thousand other photographers.[33]

John Ford served a similar role for other navy filmmakers. He did some of the most impressive work of his career in the three years before Pearl Harbor, directing *Stagecoach, The Young Mr. Lincoln, The Grapes of Wrath,* and other distinguished films. Commissioned as a naval officer during the war, Ford was seriously wounded while filming *The Battle of Midway,* one of the first wartime documentaries to show viewers in a coherent way the incoherence and relentless unpredictability of battles as perceived by those in the midst of them. In his film *They Were Expendable,* begun for Metro-Goldwyn-Mayer in the war's final months but not completed and released until three months after Japanese surrender,

Ford showed a sensitivity to the anxieties facing those in combat, whatever rank and whether allied or enemy, which was absent from films released in the first few years of the war.

These and other American creators of powerful and revealing war images were as varied in personality as were those who made distinct military contributions. Capa and the filmmaker John Huston often used Patton-like bluster to get their jobs done; the cartoonist Bill Mauldin, in the manner of General Omar Bradley, accomplished the same through more low-key but no less determined persistence. Capa traveled lightly; Margaret Bourke-White needed at least one assistant to keep her supplied with changes of clothes and cameras. Like the soldiers whose experiences they recorded, most found that their efforts were sometimes hampered by their fear of physical danger or personal failures, but these concerns were outweighed by the strong loyalty they developed toward those with whom they directly shared the dangers and hardships of war.

They had strong beliefs but did not allow them to trample over their encounters with experience. The beliefs, whether political, aesthetic, moral, religious, or some combination thereof, provided them with motivation, determination, and sensitivity to particular issues. They served as a lens focusing their observations, but not as a shutter censoring them. These men and women displayed what the English poet John Keats, writing about Shakespeare, had described as "negative capability," the capacity to acknowledge life's contradictions and uncertainties without pretending to have a definitive explanation of how everything fit together. How else to respond honestly to a war that was so necessary for Americans after December 7, 1941, and that caused such unfathomable suffering?

Those who rejected polarized ways of seeing war could incorporate a revealing sense of irony into their visions. Totalitarian states and conventional American propagandists used irony as a weapon of war. An example of this commonplace use of irony came in the film *Bombardier* when Japanese soldiers used a stretcher whose markings indicated clearly that it had been donated by the United States when Japan needed medical assistance at the time of the 1923 Tokyo earthquake. This was not the irony of self-reflection, but merely added ingratitude to the list of the enemy's sins. When a Paramount newsreel told how thread spun by the black widow spider had proven to be the ideal material for making the crosspiece for American bombsights, the narrator told the story with the unqualified enthusiasm accorded all American technical advances during the war, again without any self-reflexive irony.[34]

John Huston's 1945 film *San Pietro* offered a contrast. Early in this U.S. Army documentary he recites from a prewar guidebook that called attention to San Pietro's beautiful old church. As Huston read, the camera showed the viewer that as a result of the German occupation and American assault on this seven-hundred-year-old Italian village, the church had been reduced to an empty, half-broken shell. The film, a powerful tribute to the American soldier, made clear that modern combat required destroying many things that the war was fought to preserve. *San Pietro* acknowledged cinematically the contradictions Huston later stated in discussing the film: "Nobody ever wanted to kill Germans more than I did. And I thought it was anti-war to do it, in order to stop Hitler."[35]

Irony reminded viewers how easily human actions could lead to unexpected outcomes. Images that documented limitations on the ability of humans to predict and control thereby acknowledged the limitations present in all human products, including the images themselves. Photographers and filmmakers who felt compelled to communicate such complexities could find allies in government. Elmer Davis thought that most of the public, like most soldiers, were moved not by "flag-waving" patriotism but by their recognition of the war as "something grim, unpleasant, but unavoidable" which they wanted to end as soon as possible. Davis's lack of government experience, influential allies, and clear-cut authority often hampered his efforts to translate his convictions into official policy. Davis took the job in partial awareness of these difficulties. Like a soldier going into battle, he could not fully appreciate the obstacles until he encountered them firsthand.

Initially Roosevelt proposed to his press secretary, Stephen Early, that he become director of OWI. Because of his close personal relationship with the president, Early would have brought much more clout to the position than did Davis. Roosevelt was not even sure of Davis's name when he decided to appoint him after Early declined, but he had been impressed by qualities captured in David Brinkley's description of him: "a former New York *Times* reporter, writer, and since the war began a commentator on CBS radio and among the best on the air. He spoke in tight sentences and a dry, nasal Indiana twang. When he offered to take speech lessons to eliminate it, CBS was wise enough to refuse." Davis eventually became so frustrated by the often successful resistance to his attempts to make wartime news more forthright that he concluded, "Large elements in Congress and the public were willing to fight for victory but wanted to be very sure that the struggle was not contaminated by any moral principles." Davis could not place full blame on Congress or the military for inadequacies in public understanding of what he called the "people's war." Surveys by OWI and his many years as a newsman convinced him that some of the "people" detested each other intensely, and that some wartime decisions benefited narrow corporate interests rather than the commonwealth, but he showed little inclination to call attention to these particular truths. Nonetheless, the well-founded reputation for integrity that brought Davis to the OWI directorship gave him leverage which he sometimes used to make the "strategy of truth" more than rhetoric.[36]

The man who appointed Davis deserved part of the credit for his successes and bore part of the responsibility for his failures. To confidants Franklin D. Roosevelt revealed unapologetically that "I am perfectly willing to mislead and tell untruths if it will help us win the war." Not all of his deceptions served easily defensible political and military purposes. He shielded himself from some categories of disturbing information: he showed little interest in reports on conditions in black communities or in the Japanese relocation centers created under his authority. He shielded the public from even more, giving credence to the charge of Elmer Davis's friend, the historian and columnist Bernard DeVoto, that Roosevelt sometimes acted as if he believed that "the people are dumb."[37]

Near the end of the war the president's staff refused a request that he mention his own physical disability by way of introducing a government film made to assist in the return to normal life of soldiers who had lost legs or arms. These staff members acted in a way consistent with his strongly stated preference. Throughout his long presidency photographers honored his wish that they not depict him in a way that revealed that he wore heavy braces on his legs and needed a wheelchair or other assistance when he moved about. The Secret Service confiscated the film of those who did not comply. Roosevelt was not indifferent to the fate of injured soldiers. In his direct contact with them he was caring and open. He revealed the devastation wreaked by the polio that had nearly killed him a decade before his election as president. When visiting an amputee ward in the fall of 1944 he "insisted on going past each individual bed . . . because he wanted to display himself and his useless legs to those boys who would have to face the same bitterness."[38]

Roosevelt had a unique opportunity to support them in another way. The greatest problem facing many of them would be not their physical condition but public reactions to it. Decades later Betty Basye Hutchinson angrily remembered letters written to newspapers by residents of Pasadena complaining about the badly wounded veterans in the hospital where she worked as a nurse: "Why can't they be kept on their own grounds and off the streets? . . . Isn't it better for them if they're kept off the streets? What awful things for us to have to look at." These were extreme reactions, but many did not want to think about either the hardships these veterans had endured or the contributions they could make if given the chance. By refusing visual acknowledgment of his own disabilities although most citizens already knew of them, Roosevelt made it easier for Americans to avoid these issues. The president's decision was understandable: in addition to the deeply personal nature of such matters, he had justifiable concerns that his political opponents would exploit pictures suggesting his physical limitations. But Roosevelt's actions reflected a lack of confidence in people's ability to change when new evidence challenged their habitual assumptions.[39]

On other occasions Roosevelt acted as if he agreed with the journalist Raymond Clapper's 1944 assessment of public opinion: "Never overestimate the people's knowledge of facts [or] underestimate their ability to make wise judgments given the facts." Roosevelt made himself available to journalists to an unprecedented degree, responding to direct questions in lively press sessions rather than insisting on approved questions submitted in writing in advance as had Herbert Hoover and other predecessors. This policy was not without its public-relations rewards: although many newspaper and radio station owners opposed him, he was widely liked by the working press. Roosevelt's appointments included, in addition to Davis, such advocates of the free flow of information as Byron Price. He proclaimed on the final day of the war: "Those of us in the censorship business have consistently abhorred it just as all American citizens do. It has been one of the grim necessities of war, and we are happy to have it stop with the end of the shooting." If Roosevelt tolerated in his Justice Department some who contemplated a massive suppression of the black press during the war, he also upheld the successful attempts of another of his appointees, Francis Biddle, to combat that effort. And he chose as his military chief of staff a man, George C. Marshall, who gave Roosevelt graphic presentations on American casualties every few days, so the human cost of war "would be quite clear to him . . . because you get hardened to these things."[40]

General Eisenhower shared Marshall's desire to keep the war from becoming too abstract. Uninhibitedly foul-mouthed when among his military peers, his public reputation for decorum indicated his ability to distinguish between types of openness that would inform the citizenry and types that might diminish his own effectiveness while contributing little to public enlightenment. Advisers such as his brother Milton, who had journalistic experience and served as associate director of OWI early in the war, honed Eisenhower's instinctive gift for public relations, which served him well during the twenty years in the spotlight which began with his arrival in London as head of the army's European theater of operations in June 1942.[41]

Eisenhower well understood the political value of the appearance of truthfulness. Yet he also had a proven commitment to candor with the press, based in part on his belief that in a democracy military success in a prolonged war depended on the widespread support of an informed public. In the introduction he wrote in 1944 for an English officer's account of the war, Eisenhower praised the book because it revealed "the viciousness, futility and stupidity of war." It is not surprising that a general who could write such words for a public audience in the midst of war would take the actions he did to assure full exposure of the death camps at the war's end. On several occasions he intervened personally to keep the soldier-run newspaper *Stars and Stripes* free of interference from the military hierarchy, and he supported the efforts of frank observers such as Bill Mauldin, whom General Patton had threatened to shoot on sight. Like Mauldin, Eisenhower felt that the experience of ordinary soldiers had not gotten enough attention, and he considered devoting his postwar energies to telling their story. By the time he became president in 1953 he seemed less concerned with making known, or even learning of, the difficulties faced by those in the lower ranks, military or civilian. This should not obscure the sincerity of his earlier convictions, or the extent to which he acted on them during the war.

In modern combat, individual effort had little impact on larger outcomes unless massively supported. Without the help of many others, Eisenhower could not have provided the public with some sense of what war meant to soldiers. To give one example,

Captain Herman Wall put months of effort into coordinating the photographic coverage of D-Day. He made and carried out arrangements to send back photographs by passenger pigeon, went in with one of the initial landing groups, recorded action on the beach for an hour before being badly wounded, and managed to hang onto his camera as he lay on the beach for three hours waiting for evacuation. His high-quality photographs were the first of the landing to reach Washington.[42]

To differing degrees, everyone else also depended on an able supporting cast. Margaret Bourke-White relied on the darkroom skills of her printer, Oscar Graubner, to bring out the full power of her vision. Revealing images created during the American Civil War by photographers such as Timothy O'Sullivan and Alexander Gardner compensated somewhat for the lack of contemporary visual traditions useful to those seeking to communicate the enormities of modern war. Artists working in fields not directly related to the war also sometimes suggested through example methods of visual expression that offered alternatives to the numbing polarizations of the dominant images. The painters Mark Rothko, Jackson Pollock, Willem de Kooning, and Barnett Newman, whose works had a profound impact on artists in the United States and throughout the world during the postwar era, seldom made direct reference to the war in their paintings. They did, however, create works which, unlike most other images created during the war years, showed the possibility of combining commitment and complexity. Orson Welles did the same in film. In *Citizen Kane*, made shortly before Pearl Harbor, he presented differing perspectives of the life of an influential public figure (fictional, but based on the life of William Randolph Hearst). He invited viewers, by the nature of the film's dialogue, editing, shot selection, and other features, to participate actively in figuring out and making judgments about the meaning of that life.

Welles was a highly ambitious filmmaker who wanted to shake up Hollywood conventions. So did Preston Sturges, whose *Hail the Conquering Hero* (1944) satirized the disguised personal ambitions and fickle herd instincts that motivated some wartime expressions of patriotism. He believed most Hollywood stories would be improved if directors distributed virtues and vices more evenly among the characters. Alfred Hitchcock, driven by philosophical inclination as well as the profit motive to produce truly disturbing films, created in the midst of wartime's assertive certitudes films such as *Shadow of a Doubt* (1943), which alerted audiences to the possibility of rot at the core of apparently wholesome American families and communities.[43]

Few directors had visions as distinct as those displayed by Welles, Sturges, and Hitchcock. Films that challenged oversimplified ways of viewing were more the exception than the rule before, during, and after the war years. As the writer James Agee noted, Hollywood made most films with "the evident assumption that the audience is passive and wants to remain passive." Such movies presumed to do all the work for viewers—"the seeing, the explaining, the understanding, even the feeling." But exceptions were numerous, and drew on traditions as deeply rooted in Hollywood and American culture as were others that perpetuated narrow stereotypes. Much of *Objective Burma* fits into the narrow tradition, but it had several scenes with no equivalents in wartime films from authoritarian countries. Near the end of the movie, after one American soldier commented that their perilous fight for control of Burma might earn them medals, a buddy replied, "Medals? . . . I'll take a hamburger." The most enduringly popular film of the period, *Casablanca,* released by Warner Brothers late in 1942, was one of dozens of wartime movies whose favorably portrayed central characters were highly skeptical of wartime propaganda from whatever side, and who even after they fully committed themselves to the Allied war effort could hardly be imagined mouthing grandiloquent official pronouncements.

The pretenses of those who sought to enhance their own reputation for loyalty by questioning that of others were punctured in light-hearted but not light-headed movies such as *The Sky's the Limit* (1943). Through his portrayal of a reluctant war hero in that film Fred Astaire acted out a challenge to the neatly packaged view of human motivation visible in most war posters. In *Keeper of the Flame* Spencer Tracy and Katharine Hepburn achieved richly developed character portrayals which reminded viewers that principled individuals who wished to be decent citizens often had to choose between unclear, internally conflicting, and imperfect alternatives. Even insipid films like *Here Come the Waves* (1944) might have scenes encouraging audiences to notice the absurdities of some wartime propaganda; one of the characters left her high-paying job at an advertising agency to join the WAVES (Naval Women's Reserve) after becoming disgusted with a gum company's wartime advertising campaign theme: "Chew Your Way to Victory."

These films reflected public opinion as much as they shaped it. The populace sometimes demanded conformity and sometimes challenged polarized ways of seeing. Wartime public pressures helped bring about both the abuse and protection of the constitutional rights of American citizens, as shown by the contrasting examples of incarceration of Japanese-Americans and maintenance of a relatively free press. Before the end of the first year of American involvement an OWI survey reported on an insistent public demand "that the Censor discard his rose-tinted glasses." According to the survey many Americans resented "being treated like babies" and expected the government to recognize that "they can take bad news and want to be treated like full partners." Another survey reported that "press and public are convinced that censorship is rigid beyond any requirements of security." Wartime polls showed slightly more people in support of than opposed to publication of grim photographs. The month after the first photographs of dead Americans were released an OWI survey asked people if they wanted more pictures with this type of "realism": 45 percent responded yes, 8 percent yes with some qualifications, 42 percent no, and 5 percent had no opinion. Later in the war larger majorities responded favorably.[44]

Staffers within OWI who pushed for more forthright portrayal of the realities of combat strengthened their position by citing this and other evidence that audiences favored candor and resisted blatant manipulation. When OWI previewed Darryl Zanuck's *At the Front* in Los Angeles, "at one showing before a kid audience cries of 'fake' were forthcoming in some scenes." As noted, Roosevelt had rejected a military proposal for "complete censorship of publications, radio, and motion pictures within the U.S.A." in part because he believed the American public would not accept it. During the war the military temporarily withdrew from circulation one film in the *Why We Fight* series, *The Battle of China,* because it went so far in its attempt to show China as united and strong that it completely ignored the intense internal conflict that consumed that ally's leaders, and therefore would have no credibility for viewers with any awareness of what was going on there. The experience of the American veteran and Holocaust witness Joseph Kushlis indicated that doubts about the reliability of government-produced imagery remained strong at the war's end. He noted that audiences took his reports more seriously when they learned that his photographs of the death camps had been "taken by a strict amateur photographer in which there could be no doctoring of scenes and no faking of film."[45]

Soldiers were the toughest audience. The Marine veteran William Manchester remembered "John Wayne being booed in a Hawaiian hospital by an audience of wounded Marines from Iwo Jima and Okinawa, men who had had macho acts, in a phrase of the day, up their asses to their armpits." Manchester also reported that after seeing an advertisement in an American magazine that jauntily declared "Who's afraid of the big Focke-Wulf" [a German fighter plane], pilots at one base wrote " '*We* are" and "followed it with the signatures of every airman there, including the commanding officer, and mailed it to the sponsoring firm." Near the end of the war the most publicity-conscious of all American generals, Douglas MacArthur, refused to appear in a government-produced film explaining that American soldiers were fighting for "peace for ourselves, our children, and their children." MacArthur argued against making such films because "the reaction of the troops is cynical and resentful as they regard [them] as propaganda." A G.I. in Rome complained that "stuff like Humphrey Bogart whipping a whole German armored-car column singlehanded gives us pains in the pratt because that kind of crap gives the folks at home the wrong kind of idea about what we are up against." During the war few American soldiers made recorded comments concerning depiction of its horrors. Most who did agreed with the colonel who told George Biddle that he should draw a recently killed soldier because "the people at home ought to see things like that."[46]

At the same time, soldiers did not want to increase the anxieties of those waiting for them to return. Thus the novelist and veteran James Jones reported that almost every soldier was able "to perk up enough so that whenever he saw a reporter with a pencil or a photographer with a camera, he could be ready with the wisecrack and make the toothy smile for the folks back home." Meanwhile, back at home, soldiers' families were among those pushing hardest for full and honest disclosure of war news. In November 1942 about one hundred members of a midwestern Marine Fathers Group held a protest meeting in

Chicago to call attention to excessive censorship of news from military areas. Such protest meetings were rare during the war, although numerous individuals and groups wrote to criticize various aspects of government information policy. The controversy caused by Patton's slapping a shell-shocked soldier brought forth perhaps the largest number of letters to the government and the press; a substantial majority condemned not only Patton's action but also early attempts to suppress information about it. More unusual were letters like the one sent by Edith Huntington Snow of New York to OWI objecting that newsreel pictures of battle were "softened and made unreal" by the upbeat music that accompanied the images.[47]

Some of the messages came from individuals and organizations interested in a specific aspect of visual coverage of the war. In 1944 the editor of Baltimore's *Afro-American* protested the " 'jim-crowing' of Negro soldiers" in a picture magazine about one army camp. At about the same time "500 stage, screen, and radio performers" signed a declaration, written by Lillian Hellman, Maxwell Anderson, and Peter Lyon, calling for the entertainment industry to stop stereotyping blacks as inferiors and to start depicting them seriously and truthfully. The declaration called specifically on the motion picture industry to confront and "find a solution to the prejudices of Southern customers and theater owners."[48]

Such disagreements on fundamental issues complicated the task of those who sought to create images that communicated a consistent message to a diverse audience of more than 140 million spread out over a continent. Excluding China, where internal conflict made even the semblance of unity impossible, among the major combatants only the Soviet Union had a larger population than the United States. Stalin depended on coercion more than on persuasion to assure support for his war aims. Even in dictatorships each individual viewed images from a perspective formed by their particular experiences, beliefs, interests, and circumstances. In both the United States and Britain surveys indicated that men were more likely than women, by as much as a two-to-one margin, to look at news photographs of combat and posters with war themes. One detailed study done for the *Oregon Journal* in Portland found that 63 percent of the men and 41 percent of the women could recall something about a story under the headline "Allied Fleet Hits Sumatra," 34 percent of the men and 15 percent of the women had some memory of a map of Sumatra that accompanied the article, and 75 percent of the women and 54 percent of the men remembered a photograph showing a Pittsburgh woman looking out of a window awaiting the return of her son, a winner of the Congressional Medal of Honor. Men were more likely than women to approve of the use of pictures of American dead in bond sale posters and to react favorably to war action footage in newsreels and Hollywood films. A female respondent to one poll remarked, "A big tank or bomber gets my boy friend all excited, but it leaves me completely cold."[49]

All images of war left others cold. Juanita Loveless, a teenager in 1942 when she went to work at Lockheed and whose father had suffered from exposure to nerve gas in World War I, recalled that she was disturbed by what evidence she did see of the war's bloody results and had no desire to see more. Despite health problems, "an aversion to making anything that would hurt anybody," and excessive work demands, she continued in military production work for most of the war but had deep suspicions about wartime policies. When interviewed forty years later, her memory was that many young people had shared her feelings:

> I think when we actually began to see the boys come home in late 1943, 1944—those that had been injured had started coming back—then the rumbles grew into roars, and the young people thought maybe they were being led into this. . . .
>
> I would never have stayed as long as I did if I hadn't been motivated by the fact that in my mind war was hell. I could visualize it but I wanted to black out some of it. I never went to see a war picture and I never wanted to read a newspaper. I never wanted to know what was going on. Maybe the older people did, but the young people didn't want to hear about what was happening in the war; they just wanted to know we were winning.[50]

Attitudes such as this, which contained both skepticism and willful indifference, could help or hinder those who sought to make visible revealing wartime images. The same was true of the public in general, which could react adversely both to those who tried to challenge conventional understandings or practices and to those perceived as withholding or distorting information. If the historian Lee Kennett is correct, limits in the public ability to understand war's painful necessities sometimes cost lives, as when the U.S. Army, knowing that one death during basic training outraged the public more than a dozen during battle, established training procedures that reduced fatalities in the short term but ultimately led to more deaths by leaving soldiers less adequately prepared for combat. Kennett's claim seems plausible, but so does the wartime belief of Elmer Davis that the public desire for truth was one of the most valuable resources he had to draw on in his battle against excessive restrictions on the flow of information.[51]

Whatever the wisdom of the competing policies of restriction and openness, the war as presented gave many Americans an enlivened sense of purpose. Despite significant contributions to dialogue made by individual effort, free speech traditions, and the diversity of the American population, wartime imagery reinforced those aspects of the culture that encouraged thinking of international relations in simple terms of right and wrong. Because of its consequences, this encouragement of polarized ways of seeing must be calculated as one of the costs of the war.

War

as

Monologue

Look unpleasant, please...

THIS camera lens was built to take unpleasant pictures of Nazis and Japs . . . blasted enemy positions . . . sinking enemy ships.

From eight miles up the aerial camera's piercing eye captures needle-sharp pictures. It penetrates camouflaged positions, records the enemy's strength and movements... pictures his destruction.

The winning of battles and the lives of our men depend on such photographs. Yet camera shutters and film mechanisms were failing for want of a lubricant that would permit instant action in the 90° below zero stratosphere cold.

That day is past. No longer need our men fly dangerous missions and come back empty handed. Texaco's "LOW-TEMP" grease, unequalled in resistance to cold, now assures perfect performance.

It is a product of the same Texaco Research that has contributed so much to the nation's war supply of *Butadiene* for synthetic rubber, *Toluene* for explosive TNT, 100-octane aviation gasoline and many other critical materials.

THE TEXAS COMPANY
TEXACO FIRE-CHIEF AND SKY CHIEF GASOLINES • HAVOLINE AND TEXACO MOTOR OILS

War is what happens when interaction continues after conversation stops; it is a monologue. Bombsights are not devices for understanding (listening to) another culture but for identifying targets of destruction. Paul Fussell notes that "monosyllabic enemies are easier to despise than others. A *kraut* or *wop* is instantly disposable in a way a German or Italian isn't quite." The narrowly focused view from a bombsight is one visual equivalent (caricature of the enemy in posters and films is another) to such one-syllable epithets. This view of Tokyo is from a December 1943 Texaco advertisement in *Newsweek*.

To keep clear the distinction between clean-fighting Americans and the tricky enemy, the government did not release to the general public training posters that taught soldiers the value of sneak attacks, although verbal and visual reports of such practices sometimes reached the public. Innumerable images emphasized the treachery and, especially in the case of the Japanese, subhuman status of the enemy. As the historian Michael S. Sherry has observed, such typical posters as "Plane Warning" focused on one hated leader in their caricatures of the Germans while suggesting a more general contempt for all Japanese, and "the Japanese are rendered as cruder and visually impaired . . . [and] technologically more primitive."

JAPAN
used gas in China

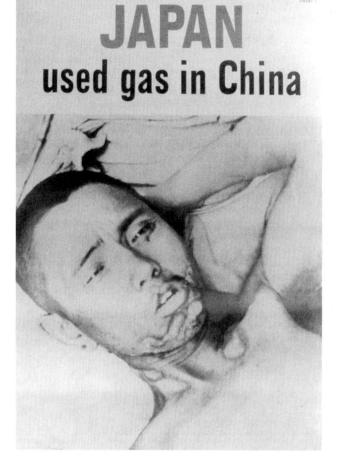

Even as American officials created posters charging the Japanese with using poison gas in China, they censored photographs of American liquid mustard gas stockpiles (never put to use during the war) and of the casualties of American experiments with chemical warfare.

Declaring that most Japanese-Americans forced to leave their homes for government relocation camps "recognized the necessity of the mass evacuation and cooperated cheerfully," OWI asked Hollywood neither to portray them as martyrs nor to "overemphasize the disloyalty of the few." In its own censorship policies the government suppressed photographs that might have challenged the premises of the relocation program. One such photograph, taken by Dorothea Lange, showed a Japanese-American reporting to the Santa Anita Park assembly center, a stage in the relocation process, dressed in a uniform testifying that he served the United States during World War I. The War Relocation Authority's internal shelf list of its negatives indicates that this photograph was one of several "impounded by Major Beasley," and as far as I know it was not released during the war years. Officials also censored most photographs that might have elicited sympathy for Japanese civilians, such as one showing an army interpreter, Sgt. Hoichi Kubo, consoling a Japanese child in an area captured by American forces on Saipan.

Maintaining a clear distinction between Allied and enemy forces required public confidence that American military personnel had things under control. If not, proclaimed policies such as precision bombing lost their meaning. Thus officials censored images of disorderly conduct. The government did not routinely censor photographs of American soldiers' consuming alcoholic beverages. But if the drinking seemed too boisterous, then it contradicted the ideal of thoroughgoing control. Photographs documenting such behavior, like the one above, ended up in the files of censored material. This policy also kept out of view photographs of soldiers in the midst of mental breakdowns. Censoring photographs of soldiers losing control of their actions displayed an appropriate respect for their privacy, but censors prohibited even pictures that obscured the identity of the soldier, such as a photograph showing Lt. Allen Enzor administer a sedative to a psychoneurotic soldier in New Guinea in 1943 while others restrained the patient. One year after the war ended John Huston completed a powerful film about the rehabilitation of soldiers with neuropsychiatric problems, *Let There Be Light,* but the army did not release it until three decades later.

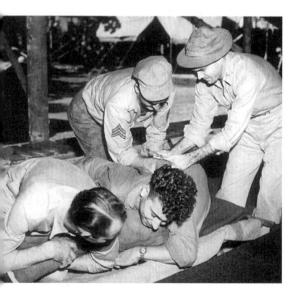

At a time when home front posters impressed on citizens the need to conserve on behalf of the war effort, officials censored images of waste within the military, such as one showing damaged cans of evaporated milk scattered about in an army warehouse in Australia. Army censors also withheld an interior shot of a hospital on Good-enough Island, perhaps because they feared that viewers would interpret the rough floor as an indication of mismanagement and inadequate care of the American wounded.

Images that reeked of sexuality also seemed subversive of
the illusion of control. The photograph at top, officially
captioned "An American couple at a party . . . somewhere
in England," November 1942, posed no such threat and
was released for publication. Army officials did censor the
second photograph, although it was taken two months after the war ended. It showed American occupation forces
in Japan in the Sapporo Club restaurant.

The American servicemen and servicewomen shown here revealed too lively an interest in sexually suggestive subjects for the photographs to get past army censors. One pictured military police taking Neapolitan prostitutes with venereal disease to a hospital for treatment and confinement. In the other, according to the the official caption, "WACS watch elephants bathe while the elephant driver stands by."

LIFE *a party...*

A CONTRIBUTION BY OUR SOCIETY REPORT

It was a charming idea of Mr. Levy, big munitions manu-facturer, to invite those of his female employees who have a friend or fiancé at the Nettuno front. He had considerately called it a "Nettuno Party". A large number of armaments manufacturers was also present.

At first the girls, of course, were somewhat reserved, but the whisky and the other drinks were so excellent that soon everybody was having a grand time. There was only one embarassing incident - when one of the girls suddenly left the party, exclaiming:

"I only hope that my Joe over there in Europe is not going to be so dumb as to risk his life or health for you profiteers and racketeers!"

Apart from this "slip of the tongue" nothing else spoiled the fun of the party.

It is very comforting for the boys at the front to know that their girls - when they are pretty - are well taken care of.

DON'T BE COY! JOE'S A COUPLE OF THOUSAND MILES AWAY!

Also censored were photographs of the army prophylaxis stations, like this one in Naples, Italy, where soldiers went to clean themselves after sexual encounters. The army used its powers of censorship to shield viewers on the home front from German propaganda leaflets such as those dropped on British and American troops at the Anzio beachhead (above), which played on soldiers' sexual deprivation as well as appealing to American anti-Semitism.

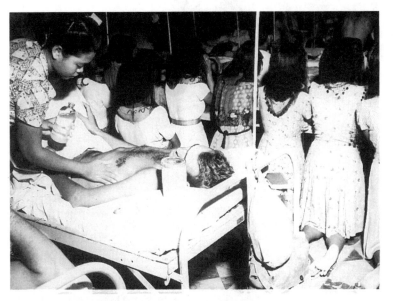

Another censored photograph (top) showed a Filipino nurse's aide giving an alcohol rub to a bare-chested American soldier hospitalized in the Philippines. The army set up the hospital in the Church of the Transfiguration (note the worshipers kneeling for a Christmas Eve mass). If officials censored photographs suggesting that the war might unleash a soldier's sexuality, they also censored those that suggested it might damage it. Thus all photographs that depicted what appeared to be genital wounds ended up in the files of censored material and remained there even after release of other images of painful wounds. The official caption to the unreleased photograph at bottom describes the soldier's wound as "in the abdomen."

Red-Handed: *In an Oakland, Calif., bar, a soldier briefly accepted the invitation of Mr. and Mrs. George L. Hites to help celebrate their two weeks of married life. After he left, a souvenir-of-the-occasion photo showed his hand in Mrs. Hites's purse. Though she says she later missed $26 from her purse, International Newsphotos blacked out the soldier's face for lack of proof that he actually stole anything.*

To the disappointment of some officials and with the enthusiastic encouragement of others, wartime circumstances, the tradition of a free press, and individual actions led to the publication of many images that did not present the war and its social impact in a manner that eliminated ambiguities. Thus photographs and motion picture images of men in drag probably received wider distribution during World War II than at any previous time. When OWI, however, circulated a picture (above) from Irving Berlin's Broadway hit *This Is the Army,* which had an all-soldier cast, it assured viewers that it was a good cause that earned "$40,000 a week for Army Relief." The caption continued, "Don't let them fool you, boys. They're chorus 'gals,' but tough as mule meat." *Newsweek* reminded readers of the fallibility of some American soldiers when it ran a candid photograph (left) of one with his hand in the pocketbook of a benefactor. Among the many other published photographs that gave a more complex view of the war than that encouraged by the usual patterns of display and censorship were those showing massive and violent home front racial disturbances, those from late in the war showings G.I.s who were involved in a crime ring in Europe, and one showing men of draft age in the State Department, run by the *Washington Times-Herald* in 1944 with this caption: "If the Army really needs ALL the young men it can get, it can find in Secretary Hull's fold an assortment of rich, able-bodied unmarried boys of no particular use to anyone."

K-ACK-ACK—"*SLEEP! LET ME SLEEP!*"

SHELL RESEARCH—

Sword of Today
Plowshare of Tomorrow

The SOLDIER Whose LETTER Never Comes

THE PARKER PEN COMPANY

JANESVILLE · · · WISCONSIN · · · U.S.A.

Advertisements, which were unaffected by most censorship provisions, sometimes made use of the special power of otherwise taboo images. No government poster or officially sanctioned photograph showed a scene of the mental stress faced by American soldiers comparable to the one that the Shell Oil Company used in a 1943 ad to promote a tranquilizer it derived from petroleum. In support of the goal of getting folks on the home front to write letters to their loved ones in the service, one 1942 advertisement by the Parker Pen Company carried another sight not found in official imagery, a soldier who seemed to be crying.

*"Fresh, spirited American troops, flushed with victory, are bring-
ing in thousands of hungry, ragged, battle-weary prisoners . . ."*
(News item)

Whatever the limitations imposed by censorship and practical problems, great effort went into the official effort to
document the war and sometimes produced informative
and moving images. Members of Edward Steichen's Naval
Aviation Photographic Unit created some of the war's
most striking pictures, such as Barrett Gallagher's November 1944 photograph "Burial at sea for the officers and
men of the *USS Intrepid* who lost their lives during the battle for Leyte Gulf in the Philippines" (left). In cartoons created as part of his army assignment and widely
reproduced in publications that reached both soldiers and
civilians, Bill Mauldin supplied funny, poignant, and candid
depictions of the experiences of enlisted men. Some of his
cartoons visually measured the gap between this experience and official reports of it.

The most revealing and memorable photographs taken by Americans during World War II were created largely by professionals employed by newspapers, the news agencies, and magazines, especially *Life*. In a 1944 photograph taken at Saipan, showing a mother and son fleeing from a cave in an area under American attack, Eugene Smith provided viewers at home with a rare glimpse of the impact of the war on Japanese civilians. Referring to his pictures of civilians on Saipan, Smith wrote, "My people could be these people, my children could be those children."

Those societies which cannot combine reverence to their
symbols with freedom of revision, must ultimately decay
either from anarchy, or from the slow atrophy of a life stifled
by useless shadows.
                              —Alfred North Whitehead, 1927

CHAPTER 4

War

Costs

AS MEASURED BY the ability to produce material goods
and to destroy lives and property, the United States
possessed unprecedented power at the end of World
War II. In 1946 the United States, with less than 6
percent of the earth's population, accounted for close
to 50 percent of its gross world product (compared to
roughly 25 percent in 1938 and 1992). Its leading role
in international affairs, challenged only by Soviet
dominance within a far poorer sphere of influence, was
acknowledged by the decision to place the headquarters of the newly created United Nations in New York.
Location of the April 1945 U.N. planning meeting in
San Francisco assured that delegates from war-torn
European lands would travel across the United States
and be awed by evidence, visible from their plane or
train windows, of the country's immense productive
capability, which had been expanded rather than diminished by the war.[1]

Victory had its costs. War brought hatred as inevitably as it brought death. Few could have carried out
wartime responsibilities without its motivation. When
it led, however, to a contempt for opponents that resulted in underestimation of them or exacerbated so-

121

cially corrosive conflicts among Americans, it hindered the war effort and placed an additional burden on the postwar world. Wartime hatreds fed on deeply rooted prejudices. Elmer Davis concluded that at the outset of World War II "there was much more domestic political bitterness in the country than there was in 1917," the year the United States entered World War I to the accompaniment of racial and ethnic strife. Monthly reports from the hundreds of people throughout the country who kept OWI informed of public opinion nudged Davis toward this debatable conclusion. The reports revealed antagonisms immune to wartime pleas for unity. At Baltimore's Bethlehem-Fairfield yard, which employed thirty-five thousand workers, whites accepted the unavoidability of working temporarily with blacks during the war, but the "universally used" saying among whites was that "when the war is over, we are going to have to fight another one against the Negroes" to regain exclusive white control of high-paying jobs at the yard. Davis's files contained hundreds of similar examples.[2]

Workplace graffiti warned "niggers" and "okies" to go home. Those who considered the war a "Jewish conspiracy" with Roosevelt's connivance defaced synagogues in Boston with the painted message "Jewnited States of America." When two black citizens from Muskogee, Oklahoma, sent a letter to the army protesting that the prophylactic station in their hometown had separate and unequal facilities for white and black soldiers, the adjutant general's office carried out an investigation that in the end focused on the letter writers. The army defended the segregated facilities, noting that racial mingling would be dangerous because troops often made use of them while intoxicated. The region's provost marshal reported that one of the letter writers was a "loudmouth" and that both were "troublemakers." He recommended that the FBI keep track of their activities. A 1945 survey found that in Monterey County "three out of four cars carry a sticker saying 'Keep All Japs Out of California.'" In 1944 a national poll revealed that 61 percent of Americans believed that after the war "white people should have the first chance at any kind of a job" before anyone of Japanese descent.[3]

Politics or ideology often motivated attempts to foment anger. Japanese advances early in the war engendered stories that this setback for white supremacy in Asia made American blacks more aggressive. These stories merged with others that associated Eleanor Roosevelt with increased black assertiveness. Such actions as her withdrawal from the Daughters of the American Revolution after that organization blocked a performance by the black singer Marian Anderson at the DAR's Constitution Hall in Washington had earned her the intense hatred of defenders of the racial status quo. Rumors that black women who did domestic work had formed subversive "Eleanor Clubs" further fueled this hatred. Members supposedly received assignments "to patrol downtown streets in other cities to bump into white people and crowd them out of store counters." Some critics echoed Adolf Hitler's claim that her "completely negroid appearance" proved she was "half-caste."[4]

Visual documents became weapons in hate campaigns. One fringe group, the Houston-based Christian American Association, distributed photographs of Eleanor Roosevelt meeting with blacks. They used the pictures to support their warning that American whites would be "forced into organization with black African apes whom they will have to call brother or lose their jobs." President Roosevelt, less disturbed than his wife by racial bigotry but more alert to the dangers her activities posed to his career, responded by keeping such ammunition away from his enemies. Late in 1943, in answer to a command from Roosevelt's press secretary, Steve Early, BPR sent to the White House all photographs and negatives showing "Mrs. Roosevelt with Negro personnel" taken during her recent visits to military bases, as well as those showing her wearing a hula skirt. The photographs might have seemed especially dangerous to Roosevelt on the eve of an election year, but his action was consistent with other official suppression of controversial visual material.[5]

Efforts to challenge public expectations often ran afoul of media policies subservient to these expectations. The Chicago businessman Dempsey Travis told what happened in early 1945 after he became manager of the first integrated PX in the state of Maryland and won first prize for the best-managed store at his base, the Aberdeen Proving Grounds. The post commander came in and said, "We're gonna have the newspapers take pictures of you, 'cause we're very proud of what you're doin.'" A few days later he came back to report that the newspapers would not do the story because "those fellas can't stand the idea of a black man being able to operate a post exchange in this manner." Travis believed that "those fellas"—the newspaper editors—refused to run the story because of fear that it would offend many of their readers. Such practices reduced the commitment of some blacks to the war effort. Many, such as John Hope Franklin, later a prominent historian, were particularly outraged when they saw German prisoners of war in the United States eating in segregated restaurants, traveling in whites-only railroad cars, and enjoying other privileges prohibited to black Americans, even those wearing military uniforms.[6]

Edward R. Murrow feared that white as well as black soldiers might have cause for bitterness when they returned home. Late in 1943 Murrow, whose tough-minded broadcasts from London had won him great prestige, warned Elmer Davis of the possibilities for misunderstanding created by the huge gap between the realities and the public perception of the military experience. Murrow anticipated that "this army of ours will return home as strangers, impatient and intolerant, and . . . the people at home ought to be prepared for it." Murrow added that "the refusal to face unpleasant facts was the primary reason for the war happening as it did." If the country continued its refusal to face facts about what the war was really like and about those who used political and financial power to benefit from it, then "a vast number of boys who are fighting this war will feel . . . they have been betrayed."[7]

Partly because of such concerns, as the war's end approached, civilians saw more images emphasizing differences between combat and domestic experiences. A powerful film made by the Army Pictorial Service in 1944, *He Has Seen War*, explained why, contrary to the message conveyed by earlier use of the home front analogy, what combat soldiers had seen had changed them: they had become "not worse, but different." The audience saw scenes a soldier might have, including wounded Americans in agony, corpses nearly indistinguishable from the mud, a recently severed limb, and the body of a little Italian girl. The 1945 War Department film *Action at Anguar*, intended for use in the Seventh War Loan campaign, brought the public slightly closer than earlier films to the language of combat by having the soldier-narrator speak of "how mad you got when the bastards hit the guy next to you." Thus by the end of the war the government incorporated into some of its own films language kept out of Hollywood films by the self-regulating codes established to forestall government regulation.[8]

Censorship and customary practice kept one particular consequence of war out of view for the duration: crying. An early example of a visual report on Americans responding to news of a combat death, a *Life* photograph of an Iowa farm family who had just learned that their son had been killed in one of the conflicts between U.S. and German naval forces in the fall of 1941 before formal declaration of war, showed the father, mother, and brother receiving the news sadly but with stiff upper lips and without tears. Indeed, during the war *Life* showed only one photograph of an American crying because of physical or emotional pain caused by the war—a mother wiping tears from her eyes as she accepted a high school diploma for a son killed in battle. A friend took her photograph, which appeared in the "Letters to the Editor" section. *Newsweek*'s first war-related photograph of an American crying, a picture of a Seattle woman weeping over the death of her son, a Marine, did not appear until August 20, 1945, after V-J Day had marked the end of the fighting. Earlier in the war a photo caption in that magazine had assured readers that "in the terrible jungle fighting in New Guinea, the wounded don't cry." Government-produced posters occasionally drew extra emotional force from the depiction of overt American grief: a billboard display captioned "Somebody Talked," warning people against divulging information, showed a woman with her head nestled in her arms and presumably sobbing after receiving a bad-news telegram. The cartoonist Bill Mauldin, one of the war's wisest visual commentators although only twenty-four years old at its end, wittily depicted an American soldier crying—after learning that Ernie Pyle had misspelled his name in his newspaper column.[9]

More tears were shed in Hollywood movies, at first almost exclusively by women. In *Army Surgeon* (1942) one army doctor cried hysterically after her first exposure to war casualties until a male doctor slapped her. She was smiling in a few minutes and married him by the film's conclusion. In *Cry Havoc* American nurses under Japanese siege in Bataan did the crying, as they did in another 1943 film on the same topic, *So Proudly We Hail*. Male soldiers comforted them in that film when, en route to assignment in the

Philippines, the nurses sobbed and looked on in horror as nearby ships exploded. In *The Fighting Sullivans* the wife of one of the five brothers rushed to her room crying uncontrollably after that family received its terrible news.

Special explanations excused male crying. A young soldier sobbed from fear while under bombardment in *Guadalcanal Diary*. An earlier scene in which the discovery of a whisker led him to conclude that he should start shaving emphasized his youth, as did the revelation that although he claimed his daily letters were to his girl, they actually were to his mom. Although an older Marine comforted him by telling him that anyone there who said he was not scared was a fool or a liar, none of the older soldiers cried. A soldier who added a touch of gender diversity to the crying in *So Proudly We Hail* earned his nickname 'Weeping Wallachek" because as a college football star he had made his greatest plays after becoming so angry that he started to cry. Soldiers cried more often in films from later in the war, such as *Objective Burma,* usually not because of their own pain, fear, or loneliness but because of their outrage at something dreadful that had befallen a friend. [10]

Years after the war one woman recalled with regret breaking up with her soldier fiancé after he had mentioned in a letter that he often cried at night. With expectations created by the images available to her she assumed that his behavior was extremely unusual: "I was convinced I had loved a coward. I never wrote him again." His behavior might have seemed less contemptible to her had she known that army psychologists studying a division of soldiers engaged in an especially intense conflict found that nearly one in four reported they had lost control of their bowels and fouled themselves during battle, an equal number had vomited, and one in ten had wet their pants. [11]

Although American editors may seem to have shown laudable discretion in not publishing photographs of Americans crying, they practiced no such restraint in running pictures of weeping Italians, Russians, and Chinese. Most wartime photographs of grieving people, however, dignify the subjects and do not seem intrusive. Examples included Robert Capa's picture of Neapolitan women mourning the loss of sons from their community, Dmitri Baltermants's of male and female relatives identifying bodies after a battle in the Soviet Union, and Edward Clark's photograph of Roosevelt's favorite musician, accordionist Graham Jackson. Jackson, a chief petty officer in the navy, had been scheduled to play "Going Home" at a picnic Roosevelt planned to attend the day he died. Instead Jackson played the tune, tears streaming down his face, while bearers carried the President's body out of the Little White House in Warm Springs, Georgia. By failing generally to produce such pictures of themselves, Americans cut themselves off from the fullest understanding of their own humanity as well as of the war's impact. [12]

This is not to suggest that revelation was always the best policy. Depending on context, manner of presentation, and the responses of individual viewers, things shown as well as things unshown could diminish understanding. Even though depiction of American death became harsher as the war grew longer, editors never presented these images in ways that dehumanized the victim. They accompanied these stark pictures with captions or narratives that fit the death into a meaningful story. Officials suppressed images not amenable to such treatment. For example, they withheld footage showing soldiers tossing onto a truck the stiff corpses of Americans killed in the Malmedy massacre. Similar unofficial and unstated rules guided depiction of western and northern European allies, but not depiction of other groups, especially Asians, whether enemy or ally. Widely circulated photographs and newsreel footage of Asians included images of burning Japanese bodies, Chinese civilians trampled to death in a rush to an air raid shelter, and a dead Chinese baby, the victim of a bombing raid, being carried like a sack of potatoes.[13]

A 1944 OWI newsreel analysis noted but did not challenge this differential presentation of death. It reported that the newsreels under review mentioned atrocities against American soldiers, but "naturally these pictures did not show any of the atrocities" even though footage was available. The newsreels did show Japanese atrocities against the Chinese. The footage used was "among the most horrible pictures imaginable as Jap soldiers were shown deeply prodding securely bound Chinese with bayonets, . . . throwing bodies haphazard into carts and laughing as they did so, and driving horses and wagons over heaps of dead." For decades before the war gruesome images of Asian death had been far more common in the American media than equivalent images of Europeans or Americans, except for those of black Americans whom lynch mobs had burned and mutilated. To give an early example, a popular turn-of-the-century stereograph showed Chinese beheaded during the Boxer Rebellion.[14]

Like images of crying, images of mass or brutal death were not necessarily a sign of disrespect. Americans appalled by lynchings often worked hardest to have the horrors of this practice made public. Newsreel reports on the 1937 "rape of Nanking" and other Japanese atrocities, and a 1937 photograph showing an injured Chinese baby crying amid the wreckage of a Shanghai rail terminal after a Japanese bombing attack, deeply affected many Americans. The Shanghai photograph and many other disturbing images of the Chinese wounded and dead appeared in *Life* in support of the owner Henry R. Luce's campaign to secure support for the government of Chiang Kai-shek. The problem was not in publication of such images if created and presented with respect for human dignity, but in the application of a double standard, or more precisely a sliding-scale standard. The more culturally distant people were from the norms of those who controlled publication of the imagery, the more likely they were to be depicted graphically as victims of mass death or horrendous mutilation.[15]

These practices defined the context in which Americans encountered pictures of death camps. At these and other sites Nazis had killed millions of Jews, and tens of thousands of political dissidents, gypsies, homosexuals, the mentally abnormal, and other groups they considered undesirable. The decision to release visual evidence of these outrages in the spring of 1945 was a brave and clear-sighted one that could as easily have gone the other way. Hollywood films had largely avoided the issue during the war. When newsreels documenting the genocide became available near the war's end, many exhibitors shared the fears of the managing director of Radio City Music Hall, who did not show them because they might sicken "squeamish persons in the audience which usually is family trade, mostly women and children." Throughout the war the U.S. government kept secret most of the increasing flow of reliable information on the Holocaust. Officials, finding it difficult themselves to believe the horrendous reports, feared publicizing them would rouse suspicions that the United States government was reviving the crude propaganda techniques of World War I. If the reports were believed, they might encourage questions about why the U.S. was not taking steps such as bombing the extermination camps. As the end of the war approached, some officials worried that death camp pictures would make it harder to convince the American public of the need to rebuild postwar Germany to counter Soviet influence in Europe.[16]

Despite such concerns political and military leaders decided to release many of these pictures. General Eisenhower pushed hard for maximum exposure although he knew that sights of the camps could sicken more than the squeamish; even after immersion in four years of horrific war General Patton came close to vomiting when he and Eisenhower visited the recently liberated camp at Ohrdruf in April 1945. At the war's end Eisenhower insisted that German civilians, international journalists, and bipartisan congressional delegations visit the camps to confront the results of programs designed to remove entire groupings of humanity from the face of the earth. Here was one instance where visual evidence was indispensable; only by seeing could the true but unbelievable become credible.[17]

Eisenhower could not bring the entire world population to view the camps. He and other like-minded officials hoped that authenticated photographs and film would be an effective substitute. By a two-to-one margin the public agreed with the decision to release these images, although one in six of those who agreed chose not to look at them. Nongovernmental organizations helped implement the policy of disclosure. In cooperation with the federal government the *Saint Louis Post-Dispatch* sponsored a well-attended exhibition, "Lest We Forget," of life-sized photo murals of the camps, supplemented by a Signal Corps documentary. The widespread display of Holocaust pictures made public expressions of anti-Semitism less acceptable in the United States, validated the war against Germany more effectively than any other evidence, and helped bring about the creation of the state of Israel. The released images also changed individual lives. Years later the writer Susan Sontag described her response when she had encountered photographs of Bergen-Belsen and Dachau in a Santa Monica bookstore in July 1945: "Nothing I have seen—in photographs or in real life—ever cut me as sharply, deeply, instantaneously. Indeed, it seems plausible to me to divide my life into two parts, before I saw those photographs (I was twelve) and after."[18]

Not all Americans were so moved. Several contemporary observers, after the initial shock of the pictures, were shocked a second time by evidence that they had little impact on the public. Gerhard E. Lenski wrote in August that the "common reaction" to the photographs seemed to be one of relative indifference. Lenski believed that Americans felt the photographs had little relevance to their lives because "all these horrors took place in Germany, and, of course, they can't ever happen here." It is impossible to know how many Americans responded that way. Further evidence that many did comes from the experience of those American soldiers who participated in the liberation of the camps. Some, like Joseph Kushlis, who had witnessed the horrors of Ohrdruf, upon their return to the United States spoke to community groups about what they had seen, and used visual materials to substantiate their testimony. But, as detailed in *Inside the Vicious Heart,* Robert H. Abzug's powerful study of American responses to the camps, other veterans stopped talking about what they had observed because they encountered too much disbelief.[19]

The disbelief had many sources. Abzug concluded that denial was a major one: people simply could not bring themselves to acknowledge the human depravity documented in the pictures of the camps. Emotional exhaustion might be another, related reason. By the end of a war so rich in horrors, the capacity of many viewers to be distressed by yet another terrible happening, even one of such immense proportions, had been used up. Because the majority of the victims were Jewish, no doubt anti-Semitism also dulled the response of some: in a Gallup poll taken shortly before the war 51 percent of Americans answered "no" to the question "Would you vote for a Jew for President who was well qualified for the position?" Perhaps as a result of such attitudes, one OWI survey (with excessive faith in the ability of social scientists to quantify emotions) found that "the impact of atrocity information on the average American was seven times stronger when it involved atrocities in general than when it referred specifically to atrocities against Jews."[20]

The visual message that films and photographs of the preceding years had transmitted was also part of the explanation. The perpetrators and victims of wholesale slaughter and dehumanizing treatment always were shown to be people very different from ourselves, with "ourselves" narrowly defined in disregard of American diversity. If this message diluted American responses to the Holocaust, it also ill prepared Americans for their responsibilities after the war, when they would be called upon to elect leaders whose choices had the potential to affect the entire planet.

Polarized ways of seeing helped define, and were sustained by, postwar relations with the Soviet Union. Although some editorial cartoonists expressed in their work their skepticism of Soviet intentions, most wartime visual imagery of the Soviet Union implied that people who were our military allies also must be like us in all other important ways. In 1943 *Life* described Russians as "one hell of a people" who "look like Americans, dress like Americans and think like Americans." It compared the Soviet secret police to the FBI. In the same year Warner Brothers' much-publicized film *Mission to Moscow,* based on a book by the U.S. ambassador to the Soviet Union, Joseph Davies, treated Josef Stalin as a grandfatherly figure and accepted without challenge his justifications of such outrages as the purge trials of the late 1930s. These "trials," based on fabricated evidence, were part of the process whereby Stalin eliminated, by arrest often followed by execution, all possible rivals for power. Among those killed were a majority of the highest Soviet military, political, police, and trade-union leaders. Many other visual messages avoided the potentially controversial question of Soviet leadership and policies, but suggested that the aspirations, beliefs, and consumer preferences of the Soviet people mimicked those of Americans. Advertisements like one captioned "Ivan Knows" run by the Monsanto Chemical Company in 1943, which showed a Soviet soldier enjoying a hot chocolate sweetened with that company's saccharine, indicated that their love of the same products bound the two country's citizens together in a community of consumption.[21]

Such imagery helps explain why Americans felt betrayed when postwar Soviet behavior conflicted with the wishes of American leaders. The polarized structure of wartime ways of seeing proved to be stronger than the content. Visual depictions of the Soviets switched from almost all positive to almost all negative within a few years of the war's end. Although more the product than the cause of a bifurcated world, polarized visual images of the Soviet Union helped entrench this perspective and put at risk the careers of those in education, journalism, and politics who wished to subject it to probing reconsideration. It also put at risk, retroactively, those involved in production of pro-Soviet or at least pro-Russian films like *The North Star, Song of Russia,* and *Days of Glory,* even though all were consistent with the wartime custom of praising allies. Depictions of China and the Chinese during the war and after the communist triumph in 1949 also underwent dramatic shifts that demonstrated the strength of polarizing tactics. Like the optical illusion that can be seen as rabbit or duck but never both at once, the Soviets and Chinese appeared as good, then evil, but seldom as both in the same image.

The Korean War came close to changing this dual view. At its outset it seemed to lend itself well to unambiguous presentation. It began with the invasion of South Korea by communist North Korea in June 1950. The United States responded under the aegis of the United Nations. The victory of Mao Tse-tung's forces in China the previous year made plausible claims that the invasion was part of a larger plan for communistic expansion in Asia. But after initial advances and setbacks, before the end of its first year the war settled into a stalemate, touching off disputes over strategy which led to President Truman's dismissal of General MacArthur and to acrimonious debate at home. As the war dragged on, the uncertainty about the U.S. role and goals limited the possibilities for clearly defined, encouraging images.

Because of these limitations President Truman had no wish to focus attention on events on the Korean peninsula. He decided not to create any OWI-type propaganda agency to build support for the war. Most American photographers in Korea had World War II experience and began their coverage of the new war with the graphically depicted suffering that had been possible only at the end of the previous war. The results were subject to military censorship, but here too the less restrictive practices in place by the end of World War II became the starting point for the Korean conflict. Images of destruction and American death appeared early in the war, as did such previously taboo images as American soldiers crying. These images communicated a more complex message than their captions. They appeared in the context of articles that usually described the war's issues in the language of a polarized worldview.[22]

This divergence might have led to a serious challenge to that worldview. It did not, however, because of the success of contemporaneous efforts to direct attention to threats to American dominance in the bipolar world. In the 1952 election the Republican party made an issue of the Democrats' alleged failure to pursue with vigor the domestic and international fight against communism. Senator Joseph McCarthy's voluminous charges of subversion within government, the academic community, and the military, although later discredited, increased the public hazard of questioning bipolarity. The Democratic party assumed a defensive posture that further discouraged such questioning. Arrangement of a cease-fire in Korea in July 1953, six months after Dwight Eisenhower's inauguration as president, ended the flow of visual images. The period of intense conflict over Korea did not last long enough to challenge seriously the polarized way of seeing nurtured by World War II.

The war in Vietnam *was* long enough. Extensive United States involvement began with the evolving decision to support French efforts to reassert control over Indochina (Vietnam, Cambodia, and Laos). France had held control since the nineteenth century, then lost it to Japan during World War II. Nationalist and communist movements in Vietnam resisted French attempts to return after Japan's defeat. In 1950, partly because of fears raised by the outbreak of the Korean War, the United States sharply increased its financial and material support to the French. By 1954 the United States was paying 80 percent of France's war costs. In that year the French gave up their effort and the Geneva Accords temporarily divided Vietnam into a communist-controlled North and a largely anticommunist, internally divided South. The United States opposed all communist efforts to gain control of the South, whether through military action or open elections. The number of American military personnel in Vietnam gradually increased in the 1950s, jumped from six hundred to sixteen thousand during John F. Kennedy's one thousand days as president, and passed the half-million mark by the end of Lyndon Baines Johnson's five years in office. Richard Nixon brought all combat troops home during his presidency while increasing bombardment of known or suspected communist strongholds and supply routes. Communist forces gained control of the entire country in April 1975, less than a year after Nixon's resignation due to scandals partly caused by his attempts to plug leaks of secret information about the war in Vietnam.

No American president ordered mobilization of the visual environment on behalf of that war. Government publicists, ever more numerous, did distribute documentaries, "white papers," and other material intended to build support for American policies in Vietnam. Each administration sought, often successfully, to influence television and other reporting on these policies. But from the murky beginnings of American involvement to the humiliating end, there was no outpouring of posters for travelers to notice on train station walls, film shorts for factory workers to view during their coffee break, or "V for Victory" stamps for citizens to place on hundreds of millions of letters. The private sector followed suit. Corporations ignored Vietnam in their advertising. No washing machine manufacturer offered wall charts instructing users how they might contribute to the effort. Neither business establishments nor private homes displayed service flags indicating the number of employees or family members who had gone off to war.[23]

Those seeking visual affirmations of American policy could turn to the press. As in World War II, when it came to American military efforts reporters considered themselves part of the team. During the 1950s and the first half of the 1960s, journalists selected and presented almost all newsreel, television, and still pictures of Vietnam in a manner intended to support the American effort. But this coverage was minimal until the massive troop buildup of 1965 and after. Coverage of Vietnam did not begin at the level of graphic violence where World War II ended, but repeated the World War II cycle. Early 1960s reports on Vietnam were restrained in their depictions of both the impact of the war on Americans and of the impact of American and allied actions on the land and people of Vietnam. As in World War II, sufferings caused by and inflicted on the enemy were shown earlier and in greater detail. And as in that war, the longer the conflict continued, the more revealing the imagery became. When the period of American involvement stretched far beyond that of the earlier war, increasing numbers of journalists questioned and eventually criticized American policies.

The nature of the war as well as its length affected its visual presentation. It lacked a galvanizing beginning, clear-cut good and bad guys, and a coherent story line that integrated the efforts of those in battle and those at home. Lyndon B. Johnson was well aware of the value of a dramatic event to unite public support behind a war effort. At the outset of World War II, in response to the stunning imperative of Pearl Harbor (and in response to campaign promises from which he could not extricate himself), Johnson briefly left

Washington, where he was a U.S. congressman from Texas, to go off to war. Twenty-three years later, as president, he tried to provide an equally compelling justification for escalation of the American presence in Vietnam. But even before subsequent revelations of the deceit involved in Johnson's report of allegedly unprovoked attacks on American ships by the North Vietnamese in the Gulf of Tonkin in August 1964, it was apparent that this incident was no Pearl Harbor.[24]

Pearl Harbor remains the most devastating single naval defeat ever inflicted on the United States. Although in reporting on the attack President Roosevelt intentionally withheld specific details, he revealed that the Japanese had severely damaged the country's Pacific fleet and that "very many American lives have been lost." In the twenty-four hours after Pearl Harbor, Japan attacked Malaya, Hong Kong, Guam, the Philippines, Wake Island, and Midway Island. In the Gulf of Tonkin incident the North Vietnamese did not kill any Americans, sink any ships, or attack any American territory. No coordinated attacks were made either by them or by their allies within South Vietnam, the National Liberation Front (NLF or Viet Cong). Johnson successfully used the incident as the pretext for getting congressional approval for taking "all necessary actions" to resist North Vietnamese and Viet Cong aggression. But no American president is likely to travel to the Gulf of Tonkin in 2014 to commemorate the event, as George Bush visited Pearl Harbor on the fiftieth anniversary of the Japanese attack.

Providing visual indicators of American successes in Vietnam presented another problem. By 1943 World War II newspapers showed maps recording monthly, weekly, even daily gains of territory as the Allied forces made visible progress toward the objective of gaining control of the enemy homeland and thus bringing an end to the war. In Vietnam almost all of the fighting took place within the allied South, which meant maps could only show areas that had once fallen out of government control and were now being regained. Depictions of military actions within the cartographic outline of an S-shaped country less than forty miles wide at its waist did not provide the visual satisfactions of World War II campaigns that swept over oceans and continents. Often after American and South Vietnamese forces captured an enemy area within the South they soon abandoned it, because the goal was not so much to control acreage as to build support for the threatened government and destroy effective opposition. This made the chief measure for success in the war the "body count" of the number of enemy dead. The body count in a particular engagement could be expressed graphically by pictures of the bodies. But to represent the cumulative effect of the American effort, the visual equivalent of maps showing Allied forces closing in on Berlin or Honshu would have been a pile of bodies physically documenting the million or so enemy deaths reported during the course of the war.

Visually distinguishing friend and foe was another problem confronting the war's publicists, and American soldiers as well, whether in the field or in a brothel in Saigon. The problem was compounded by the absence of a caricaturable enemy leader, a role that all the

Axis leaders, especially Hitler, played so well in World War II. In 1945 many Vietnamese considered Ho Chi Minh a hero owing to his identification with Vietnamese independence; by the time he died in 1969 opinion was deeply divided in both Vietnam and the United States as to whether he was an enlightened revolutionary and nationalist leader or a brutal dictator. Whatever his actual characteristics, visually the white-bearded Ho, the president of North Vietnam until his death and the only Vietnamese communist recognizable to a sizable portion of the American public, looked more like a sagacious village elder than a vicious opponent.

Absence of visually memorable leaders like Ho complicated attempts to reassure the public about the stability and probity of the government Americans fought to defend. President Ngo Dinh Diem was the first South Vietnamese leader to receive massive U.S. support. Officers in his military deposed and murdered him in a 1963 coup carried out with American approval (although Americans had not consented to his murder) three weeks before the assassination of John F. Kennedy in Dallas. South Vietnam then went through a series of rapid changes in leadership before Nguyen Cao Ky and Nguyen Van Thieu, and later Thieu alone, remained in office long enough to become recognizable to Americans. The pilot and air marshal Ky, his aviator's jacket accented by a silk scarf, was the most striking visually of the South Vietnamese leaders. But his zest in telling the American press that his greatest hero was Adolf Hitler indicated that he was not well suited as a symbol to reconcile the American public to the lives lost, to the $80 million spent on the war every day by 1968, or to the stresses the war placed on the American and Vietnamese economies, political systems, and social orders.

American leaders responded to problems inherent in presenting the war positively by trying to minimize presentation of any sort. This is one reason why no president requested a formal declaration of war. Secretary of State Dean Rusk explained after the war that Kennedy, then Johnson, had decided not to have soldiers on the way to or from Vietnam marching through American cities, or movie stars selling war bonds, because they considered it dangerous to whip up "war fever" in a world that had "thousands of nuclear weapons lying around." This was hardly the entire story. The persistence of the communist effort, the lack of Vietnamese popular support for the governments kept in power with American aid, and the danger of provoking an increased Russian or Chinese response led each American president to conclude that prevention of communist control of South Vietnam during their term in office was a more plausible objective than total victory. This seemed a less satisfying goal than the World War II quest for unconditional surrender. The desire to assure citizens that they could have butter as well as guns, that the effort in Vietnam would not require domestic sacrifices, was a further reason to downplay the war. Ultimately officials failed in their attempts to keep Vietnam out of sight. The war Americans saw looked very different from World War II.[25]

These differences emerged slowly, as in the depiction of atrocities. Staff members at the

Office of Facts and Figures warned at the outset of World War II that reports of atrocities against Americans might incite reprisals against Americans of actual or presumed German or Japanese descent and would alarm Americans with relatives in danger zones. They observed that such reports would have the most bracing effect if the victims could be shown to have resisted bravely. They worried over the public tendency to be more outraged by atrocities when the victims were British than when they were Chinese. Widespread knowledge that propagandists had concocted outrages during World War I, as when they claimed that Germans had cut off the hands of Belgian babies, encouraged skepticism. This remained a concern throughout World War II; a month before V-E Day OWI warned the Treasury Department that "the credence of the American people in the authenticity of atrocity information will be broken down by a sudden whooping up of atrocity stories . . . for the obvious . . . purpose of selling bonds." Plausible atrocity stories, however, could make bond sales "soar." Officials released the first vividly detailed stories in the fall and winter of 1943–44 to reinforce the effect of newly released images of death. Hollywood practices remained synchronized with those of the government. The first film to focus on Japanese atrocities against Americans, *Purple Heart*, Darryl Zanuck's imaginative re-creation of the mistreatment and execution of American fliers captured during the Doolittle raid over Tokyo, came out in 1944. It depicted the results of Japanese torture without explicitly showing the process, and it became one of the year's most widely viewed films.[26]

Censors strictly prohibited visual or written depictions of atrocities committed by American troops or their allies. Other countries had similar policies. In his study of war journalism, Phillip Knightley reported that he had been "unable to find any report in the Allied press of an atrocity committed by an Allied soldier." A few published stories of American soldiers collecting body parts as trophies were rare exceptions. Chief of Staff George C. Marshall sent Pacific commanders a cable in October 1943 urging them to stop their soldiers from such practices as making necklaces out of Japanese teeth and taking photographs documenting the steps required to remove the flesh from a skull. Marshall instructed the officers to "give this matter your immediate attention and take action to suppress photographs as well as stories of this nature." The suppression was largely successful, although *Life* published in its May 22, 1944, issue a photograph of a prim woman from Arizona looking at a Japanese skull that her navy boyfriend had managed to smuggle home to her. He and thirteen friends had signed it and added an inscription: "This is a good jap—a dead one picked up on the New Guinea beach." *Life* noted that "the armed forces disapprove strongly of this sort of thing."[27]

Depiction of atrocities in Vietnam followed the World War II pattern. The first published pictures showed only atrocities committed by Asian enemies against Asian allies. Late in the war depiction of atrocities committed by American allies broke the pattern. Later still a few photographs and televised reports of American atrocities received wide attention, most notably army photographer Ronald L. Haeberle's photographs of the March 16, 1968, massacre at My Lai, in which American officers and enlisted men murdered at close range several hundred Vietnamese civilians, mainly women and children. After initially successful army efforts to suppress news of the incident, these photographs appeared in the *Cleveland Plain Dealer* in November 1969, and then in many other publications. Images visually documenting the torture and mutilation of American soldiers never appeared in any of the mainstream media, although some were depicted in Hollywood films released after the war and in *Hustler.* The publisher of *Hustler,* Larry Flynt, presented himself as a champion of free expression, but the context he devised for the images suggested that more than anything else he wished to profit from the images' exploitable shock value.

Differences in the presentation of the two wars obscured similarities in the military experience. World War II films suggested that soldiers' language habits resembled those of kids who had just learned their first swearwords. In *Abroad with Two Yanks* (1944) William Bendix teased the audience with the phrase "war is . . ."—but he never completed it, instead singing, "I'm only quoting General Sherman." Lester Cowan struggled to get approval from the Hays Office of the Motion Picture Producers and Distributors of America to include some mild profanity in his gritty 1945 film *The Story of G.I. Joe,* arguing that the dialogue was spoken "with such deep feeling and conviction that it could not be construed as blasphemy." The Hays Office refused, and Cowan removed the offending dialogue. Hollywood left cinematic depiction of the niceties of soldierly discourse to the Vietnam era, even though it was the World War II combat soldier whom James Jones referred to as "about the foulest-mouthed individual who ever existed on earth. Every other word was fucking this or fucking that." Films made during World War II, in contrast to those made by the end of the Vietnam War, also failed to reveal that American soldiers used derogatory terms for allies as well as for enemies. In practice "the soldiers made little distinction among the occupied, the liberated, and the Allied countries, since the people in all of them were foreigners—that is frogs, limeys, heinies, ginsoes, yellow bastards, wogs, flips or gooks."[28]

Television helped account for differences in presentation of the two wars. Millions of visitors first encountered television at the 1939–40 New York World's Fair, and it was used experimentally for training purposes during World War II. It did not, however, find a place in most American living rooms until the 1950s. Early television reporters went to the war in Vietnam to present the American side of the issue, as journalists had done in World War II. Such reports as Morley Safer's controversial 1965 story on the American burning of the village of Cam Ne differed significantly from anything shown during World War II and must have provoked doubts about U.S. policy in the minds of many viewers. Photographs published in *Newsweek* on 26 April and 21 May 1965 showing South Vietnamese soldiers kicking and tormenting captured enemies perhaps did the same. But at that time they "were minor currents in a general flow of reporting that was strongly supportive of American actions in Vietnam." Although critical reports were more common by 1966 and 1967, they remained the exception.[29]

After the early 1968 Tet offensive, television segments that used words and visual images to question claims by the American government became commonplace. During this offensive Viet Cong and North Vietnamese forces attacked thirty-six out of forty-four South Vietnamese provincial capitals, sixty-four district capitals, including five out of the South's six major cities, and temporarily occupied the grounds of the American embassy in Saigon. It was a military defeat but a public-relations victory for the communists, not only because the press failed to realize the dimensions of the military setback suffered by these forces, but also because Tet revealed the inaccuracy of American government claims that it would be impossible for the enemy to carry out such a major offensive. By that time a vigorous antiwar movement had long been in the streets. In Tet's aftermath many others grew dissatisfied with U.S. government policies in Vietnam, although those who favored lifting all restraints on American actions (sometimes including actions taken against antiwar demonstrators) were as numerous as those who wanted complete withdrawal.

The impact of television coverage of Vietnam, like that of any other visual image, depended on context. Television images showing pain caused by that war did not invariably lead to opposition to government policies. In 1967 a majority of Americans polled reported that images of the American dead in Vietnam made them more supportive of the American war effort there. Tet created a new context. David Culbert argues convincingly that timing increased the impact of the footage (and the still photograph) showing General Nguyen Ngoc Loan, the head of the South Vietnamese National Police, shoot a Viet Cong suspect in the head in the streets of Saigon. Its appearance on American television screens on the third day of the Tet offensive had the negative effect on public support feared by the Johnson administration and hoped for by the antiwar activists. It was one reason why a few weeks later polls showed for the first time that a majority of Americans disapproved of Johnson's Vietnam policy. Television is only part of the story of the loss of public support for American policies in Vietnam. During the war network executives, like their predecessors during World War II, never showed American soldiers with brains or intestines oozing out, or anyone who had just issued himself a reprieve from combat by shooting off his foot, or the mutilated body of a Vietnamese rape victim. Such censorship can be defended, but it shows the emptiness of claims that television brought home to viewers the full reality of war. Television reassured before it questioned, and mobilized support for the war before it contributed to a growing opposition.[30]

Fully engaged participants in the antiwar movement had the home front experiences that most resembled those common during World War II. They organized "school, work, and everything else" around activities related to the war. In 1988 a Vietnam-era activist wrote that opposing American policy in Vietnam "gave a clarity and purpose to our lives that, for many, has been missing ever since." Powerful symbols emerged from the government's opponents rather than from its supporters: the peace symbol, the dove, the "V" hand signal which the antiwar movement appropriated despite Richard Nixon's attempts to keep it as his own. The most widely known visual images of the war, although not always meant to be antiwar statements, were mobilized in support of that position: the Buddhist monk Thich Quang Duc's self-immolation to protest policies of the U.S.-backed regime in South Vietnam; the twelve-year-old Kim Phuc running down a road after being napalmed; General Loan's fateful shot to the head; a fifteen-year-old runaway from Florida expressing grief over the killings at Kent State.[31]

Public figures running conspicuous risks to their careers were also most often associated with the antiwar movement. During World War II movie stars such as Jimmy Stewart, Clark Gable, and Henry Fonda, as well as four thousand out of the fifty-seven hundred active major- and minor-league baseball players, including Ted Williams, Joe DiMaggio, and Hank Greenberg, went to war. Sons of Roosevelt's closest adviser, Harry Hopkins, and of Republican senator Leverett Saltonstall were among those killed, as was the future president John F. Kennedy's older brother, Joe. During the war in Vietnam, movie stars traveled to that country to entertain the troops, but very few of the famous and powerful or their children entered into combat. I know of no equivalent from Vietnam to the letter that Harry Hopkins wrote to General Eisenhower saying that he did not want his son to be given any special privileges because of his father's high position, although many without Hopkins's scruples did pull strings to win special privileges in the earlier war.[32]

Some who could have used their position to avoid fighting in Vietnam did not choose to do so—but not many. As of 1970 Clarence Long, whose son was wounded twice in the leg, was the only one of 535 senators and members of Congress whose child had been a combat casualty in Vietnam. None of the young men in Congress gave up his seat to take part in the fighting, as twenty-seven had done in the earlier war. The best-known American athletes who fought in Vietnam were those obligated to serve because they had gone to one of the military academies. Perhaps the most famous athlete in the world at the time, the boxer Muhammed Ali, risked his career by refusing induction into the U.S. Army. Many considered his act a cowardly one, but it received massive press attention, as did the rapid decision of boxing authorities to strip Ali of the heavyweight championship title because of his refusal. No celebrity who supported the war paid such a dramatic and conspicuous professional price for his or her position.[33]

With the government hoping to deemphasize the war, participants in the antiwar movement did most to keep alive a polarized way of seeing. Visual material distributed by the movement almost always presented the issues in stark terms of good and evil. Marchers held posters showing Vietnamese children maimed by American actions rather than victims of all sides in the war; antiwar cartoonists caricatured only American and South Vietnamese leaders; in an inversion of the home front analogy critics compared American military efforts not to what went on at factories and farms but to the actions of gangsters and Nazi storm troopers.

Promotion of this type of polarized view of the world focused the attention of many on the excesses of the antiwar movement rather than on troubling aspects of U.S. policy. It gave aid and comfort to later apologists who sought to defend American actions in Vietnam without taking the trouble to examine closely what actually happened. These apologists found it easier to argue against the view that Americans were carrying out genocide in Vietnam than to explain what positive consequences reasonably might have been expected from American decisions to support the French effort there, easier to point out the flaws in uncritical acceptance of everything the North Vietnamese government stood for than to justify the behavior of leaders in the South, easier to condemn the protesters who threw rocks at prowar speakers than to answer the questions raised by the far larger number who wanted to encourage debate.

Participants in the antiwar movement disagreed among themselves over whether they should present their position in simple terms of right and wrong. But the implication that all the right was on the side of the antiwar position dominated the visual legacy of the movement. Polarized ways of seeing nurtured by World War II helped get the United States into the Vietnam conflict and helped promote initial faith in the government's assurance of the necessity for this involvement. To the extent to which dissenters influenced the visual associations Americans had with the war in Vietnam they worked within the same polarized structure, inverting only content. If World War II was the straightforward movie everybody could be in, Vietnam was the sequel that was so confused that it demanded a review of the original. Perhaps the seeds of a later confusion were present in the midst of seeming clarity.

War

Legacies

Although Americans probably have seen more of World War II than of any other event, much remains concealed. The bones of American fliers who died in 1943 when their bomber, *Lady Be Good,* crashed in Libya were part of the war's invisible legacy until found by a U.S. Army search team as part of Operation Climax in May 1960. The army's decision to censor photographs of the team's findings prolonged this invisibility.

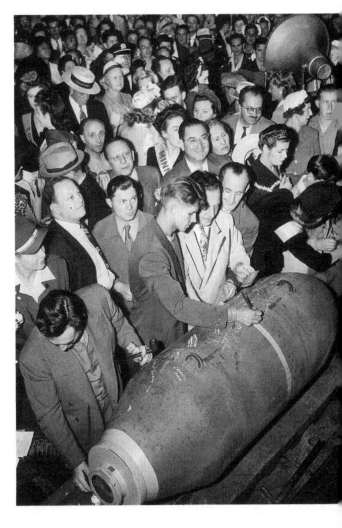

Will Chicago Be Bombed?

**Study this map and decide for yourself!
Look at a globe and note the probable route
of bombers from Norway's coast to Chicago!**

A study of this map will show you that the Chicago area, a
vast industrial city, vitally important to war production, is
as near to enemy bases as New York City, Detroit or Boston.
Chicago is nearer the enemy than Washington and the bomber
route over Greenland and Canada is less well protected.
Chicago is only a few hours flying time from Nazi bases in
Norway. Yes, it *can* happen *here.* Preparedness is the only
reasonable, sensible attitude to take! Chicagoland must be
ready!

The war gave a focus and intensity to American visual experience not matched for any sustained period before or
since. The government arranged constant reminders that
everything citizens did, including lowering their driving
speed to conserve gas, had an impact on the war effort,
and displayed incentives to visual alertness such as a map
reminding Chicagoans that their city was vulnerable to direct attack by German planes stationed in Norway and
flying over the Arctic. The Office of War Information distributed a photograph of a public bomb signing with this
caption: "The Greater New York War Bond Pledge Campaign neared its end in Times Square where pledgees
signed their autographs to big and little bombs with the
happy thought that the missiles might fall on the Japanese
capital."

In order to maintain the unrelenting commitment of civilians to the war effort demanded by official imagery, censors withheld photographs that sent contradictory messages, such as one showing a general and aide fishing during a break from military duties.

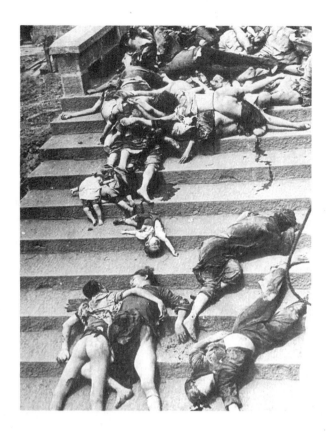

In part because of cultural assumptions that life was held more cheaply in the East than in the West, wartime visual imagery usually associated mass death with the non-Western world. Thus a photograph showing Chinese trampled to death while rushing for bomb shelters during a Japanese air raid on Chungking (above) appeared in numerous publications and was made into an anti-Japanese poster. In contrast, even late in the war the army censored photographs like one taken in 1944 (left) showing "American dead piled up in a buffalo on Lorengau Beach, Manus Island in the Admiralty Gp., awaiting movement for burial." This visual tradition of associating mass death with remote cultures complicated for Americans the already difficult task of comprehending the human suffering caused by Nazi extermination policies or by Allied bombardment of cities in distant countries.

The German attack on the Soviet Union in June 1941 won that country the sympathy of many Americans, although many others maintained the hostile attitude toward the belligerents expressed in a *Chicago Tribune* cartoon that appeared two days before Pearl Harbor (above left). Some anti-Soviet feelings remained even after American entry into the war made the United States and the Soviet Union allies. Most wartime imagery, however, presented the Soviet Union and its peoples favorably (above right) and emphasized the similarity between their values (and even preferences as consumers) and those of Americans. Soon after the war ended, escalating tensions between the former allies meant that depictions of the Soviets in American media became almost as consistently negative as those of the Axis powers had been during the war. A Fitzpatrick cartoon in the *St. Louis Post-Dispatch* (left) drew on visual imagery from World War II to warn against present dangers.

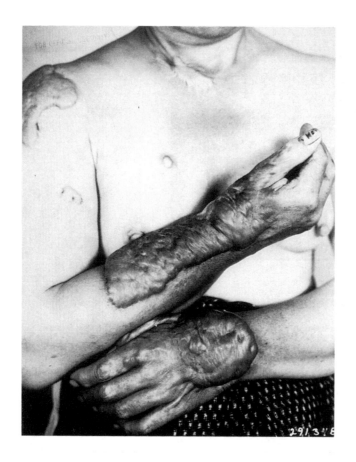

Although the government dismantled the civilian Office of Censorship as soon as the war ended, Soviet-American tensions provided one impetus for continuation of military censorship. Much of the visual evidence of the human impact of atomic bombs remained in the files of censored material for decades after the bombing of Hiroshima and Nagasaki, as is this photograph of the arms and hands of a survivor of the Nagasaki bomb. During the cold war officials continued their practice of censoring material that documented conflicts among Allied soldiers. One censored photograph from 1946, for example, showed the bloody door of the Rome apartment of an English captain who had allegedly been assaulted by two American soldiers. The caption noted that "the base of the lamp, which was one of the weapons used in the assault, rests on the table." For an account of how film footage of the devastation caused by the atomic bombings reached the American public after more than two decades of censorship, see Erik Barnouw, "The Hiroshima-Nagasaki Footage," *Historical Journal of Film, Radio, and Television* 2 (March 1982): 91–100.

Perhaps because the war in Korea began less than five years after the end of World War II, published pictures from the beginning of the Korean War matched the candor of those from the end of World War II and soon surpassed it. For instance, although officials did not release any photographs of crying American soldiers during World War II, such photographs were published during the first months of the war in Korea. Moreover, the caption to the photograph above also had a tone that would not have appeared in the early phase of World War II: "A grief stricken American infantryman whose buddy has been killed in action is comforted by another soldier. In the background of the picture a corpsman methodically fills out casualty tags." Although the government did not set up a censorship apparatus as formal and elaborate as that which existed during the two world wars, officials did censor many visual images from Korea, such as the one at left: "This Korean boy was a victim of Allied bombing of a Korean village where Chinese Communist forces made their Headquarters." This policy probably added to the impact of similar photographs which appeared during the war in Vietnam.

In World War II officials also censored photographs documenting questionable American treatment of the enemy. Army censors, for instance, withheld a photograph showing the severed head of a Japanese soldier hanging from a tree in Burma, presumably put there by American troops or their allies and intended, according to the Army Signal Corps caption, as "a symbol of the Japanese defeat in Northern Burma." They also kept out of view another 1945 photograph, captioned "This patrol captured two Nips alive," which might have been interpreted as documentation of rough treatment of prisoners. Both the government and the press followed the practice of withholding similar images during the early phases of American involvement in Vietnam. The longer the war there continued, the more people, soldiers as well as journalists, thought it important to bring to the attention of the public that Americans as well as Vietnamese often committed atrocities. By late in the war the army's attempt to suppress photographs of the American massacre at My Lai failed, resulting in the publication, eighteen months after the incident, of photographs very different from any released during World War II.

CHRISTMAS '69

Just a little "Piece" from the "NAM"

Soldiers in Vietnam did not have to make their letters home conform to the tight restrictions imposed on G.I.s during World War II. Censors in that war would not have tolerated the Christmas card that the navy hospital corpsman Andrew T. Gerstmyer sent from Vietnam in 1969, in which he is holding a Vietnamese boy's amputated foot. His medical unit had toiled for three days to save the foot, injured during a Vietcong rocket attack on Quang Tri City Northern I Corps in November 1969, before concluding that they had to amputate it. Inside the card Gerstmyer wrote, "I hope your Christmas is better than mine," and "WHY ME?" Sustaining a complex vision of war has proved as difficult a challenge with regard to Vietnam as it was for earlier wars. But unlike in World War II, images of pain inflicted by the United States and its allies remain the most widely remembered visual legacy of the Vietnam War. Images showing suffering caused by actions of North Vietnamese and Vietcong fighters have not retained any hold in public memory, although in the early years of the American buildup the news media showed such images far more often than they showed pictures of suffering caused by the actions of Americans and their allies. One example of a "disremembered" image is this photograph (left) showing Pham Tong mourning the death of his eight-year old daughter, Pham Thi Hai, who was shot by Vietcong guerrillas in Binh Dinh Province, Central Vietnam, in September 1964.

If visual imagery helped build wartime hatreds, it also recorded and sometimes contributed to postwar reconcilia-
tions. The photograph at left documented that Italian-
Americans shared the relief felt by most other Americans
upon the final victory of the Allied powers over an Axis
coalition that had included Italy. In September 1945, the
month when Japan signed formal documents of surrender,
one of the first American soldiers to arrive in Tokyo found
that a shared fascination with the camera's magic contributed to the replacement of war's monologues by more
promising forms of human interaction.

Among their other legacies, visual images left unforgetta-
ble testimony to what can happen to populations that find
themselves compelled to view one another only through
bombsights. Decades in the files of censored material have
not diminished the power of this photograph of American
servicemen who died on the liberty ship *Matthew P.
Deady* in the Philippines on 3 November 1944.

• • • • • • • •

The war came as a great relief, like a reverse earthquake, that in one terrible jerk shook everything disjointed, distorted, askew back into place. Japanese bombs had finally brought national unity to the U.S.

—*Time*, 15 December 1941

EPILOGUE

Fifty years after *Time* editors wrote those words, World War II continues to provide Americans with a vision of unity. Seven of the last eight U.S. presidents served in World War II, counting the one whom the army assigned to Hollywood. The one who did not serve, Jimmy Carter, was preparing for duty at the United States Naval Academy at the war's end. Although Bill Clinton's 1992 victory ended the era of leaders who had participated in World War II, the war will retain a prominent role in popular culture and public discourse because there is no other event or era that serves the purposes it does.

This does not mean that Americans have a precise knowledge of the history of the war. V-E Day parades and other such commemorations are not as integral a part of national life as they are in areas more directly affected by its ravages, such as Russia. But even among generations whose understanding of World War II includes the impression that, to quote one student, Pearl Harbor is "that place the Vietnamese bombed," World War II is recognized as a very important event during which America was on the right side. Hence politicians and historians, advertisers and teachers,

153

filmmakers and novelists, will continue to call on their particular readings of the message of World War II to bolster their authority, support their causes, and offer moral guidance to their listeners, readers, and viewers.

It will be an honest guide to the extent to which the war as actually experienced—in combat and at home, by Americans as well as Japanese and Germans, Romanians and Wake Islanders—serves as the basis for assessing its meaning. During the war the images that best communicated experiential realities of the war were ones that revealed their own limits. As Annette Insdorf has noted, *The Pawnbroker* (1965) was one of the most revealing films about the Holocaust because it did not pretend that any one human consciousness could comprehend the enormity of that horror, but shared with viewers some of the fragmentary glimpses of it burdening the memory of the central character. Less can be more.[1]

The impact of images depended on their interaction with context. Some images that gave a misleading impression of the war were faked or falsely captioned, but more misled because they were partial truths presented as whole truths. Wartime images of Japanese brutality accurately documented that such behavior was common, but by being placed in a visual context lacking depiction of Allied brutality they falsely suggested that only the enemy behaved in such a way. Misperceived partial truth continues to be a greater obstacle than falsehood to a clear understanding of World War II.

Experience contributes to such an understanding when it is neither idealized nor idolized. Some use it, however, as a weapon of intimidation. Paul Fussell asserted on the basis of his World War II experience the right to deliver unchallengeable judgments on everything from the moral character of public officials to the wisdom of the decision to use two atomic bombs in the war. Fussell's *Wartime* becomes one of the most powerful books about the war if accepted as the testimony of an exceptionally smart and well-informed writer writing from the particular viewpoint of an angry combat veteran. Fussell's anger, nurtured over four decades, allowed him to expose the horrors, hypocrisies, and absurdities of wartime as few others have. But his book obscures more than it clarifies if mistaken for a reliable analysis of the motivations, beliefs, and experiences of all the civilians who had to make key decisions regarding the war and its presentation, or of all the photographers, journalists, and others who tried to record it. Americans who filtered direct encounters with combat through sensibilities less adversarial or more theistic than Fussell's had a different story to tell.

Fussell had no obligation to dilute the force of his statement by warning readers of its limitations, but readers who seek understanding in addition to the satisfactions of shared or vicarious outrage must be alert to them. Marine corporal J. B. Sacks, in a letter to his family in July 1944 describing his landing at Saipan, recorded the type of war experience Fussell's book could not accommodate. Sacks wrote that he had been shaken by seeing for the first time dead American Marines, then had gotten over the crisis with the help of the "wel-come" sight "of *many good japs* (dead ones) strewn all over the place." He continued, "When we were heading for Carapan, we all talked about how we were going to kill any jap we saw. Young or old, male or female. But, we really changed our minds when tattered, terror and hunger stricken kids, the age of Harvey, Linda, and even carrying babes as young as Bobbie, came out of holes and caves waving a torn white rag. Well this was really a sight that put a lump in your throat. The killing was confined to those japs who preferred dying for their emperor rather than surrender."[2]

This extraordinary letter shows the inadequacy of accounts that sanitize war, but also of those that speak only of its brutalizing effect. The casual and stereotyped attitude toward killing Japanese soldiers expressed in the final sentence was often displayed in wartime visual imagery, but photographs, newsreels, films, advertisements, and posters never suggested that Americans might consider indiscriminately killing civilians. Indeed, these images almost never reminded viewers that there were Japanese children, women, old people, and gentle men. When Americans at home did get a glimpse of Japanese children, as in Capra's propaganda films, they saw their elders training them for military duty. Those on the home front who formed their understanding of the war's meaning through such imagery were not likely to undergo the type of transformation experienced by Sacks, nor make any emotional connection between the Harveys, Lindas, and Bobbies in their lives and those feeling the consequences of American military force.

An understanding of the war grounded in study of the experiences it engendered cannot fail to recognize its complexity. I have argued in this book that wartime visual imagery understated this complexity. It thereby encouraged polarized ways of seeing that affected postwar American attitudes and policies. The appeal of such formulaic ways of seeing, and the assumptions about history associated with them, is powerful in part because of the psychological satisfactions and conveniences they afford. It is easier to remember a formula, whether it be that Americans were precision bombers or Americans were indis-criminate mass killers, than to engage in sorting out the truth about specific cases. Sifting the truth requires that we enter into a dialogue between beliefs and evidence; relying on formulas requires only that we impose beliefs on evidence. The visual presentation of World War II was more a reflection than a cause of formulaic ways of thinking deeply embedded in human behavior and American culture, but it helped reinforce them.

Vietnam was the most tragic result. Had Americans seen more of World War II perhaps they would have had less war to see in Vietnam. This is not because full exposure to the horrors of war would have made Americans more reluctant to become involved in another one: some of the most shocking of all the pictures to emerge from World War II, those of Nazi concentration camps, suggested that delay of an unavoidable war can bring the most obscene outcomes. Rather, it is because more exposure to the ambiguities of war and of relations among nations might have encouraged more rigorous questioning of subsequent policies based more on overgeneralized assumptions about a world divided into "free" and "communist" blocs than on critical analysis of particular cases. The numbing casualty statistics of modern war make it easy to forget that the death of each individual is a brutally specific fact in the lives of those who loved them. Those making, answering, or resisting the call to war would do well to be sure they are as certain of their facts as will be the mourners who greet the returning coffins.

Elusive but fundamentally important truths about individual lived experiences, such as those revealed by Fussell and Sacks, must be included among the requisite facts. Understanding and communicating the many ways World War II was experienced, though difficult at the time, is no less difficult fifty years later. If one of the obstacles to such an effort is the polarized way of seeing encouraged by World War II, the war also left other legacies which contributed to more open-eyed ways of seeing. Perhaps the most important was the civil-rights movement of the postwar decades. This movement grew in part from the enhanced motivations and means for resistance to injustice and from the new opportunities which many black Americans encountered during World War II.

The war in the Persian Gulf demonstrated the impact of the civil-rights movement on depiction of later wars. Analysis of coverage of the Gulf War has placed emphasis on the high degree of military control maintained over the media, especially the visual media. But comparison of the coverage of that war with coverage of World War II shows how the options available to propagandists and censors have changed and in some ways narrowed. Not only the presence of a black, Colin Powell, as head of the Joint Chiefs of Staff, but the circumstances that made his appointment possible, made it difficult to imagine the United States government in 1991 issuing statements like the ones in the World War II propaganda film *Action at Anguar*: "By this time we had shot, blasted, or cooked six hundred of the little apes." Such lines also were absent from official government material on Vietnam, partly because the Vietnamese were allies of the United States as well as enemies, but also because that war reached its peak soon after the civil-rights movement had transformed American life and government. However easily American soldiers in Vietnam took to the term *gook* to describe their Asian enemies and allies, and however easily some Persian Gulf troops made similar use of *sand nigger* to describe Arabs, the absence of such language from official propaganda is a significant change. Despite the persistent exploitation of racial fears and hatred in American political campaigns, it seems unlikely that in the foreseeable future either the government or large private organizations will revert to the practice, common in World War II, of creating visual imagery that crudely and viciously distorts the physical appearance of various racial and national groups.[3]

Although officially sanctioned visual racism has decreased, other forms of visual obfuscation have flourished. As during World War II, the most misleading images to come out of the Gulf War were not faked or doctored ones but those placed in a context that overstated, or understated, how representative they were. Obvious examples were images taken from the monitors that allowed military personnel to direct laser-guided "smart bombs" at precise targets and observe the results. In the tradition of the World War II emphasis on the accuracy and humanitarianism of American bombing, imagery released by the U.S. government depicted the material, rather than human, destruction caused by these explosives, and left the impression that such precision weapons accounted for a majority, rather than a small fraction, of the bomb tonnage that U.S. forces dropped during the war. The weapons themselves, and the satellite technology that allowed images they generated quickly to be transmitted to television screens in American living rooms, indicate how greatly human choice can now shape what there is to see in the world, and who gets to see it. This condition of choice presents unprecedented possibilities for deception and revelation.

Only long struggle is likely to determine which becomes dominant. Images created and made public during World War II through the efforts of Bill Mauldin, John Huston, Margaret Bourke-White, Carl Mydans, Elmer Davis, Dwight David Eisenhower, and thousands of others unmentioned in this book remain useful to those who favor revelation. Nothing that those people did could make certain that Americans in battle or at home would act wisely. But those who mustered the courage, imagination, and skill to broaden awareness of the diverse consequences of the American war effort made it more likely that Americans would act knowingly. If knowledge does not assure wise action, its absence makes it less likely. More generally, those who give clear and forceful expression to the experiences of one part of the population in ways that make this experience more understandable to others serve the needs of peacetime as well as of wartime. Such understanding encourages both collective action and toleration of differences. Failure to take collective action on the basis of strong commitments will lead to irreversible degradation of the environment, which sustains life on earth. Inability to tolerate the uncertainties and frictions engendered by the interaction of people of many different beliefs and preferences tempts some to seek the solace of nuclear silence or the illusory clarification promised by repression, which in a world with limitless capacity for self-destruction ultimately assumes the form of genocide.

One-half century after the attack on Pearl Harbor World War II continues both to blind and to illuminate. The intertwining of all human lives displays the great variety of patterns that can be woven out of its mixed legacy. With the world's military arsenals containing explosive power equivalent to many tons of TNT for every person on earth, we all go about our daily tasks caught in a bombsight as were the citizens of Dresden and Coventry, Tokyo and London, Hiroshima and Nagasaki. In such a world we cannot ignore, except at everyone's peril, the disturbing yet life-affirming images furnished by those photographers, filmmakers, graphic artists, and others who saw in war and through war our capacity for brutality and dignity, and who did what they could to help us tell the two apart.

NOTES

PROLOGUE

1. *Life,* 14 May 1945, pp. 40B–C. Capa took the photograph in Leipzig on April 18, shortly before the city surrendered to Allied forces. The phrase "chamber of horrors" is mentioned on p. 7 of an internal study of the Pictorial Branch of the News Division, War Department Bureau of Public Relations (BPR), undated but with a cover letter of 3 November 1942, 020.4–5, Gen Rec of the Army Staff, PR Div, RG165, entry 499, box 10, National Archives (NA). The army began construction of the Pentagon in September 1941 and completed it early in 1943. Although Capa's was the first photograph in *Life* to record such a bloody scene with an American soldier, earlier the magazine had reproduced paintings showing an abundance of American blood. See the Tom Lea painting of a Japanese attack on the *Hornet,* in *Life,* 2 August 1943, p. 47.

2. Callaway interview in "Search for Tomorrow," *Chicago Times Magazine,* September-October 1988, p. 37. Courtesy John D. Callaway, Senior Correspondent, WTTW (PBS) Chicago.

3. Geoffrey Perrett, *Days of Sadness, Years of Triumph: The American People, 1939–1945* (Baltimore, 1974), 330–35; James MacGregor Burns, *Roosevelt: The Soldier of Freedom, 1940–1945* (New York, 1970), 54.

4. *Life,* 26 October 1942, pp. 127–28. The final quotes are from Susan Moeller, *Shooting War: Photography and the American Experience of Combat* (New York, 1988), 181.

5. Studies attempting to measure the impact of propaganda and other forms of verbal and visual persuasion on audiences number in the tens of thousands. Some of those most pertinent to the study of the American experience in World War II are discussed in Frank W. Fox, *Madison Avenue Goes to War: The Strange Military Career of American Advertising, 1941–45* (Provo, Utah, 1975), 3–9, and in David Culbert, ed., *Film and Propaganda in America: A Documentary History,* vol. 2, *World War II: Part 1* (New York, 1990), xxii–xxiv.

6. George Will, "The Price of Power," *Newsweek,* 7 November 1983, p. 142. Critic Walter Goodman reached a conclusion similar to Will's: "When focused on distant pinpoint hits, military briefings, parades and enemy aggression, the camera can rally a spirit of combat. But when it turns toward the down and dirty consequences of war, it becomes the super weapon of pacifism." See Goodman, "How Bad Is the War? Depends on the Images," *New York Times,* 5 November 1991, p. B3.

CHAPTER I: *RATIONING DEATH*

1. Official War Review No. 19 in CPI film series, issued by Division of Films, CPI, 1918, NA.

2. *Time,* quoted in Gary R. Hess, *The United States at War, 1941–1945* (Arlington Heights, Ill., 1986), 44. Three out of ten figure in supplementary material attached to part 5 of "Government Information Manual for the Motion Picture Industry" (first version, summer 1942), RG208, entry 285, box 1517, NA. This version of the manual is reprinted in *Historical Journal of Film, Radio and Television* 3, no. 2 (1983): 171–80. Of respondents to a March 1942 poll, 62 percent wanted the United States to put the most effort into the fight with Japan; 21 percent thought Germany should be the main target (cited in Hess, *United States at War,* 42). As late as March 1943 an OWI observer in Chicago reported that because of uneasiness over the wartime alliance with "Bolshevist Russia" a "sentiment for a negotiated peace is crystalizing." See undated memo, "War, War Aims and Post-war World," with 1 March 1943 report from Chicago, Records of the Office of Government Reports, United States Information Service (USIS), Bureau of Special Services (BSS), RG44, entry 149, box 1710, NA.

3. War Department (WD) Training Circular No. 15 (16 February 1943), Army Adjutant Genereal (AG), RG407, entry 360, box 2806, NA; Roosevelt memo, 20 February 1941, AG 000.7, 22 January 1941, AG, RG407, entry 360, box 3, NA.

4. Roosevelt put FBI director J. Edgar Hoover in charge of national censorship the day after Pearl Harbor, but by 16 December he had appointed Byron Price as head of the Office of Censorship, and Price took over those responsibilities. See Richard Gid Powers, *Secrecy and Power: The Life of J. Edgar Hoover* (New York, 1987), 248.

5. See BPR internal study cited in prologue, n. 1; Moeller, *Shooting War,* 181–82; *Purple Heart Valley,* 107. In my research I have not found a single example of a censor being reprimanded for *not* letting material through, although sometimes censors would receive directives telling them to start releasing

certain categories of previously withheld material. For an example of censors being "disciplined" for letting too much through see Sec of War Stimson to Sec of Navy Knox, 29 September 1942, AG 000.73, RG407, entry 360, box 3, NA. On the actions of British censors to withhold pictures of victims of Allied bombing raids, see Vicki Goldberg, *Margaret Bourke-White: A Biography* (New York, 1986), 269.

6. Elmer Davis and Byron Price, *War Information and Censorship* (Washington, D.C., 1943), 46.

7. Creel to Davis, 4 August 1942, Elmer Davis papers, Library of Congress (LC). To the best of my knowledge no public mention was made of the Chamber of Horrors until the appearance of my article "A Note on U.S. Photo Censorship in World War II," *Historical Journal of Film, Radio, and Television* 5, no. 2 (1985): 192. Davis's handwritten note is on the copy of the letter in his records at LC. On internal changes and struggles at OWI see Allan Winkler, *The Politics of Propaganda: The Office of War Information, 1942–1945* (New Haven, 1978), esp. 37.

8. Creel to Davis, 4 August 1942, Elmer Davis papers, LC.

9. For the adjutant general asking for more see memo dated 30 June 1942, in file marked AG 062–31 March 1945, RG407, entry 360, box 1103; OWI memo, unsigned and undated but c. spring 1943, in file Memo to Staff, RG208, entry E-79, box 241, NA. It is worth noting that despite his remarks two decades later in the Chautauqua speech, Roosevelt's correspondence in 1918 when as assistant secretary of the navy he visited World War I battle fronts displayed more enthusiasm than aversion for war. See Geoffrey C. Ward, *A First-Class Temperament: The Emergence of Franklin Roosevelt* (New York, 1989), 386. Although navy policies often gave credence to Davis's characterization of King's attitude, King himself sometimes was a candid source of information for reporters whom he trusted.

10. *Newsweek,* 17 May 1943, p. 25; Charles L. Allen of OWI News Bureau to Palmer Hoyt, Director, Domestic Branch, 16 August 1943, 062.11–186, Public Information Div, RG165, entry 499, box 25, NA.

11. "Minutes of Meeting of War Informa-

tion Board," 30 August 1943, RG208, entry 16, box 105, NA; reprint of Davis's final "Report to the President" on OWI, in *Journalism Monographs,* no. 7 (August 1968): 23. On OWI's mandate see "OWI Information Guide, May, 1943," USIS, BSS, RG44, entry 149, box 1713, NA.

12. Memos from Corr Panel Sections to Clyde W. Hart, 23 August 1943, and Clarence Glick, 30 August 1943 ("Lack of Realism about the Fighting Front—Its Effects"), ibid., box 1710; "Current Surveys," OWI, no. 16 (11 August 1943), ibid., box 1715.

13. I base my estimate of the number of photographs reviewed and released by BPR on three memos in Public Information Div, RG165, entry 499, NA. Two, dated 3 September 1943 and 22 September 1943, are in 062.1, box 23; the other, dated 2 September 1943, is in 062.1–689, box 25. See also, in box 25, memo from K. B. Lawton, Chief, Army Pictorial Service, to Captain B. W. Hellings, 31 August 1943.

14. See draft of this radiogram with cover memo dated 1 September 1943, in file marked "AG 062 1 September 43" in RG407, entry 360, box 1103, NA.

15. *Time,* 22 June 1942, quoted in Robert E. Summers, *Wartime Censorship of Press and Radio* (New York, 1942), 190; Winston S. Churchill, *The Grand Alliance* (New York, 1962), 582; letter to Edgar Newton Eisenhower, 26 September 1944, in Alfred Chandler, Jr., ed., *The Papers of Dwight David Eisenhower,* vol. 4, *The War Years* (Baltimore, 1970), doc. 1999. On military complaints about press maneuvering see Loudon Wainwright, *The Great American Magazine: An Inside History of Life* (New York, 1986), 153–54.

16. *Journal American* and *Iron Age* quoted in Office of Facts and Figures (OFF) "Weekly Media Report," nos. 7 and 8 (20 and 27 March 1942), USIS, BSS, RG44, entry 149, box 1720, NA; on tapping and planting see Thomas Fleming, "The Big Leak," *American Heritage,* December 1987, p. 71. On press and Roosevelt see David Brinkley, *Washington Goes to War* (New York, 1988), 170–71, 182.

17. Drew Pearson and Robert S. Allyn, "Merry-Go-Round," *Washington Times-Herald,* 17 April 1941; E. D. Canham, "The Battle for News," in F. L. Mott, ed., *Journalism in Wartime* (Washington, D.C., 1943), 44–47. For one early report on high respect for Davis despite dissatisfaction with government restrictions, see 13 November 1942 memo on "Developing Situation—Governments Information Policy Antagonizes Public and Press," USIS, BSS, RG44, entry 149, box 1710, NA.

18. James L. Baughman, *Henry R. Luce and the Rise of the American News Media* (Boston, 1987), 60; *Daily News* editor quoted in *Newsweek,* 20 September 1943, p. 98; *Life* truth statement quoted in Ross Gregory, *America 1941: A Nation at the Crossroads* (New York, 1989), 2; sports comparison in *Life,* 20 September 1943, p. 34. Before the war mainstream magazines occasionally ran shocking pictures, as when *Time* showed the naked corpse of a lynched man in the early 1930s, but such images were rare. See Baughman, *Luce,* 83. Prior to the lifting of censorship of photographs of dead American soldiers, *Life* and other publications occasionally ran photographs of American dead covered by blankets or of their flag-draped caskets. See *Life,* 25 January 1943, p. 38, and 2 August 1943, p. 23.

19. Letter to the editor, *Life,* 11 October 1943 ("made a mockery of sacrifice"); editorial, "War Information," *Washington Post,* 11 September 1943; telegram to OWI from Clark Salmon, New Orleans, undated but c. 22 September 1943, in RG208, entry 236, box 4011.

20. Memo from Corr Panels Section to Herman Hettinger, 22 September 1943, USIS, BSS, RG44, entry 149, box 1710, NA (". . . war closer home"); "OWI Current Surveys," no. 24 (6 October 1943), ibid., box 1715; "Appraisals of the Third War Loan Drive," Div of Research Report No. C16 (10 October 1943), ibid., box 1718.

21. "Minutes of Meeting of War Information Board," 26 January 1944, RG208, entry 16, box 105, NA; report, "Over-the-Hump Psychology," in the file "Information Roundup," 23 December 1943, USIS, BSS, RG44, entry 149, box 1713, NA. On connections between censorship, attitudes toward Japan, and American bombing policy, see Michael S. Sherry, *The Rise of American Air Power: The Creation of Armageddon* (New Haven, 1987), 242.

22. Copies of Marshall cable to Eisenhower, 5 January 1944, with identical cables to other commanding generals, are in 062.2 (case 2), Army Chief of Staff, RG165, entry 13, box 133, and in AG 062.2, 30 December 1943, RG407, entry 360, box 1104, NA. The cable seems to have been based on a memo, 20 December 1943, by Undersecretary of War Robert P. Patterson in the file just cited. For examples of continuing official concern over public apathy see Stephen E. Ambrose, *The Supreme Commander: The War Years of Gen. Dwight D. Eisenhower* (Garden City, N.J., 1970), 538, and confidential OWI pamphlet, "V-E Day," in "OWI Records Relating to War Bond Drives," RG208, entry 54, box 176, NA. Many conflicting goals influenced how the war was depicted in its closing months. Immediately after the German surrender photographs of Allied leaders shaking hands with Goering and other Nazi leaders sparked "violent protests" and led to this cable to Eisenhower's headquarters: "Urgently desire that you immediately stimulate pictures showing stern attitude of American military personnel and resulting conditions surrounding German prisoners of all ranks." See messages of 13 and 14 May 1945 in 000.7–112, Public Information Div, RG165, entry 499, box 58, NA.

23. Davis quoted in unsigned covered letter, 5 June 1944, unsigned memo to War Loan Committee in "OWI Records Relating to War Bond Drives," RG208, entry 54, box 177, NA. John Huston, *An Open Book* (New York, 1980), 110.

24. Drafts of Marshall cable to Eisenhower, 5 January 1944, in 062.2 (case 2), Army Chief of Staff, RG165, entry 13, box 133, and in AG 062.2 (30 December 1943) in RG407, entry 360, box 1104, NA; censorship guidelines in "SHAEF Press Censorship Guidance #16" (1 June 1944), 000.7–313, in PR Div, RG165, entry 499, NA; memo from Eisenhower to WD, 9 February 1945, 062.1–52, Public Information Div, RG165, entry 499, box 67, NA. Return memo, 14 February 1945, ibid., stated that the War Intelligence Division had no objection to continuing the policy.

25. Office of the Inspector General to Assistant Chief of Staff, 16 December 1944, 000.7–28, Public Information Div, RG165,

entry 499, box 57, NA; Director, BPR, to Commanding Generals in all Theaters of Operation, 30 April 1944, 000.7–77, Public Information Div, RG165, entry 499, box 32, NA; the Surgeon General's report is described in Martin Gilbert, *The Second World War: A Complete History* (New York, 1989), 599.

26. Richard A. Gabriel, *No More Heroes: Madness and Psychiatry in War* (New York, 1987), 4, 72–74, discusses the screening efforts. One stated intention of the screening was to eliminate homosexuals, but in fact it infrequently served this purpose. Of the nearly 18 million men examined, the military explicitly rejected less than five thousand as homosexual. See Allan Bérubé, *Coming Out Under Fire: The History of Gay Men and Women in World War II* (New York, 1991), 33. On the "enormous" volume of mail elicited by Patton's action, and for summaries of public and editorial responses to that incident, see the file marked "Editorial Analysis Extras 6/25/43–12/24/43," USIS, BSS, RG44, entry 149, box 1712, NA. Fellow military officers as well as the public disagreed with Patton's action. When the army surveyed different groups of company grade officers to find out what they believed should be done with "men who get shell-shocked, blow their tops, go haywire," at the most 6 percent, and in some cases only 1 percent, agreed they "should be treated as cowards and punished." See Moeller, *Shooting War*, 176.

27. All quotations are from "Analysis of Editorial Opinion #31" (14 January 1944) and "Analysis of Editorial Opinion #42" (31 March 1944), USIS, BSS, RG44, entry 149, box 1712, NA. Official handling of the Patton story caused much distrust. Although the military took most of the heat, members of the press participated in the early suppression of the Patton incident, having been convinced by Eisenhower that breaking the story might force him to remove Patton from his command and thereby do great damage to the Allied war effort. See Stephen E. Ambrose, *Eisenhower*, vol. 1, *Soldier, General of the Army, President-Elect, 1890–1952* (New York, 1983), 251.

28. Denis Winter, *Death's Men: Soldiers of the Great War* (New York, 1979), 207–8.

29. Steinbeck quotation from *Washington*

Post, 27 September 1943. The decision in the 1922 New York case *Pathe Exchange Inc. v. Cobb* is summarized in Jonathan Green, *The Encyclopedia of Censorship* (New York, 1990), 332.

30. Lee Kennett, *For the Duration: The United States Goes to War, Pearl Harbor—1942* (New York, 1985), 155 (on NBC); Raymond Fielding, *The American Newsreel, 1911–1967* (Norman, Okla., 1972), 289; Baughman, *Luce,* 81.

31. Memo from Jesse O. Irvin to George H. Lyon, "Newsreels of October 13, 1943," in RG208, entry E-79, box 241, NA; "it is expensive" quoted in Fielding, *American Newsreel,* 109; Richard W. Steele, "The Great Debate: Roosevelt, the Media, and the Coming of the War, 1940–1941," *Journal of American History (JAH)* 71 (June 1984): 73.

32. OWI Bureau of Intelligence, Media Div, "Special Intelligence Report #51" (2 July 1942), RG44, entry 171, box 1845, NA.

33. "Newsreel Critique" for 9 January 1943, RG208, entry 285, box 1518, NA; memo, 6 December 1940, AG000.7, Army-Navy Unclassified Decimal Files of General Correspondence, RG407, box 4, NA; Claude R. Collins, Newsreel Coordinator, War Activities Committee, Motion Picture Industry to Harold Jacobs, 14 May 1942, file marked "Newsreel Coverage," RG208, entry 285, box 1518, NA; OWI Bureau of Motion Pictures to Navy Dept., Bureau of PR, 8 October 1942, in file marked "War Dept.," ibid., box 1520. Gallup polls taken early in the war indicated that Americans who thought that the newsreels did not show enough of the war outnumbered those who thought they showed too much by as much as two to one. See George Gallup to Nelson Poynter, 25 April 1942, in file marked "CPS. The early days in OFF," USIS, BSS, RG44, entry 149, box 1711, NA.

34. "Newsreel Critique" for 31 October 1942, RG208, entry 285, box 1518; memo from Jesse O. Irvin to George H. Lyon, "Newsreels of October 13, 1943," RG208, entry E-79, box 241, NA; memo from John T. Gibbs to George H. Lyon, "Newsreels of Dec. 8, 1943," ibid.

35. Statistics from Joe Morella, Edward Z. Epstein, and John Griggs, *The Films of World War II* (Secaucus, N.J., 1973), 11. For an ex-

cellent, highly detailed account of wartime relations between Hollywood and Washington see Clayton R. Koppes and Gregory D. Black, *Hollywood Goes to War: How Politics, Profits and Propaganda Shaped World War II Movies* (New York, 1987).

36. Roosevelt to Mellett, 18 December 1944, in file marked "Coordinator of Govt. Films," Gen Rec of the Treasury Dept, Office of the Sec, Gen Corr, RG56, box 48, NA; "Report of the Director to the Sec of War, April–June, 1941," BPR, in Public Information Div, RG165, entry 499, box 3, NA (this report claims close ties between BPR and private sectors involved in the production of both still and motion pictures); Robert H. Denton, Paramount, to Lt. Col. Mitchell, 6 January 1943, in file marked "Advance Agent to Africa," ibid., entry 493, box 5, NA.

37. Memo from Lasky, 4 August 1932, in Claude Binyon Papers, box 1, State Historical Society of Wisconsin (SHSW). Special Intelligence Report No. 77, "The Enemy in the Movies," 25 November 1942, p. 4, USIS, Bureau of Intelligence, OWI, RG44, entry 171, NA.

38. "Government Information Manual for the Motion Picture Industry" (first version, summer 1942), RG208, entry 285, box 1517, NA.; 16 November 1942 report by Nelson Poynter and Dorothy Jones, in file marked "miscellaneous," RG208, entry 285, box 1518, NA; on *Corregidor* see Clayton R. Koppes and Gregory D. Black, "What to Show the World: The Office of War Information and Hollywood, 1941–1945," *JAH* 64 (June 1977): 95; on *Tokyo* see Lawrence Suid, *Guts and Glory: Great American War Movies* (Reading, Mass., 1978), 59–60; "blood and thunder" and "mortal realities" in undated supplements from file marked "Hollywood Information Manual," RG208, entry 285, box 1517, NA. For a well-documented argument suggesting that OWI had a more significant impact on Hollywood's wartime movies than the one attributed to the agency in this chapter, see Koppes and Black, "What to Show the World."

39. On the box office success of *Shores of Tripoli* and *Guadalcanal Diary* see Aubrey Soloman, *Twentieth-Century Fox: A Corporate and Financial History* (Metuchen, N.J., 1988), 61, 63. The "send us more Japs" story was not

discredited until after the war. See Ronald H. Spector, *Eagle against the Sun: The American War with Japan* (New York, 1985), 103. Tregaskis's description of dead soldiers is quoted in Clyde Jeavons, *A Pictorial History of War Films* (London, 1974), 131.

40. Travesty and West End quotes from Ian Jarvie, "The Burma Campaign on Film: *Objective Burma* (1945), *The Stilwell Road* (1945) and *Burma Victory* (1945)," *Historical Journal of Film, Radio and Television* 8 (no. 1, 1988): 55. Jarvie provides an account of how wartime filmmaking practices and the complexities of Anglo-American relations interacted to shape the production and reception of *Objective Burma* and two other 1945 films. See also Jarvie, "Fanning the Flames: Anti-American Reaction to *Objective Burma* (1945)," *Historical Journal of Film, Radio and Television* 1, no. 2 (1981): 117–37.

41. Brutality and moral idiots quotes from Bernard F. Dick, *The Star-Spangled Screen: The American World War II Film* (Lexington, Ky., 1985), 228, 227.

42. Paul Fussell, *Wartime* (New York, 1989), 270–72. Censored material is scattered throughout public and private collections, but for especially revealing and voluminous files of photographs censored by the military see material classified under RG319-CE in the Still Pictures Branch of NA. A 1945 film produced by the Army Pictorial Service for the War Finance Division of the Treasury Department, *Diary of a Sergeant,* available at NA, does tell the story of a sergeant who lost both of this hands in a military accident in North Carolina.

43. Barry D. Karl, *The Uneasy State: The United States from 1915 to 1945* (Chicago, 1983), 209; Shell ad in *Life,* 7 June 1943, p. 69. On the New Haven ad see Richard R. Lingeman, *Don't You Know There's a War On?: The American Home Front, 1941–1945* (New York, 1976), 296, and Fussell, *Wartime,* 194. Lingeman writes that it was "widely considered the best example of war-message advertising," and Fussell calls it "the most famous magazine ad of the war." For a discussion of the initial fears and eventual triumph of the advertising industry, see Fox, *Madison Avenue Goes to War.* For the Tom Lea reproductions, see *Life,* 11 June 1945, pp. 61–67.

44. OWI to Advertising Council in "Minutes of Meeting of War Information Board," 21 July 1943, RG208, entry 16, box 105, NA; *Washington Evening-Star,* 7 September 1943 (dead paratroopers ad); *Washington Shopping News,* 9 November 1943, 18 January 1944—copies of all are in Treasury Department scrapbooks with the clipping on War Loan drives, CRG 44 NN 375–181 in RG56, NA.

CHAPTER 2: *A CAST OF MILLIONS*

1. For other comparisons of war and movies see Paul Fussell, *The Great War and Modern Memory* (New York, 1975), 221–22.

2. H. F. Gosnell case study of OWI pamphlet and letter to Dr. E. Pendleton Herring, 13 February 1943, La Mar Seal Mackay papers, box 1, Hoover Institution on War, Revolution and Peace (Hoover), Stanford, Calif.

3. Roosevelt made his comment in December 1943. In *Days of Sadness* Perrett argues that despite the rhetorical shift away from reform, wartime circumstances led to the achievement of many reform goals unsuccessfully pursued during the previous decade.

4. Statistics from OWI Current Surveys, no. 11 (7 July 1943), USIS, BSS, RG44, entry 149, box 1715, NA. Flying cadet statement quoted in Perrett, *Days of Sadness,* 37.

5. On Barclay see Brinkley, *Washington Goes to War,* 247–48, and reference to "Liberia's Chief Feted in New York (6/25/43)" in folder marked "All American Newsreel," RG208, entry 285, box 1517, NA. On Allen see H. F. Gosnell case study of OWI pamphlet and letter to Dr. Herring, 13 February 1943, in La Mar Seal Mackay papers, box 1, Hoover. South Carolina resolution cited in William Manchester, *The Glory and the Dream: A Narrative History of America, 1932–1972* (New York, 1975), 243.

6. Letters in *Life,* 6 July 1942, p. 2.

7. On *Sahara* see Thomas Cripps, "Racial Ambiguities in American Propaganda Movies," in K. R. M. Short, ed., *Film and Radio Propaganda in World War II* (Knoxville, Tenn., 1983), 130; on *Bataan* see Suid, *Guts and Glory,* 45; Emerson ad in *Washington Post,* 24 September 1943, copy in Treasury Depart-

ment scrapbooks with clipping on War Loan drives, CRG 44 NN 375–181 in RG56, NA.

8. Morton's ad from unspecified Washington, D.C., newspaper, 31 May 1945, in ibid.

9. Manchester, *Glory and the Dream,* 283. For one account of differing black and white responses to a Louis victory see Russell Baker, *Growing Up* (New York, 1982), 258–60. On *The Negro Soldier* see Thomas Cripps, *"Casablanca, Tennessee Johnson* and *The Negro Soldier:* Hollywood Soldiers and World War II," in K. R. M. Short, ed., *Feature Films as History* (Knoxville, Tenn., 1981), 138–56, and Thomas Cripps and David H. Culbert, *"The Negro Soldier* (1944): Film Propaganda in Black and White," *American Quarterly* 31 (Winter 1979): 616–40.

10. Patrick S. Washburn, *A Question of Sedition: The Federal Government's Investigation of the Black Press during World War II* (New York, 1986), 55, 223; on Louisiana State University's "V" see Richard Polenberg, *War and Society: The United States, 1941–1945* (New York, 1972), 134.

11. Item US-6031 in war poster collection, Hoover.

12. For details on the salary cap see Polenberg, *War and Society,* 89. For discussion of the politics of the cap, see Mark H. Leff, "The Politics of Sacrifice on the American Home Front in World War II," *JAH* 77 (March 1991), 1300.

13. For OWI suggestions of depiction of workers and bosses see "Government Information Manual for the Motion Picture Industry" (first version, summer 1942), RG208, entry 285, box 1517, NA.

14. Carl N. Degler, *At Odds: Women and the Family in America from the Revolution to the Present* (New York, 1980), 420. For evidence that most women engaged in war work needed the wage see Maureen Honey, *Creating Rosie the Riveter: Class, Gender, and Propaganda during World War II* (Amherst, Mass., 1984), 19–23.

15. Paired photo example, RG 208, #208-N-3314 in SPB, NA; Veronica Lake in *Life,* 8 March 1943, p. 39; for bus driver's badge see undated photograph from RG 208, #AA 354L-1 in SPB, NA. On Veronica Lake see Lingeman, *Don't You Know,* 158.

16. Director, BPR, to Col. R. Ernest Dupuy, PR Officer, Supreme Headquarters, Allied Expeditionary Force, 23 February 1944, PR Div, RG165, entry 499, box 33, NA. For a more detailed analysis of these issues see Bérubé, *Coming Out Under Fire,* esp. chap. 3, "GI Drag: A Gay Refuge."

17. Memo from Philleo Nash to Lucien Warner, Special Services Div, 23 January 1943, in folder marked "Organizational . . . Bureau of Special Services," Records of the Director, RG208, entry 1, box 3, NA; undated supplement from file marked "Hollywood Information Manual," RG208, entry 285, box 1517, NA.

18. For key documents related to the *Why We Fight* series, see David Culbert, ed., *Film and Propaganda in America: A Documentary History,* vol. 3, *World War II: Part 2* (New York, 1990), 79–225.

19. Fussell, *Wartime,* 127; Peter Roffman and Jim Purdy, *The Hollywood Social Problem Film: Madness, Despair, and Politics from the Depression to the Fifties* (Bloomington, Ind., 1981), 237.

20. Gerald Linderman, *Embattled Courage: The Experience of Combat in the American Civil War* (New York, 1987); Winter, *Death's Men,* 208; David Nichols, ed., *Ernie's War: The Best of Ernie Pyle's World War II Dispatches* (New York, 1986), 33. Spector, *Eagle against the Sun,* 383, reports that "of the army and air force troops serving in the Pacific, approximately 40 percent of the officers and 33 percent of the enlisted men spent some time in combat." Gabriel, *No More Heroes,* 74–76, estimates that approximately eight hundred thousand ground soldiers, less than 10 percent of those who served during the war, saw direct combat. David M. Kennedy, *Over Here: The First World War and American Society* (New York, 1980), 205, writes that approximately one in three American servicemen came under enemy fire during World War I.

21. War Department "Instructors Training Film Reference Pamphlet FR TF 7–1446," in AG Unclassified Decimal Files, RG407, box 3250, NA; see posters for soldier training in World War II poster collection, Special Collections Division, UCLA Research Library, including "Tarawa" as an example of gruesome Japanese dead and "Surprise . . .," which is

part of the Newsmap Series and is dated 29 November 1943. Following the convention that words could go further than pictures, scenes like the one depicted in the poster were reported by candid observers such as Bill Mauldin. See Mauldin, *Up Front* (New York, 1945), 13–14. I know of no wartime movie or poster for civilians that depicted an American soldier killing an enemy by a sneak attack from the rear. *Life,* March 22, 1943, pp. 4–6, showed such an attack as part of an article on Gjon Mili, who took the photographs for "Surprise—A Powerful Weapon." The *Life* article reproduced photographs in which Mili compared the movements of an effective soldier to those of a stealthy cat.

22. On the stage set see George Raynor Thompson and Dixie R. Harris, *The Signal Corps: The Outcome* (Washington, D.C., 1966), 549; on restriction of *Easy to Get* to male personnel see 20 August 1945 memo in AG, RG407, box 3237, NA; *Easy to Get* may be viewed at NA (RG111 TF 8.1423, 1945 in A-V section). Except as otherwise noted, I viewed all government films mentioned in the text at NA. Official presentation of Louis as a symbol of sexual abstinence might be measured against his own observation that "I didn't resist one pretty girl who had a sparkle in her eye." Quoted in Gregory, *America 1941,* 262.

23. "Minutes" of OFF Board Meeting, 22 April 1942, in Archibald MacLeish papers, box 52, LC.

24. 111–SFR–44 (1945) in *Staff Film Reports* series, NA.

25. Government officials made use of descriptions of the sufferings of American soldiers to try to dissuade businessmen from raising prices as well as to discourage workers from striking. See Brinkley, *Washington,* 135.

26. Mark Jonathan Harris, Franklin D. Mitchell, and Steven J. Schechter, *The Homefront: America during World War II* (New York, 1984), 68.

27. Confidential survey of Fourth War Loan Drive, prepared by U.S. Department of Agriculture, 13 March 1944, RG208, entry 54, box 177, NA; Morgenthau quoted in John Morton Blum, *V Was for Victory* (New York, 1976), 17–18.

28. See Spaulding story in file of material

for "Negro press" in RG208, entry E-79, box 241, NA; on complaints about journalistic segregation see 12 July 1944 memo on newspaper items referring to minority groups in file marked "Nash Report—Minority Groups," USIS, BSS, RG44, entry 149, box 1714, NA.

29. On black and white versions of advertisement see file of material for "Negro press" in RG208, entry E-79, box 241, NA; "Study of the Pictorial Div, BPR," undated but with cover letter of 3 November 1942, 020.4–5, PR Div, RG165, entry 499, box 10, NA. Cripps, "Racial Ambiguities," 139, reports that in at least one instance Warner Brothers created different versions of a film for general release and for projection in places such as churches and union halls: "in 35mm use children without Negroes in group. Use Negroes in 16mm."

30. "Newsreels and OWI Campaigns and Programs," November 1942 report of OWI Media Div, USIS, RG44, entry 171, box 1845, NA; "Newsreel Weekly Report" for 30 October 1942, RG208, entry 285, box 1518, NA. See letter, 26 January 1944, Sec of War to Army Chief of Staff, which reported that *All-American News* had been shown to black soldiers; in 062.2 (case 7), Army Chief of Staff, RG165, entry 13, box 133, NA.

31. OFF "Weekly Media Report #11" (18 April 1942), USIS, BSS, RG44, entry 149, box 1720, NA.

32. Chicago and New Hampshire examples from undated memo, with excerpts from March 1943 reports, "War, War Aims and Post-War World," in ibid., box 1710. For examples of images honoring "unconquerables" see January 1944 items in Treasury Department scrapbooks with clipping on War Loan drives, CRG 44 NN 375–181 in RG56, NA. A memo from Philleo Nash to Lucien Warner, Special Services Div, 23 January 1943, in folder marked "Organizational . . . Bureau of Special Services," Records of the Director, RG208, entry 1, box 3, NA, provided an overview of government attempts to monitor different groups of Americans, including ethnic groups, and concluded that because these attempts were modest and unsystematic, government knowledge was very limited for most groups (historically most of this effort went into keeping tabs on groups considered to be politically subversive).

33. Claude R. Collins to Harold D. Jacobs, 2 March 1942, RG208, entry 285, box 1520, NA; *Daily World* in memo "Newspaper Clippings from June 12–Aug 15, 1944," USIS, BSS, RG44, entry 149, box 1714, NA. On Lena Horne see Allen L. Woll, *The Hollywood Musical Goes to War* (Chicago, 1983), 122. On the limits regional ties continued to place on cultural and political nationalism during this period, see Barry D. Karl, *The Uneasy State: The United States from 1915 to 1945* (Chicago, 1983).

34. On interracial dancing at canteens, author's interview with Timmie Gallagher, July 1988; when as a young actress at the canteen Gallagher danced with black servicemen Mary Halsey said to her, "Good, that's right."

35. Robert E. Summers, *Wartime Censorship of Press and Radio* (New York, 1942), 194–95; memo from Office of Censorship to postal censors, 27 April 1942, in file marked "AG 000.73–5/2/42," RG407, entry 360, box 5, NA.

36. David Brion Davis, "World War II and Memory," *JAH* 77 (September 1990): 584–85; memo BPR to CG, USFOR, ETO, London, 2 August 1943, 062.1–589, Public Information Div, RG165, entry 499, box 25, NA; Supreme Hdq Allied Expeditionary Forces to BPR, 6 March 1945, and related memos in 062.1–104, ibid., box 67. On black protest see ibid.; on the Ninety-second see Allied Force Hdq, Caserta, Italy, to WD, 26 January 1945, in ibid., 062.1–6; on "radicals" see John Bissell, Gen Staff to Col. Page, BPR, 19 December 1942, in ibid., box 6, 000.77–126. On the policy of also restricting written descriptions of black troops "intermingling" with whites in England see staff memo of 23 February 1945, 000.73–13, Public Information Div, RG165, entry 499, box 61, NA. On official films and articles that sought to prepare American soldiers for the greater degree of racial mingling permissible in Britain see Neil A. Wynn, *The Afro-American and the Second World War* (London, 1976), 32–35. On p. 34 Wynn notes that "some two thousand 'brown babies' were born to British women as a result of their wartime friendships with black soldiers."

37. Confidential memo on "The Detroit Race Riot," 6 July 1943, USIS, BSS, RG44, entry 149, box 1715, NA. On the declining support for social activism within OWI by later in the war, see Winkler, *Politics of Propaganda,* esp. 37. Even after this decline OWI did more than most agencies, through its internal arrangements and public policies, to challenge conventional racial practices. One staffer, Mrs. Elizabeth Nichols, quit early in 1944 in part because "she wouldn't work in any office in which a Negro man [an OWI research analyst] called her by her given name." See entry from 10 March 1944 in file marked "Minutes of Staff Meeting," USIS, BSS, RG44, box 1715, NA. For examples of candid photographs of racial conflict in Detroit that were published, see *Life,* 16 March 1942, p. 41, and 5 July 1943, pp. 93–102.

38. Author's interview with Gallagher, July 1988.

39. Marshall's comment, made in the spring of 1945, quoted in Ambrose, *Supreme Commander,* 621; on shooting King, see Ambrose, *Eisenhower,* 1:141.

40. Undated memos, Herb Miller to Lowell Mellet and Milton Starr to Barry Bingham, in file marked "Newsreel Material—Miscellaneous," RG208, entry 185, box 1519, NA; "Special Directive on Treatment of Negro and Other Minority Problems," 9 October 1944, RG208, entry 359, box 116, NA; H. F. Gosnell to Dr. Herring, 13 February 1943, in La Mar Seal MacKay Papers, Hoover. Prof. Thomas Cripps of Morgan State University provided me with additional biographical information on Stark, who also went by the name Milton Starr. Wynn, *Afro-American,* 86, noted that Fox Movietone decided never to show its item on the Harlem riot of 1943.

41. "Get the Wounded Out of Sight," *New Republic* 110 (31 January 1944): 132 (the *New Republic* based this article on another written for *PM* by I. F. Stone); accident statistics from Lee Kennett, *G.I.: The American Soldier in World War II* (New York, 1987), 123. On "basket cases" see Perrett, *Days of Sadness,* 340.

42. Memo from Col. A. Robert Ginsburgh, Chief, PR Branch, to OFF 19 May 1942, in 000.7, AG, RG407, box 4, NA.

43. Newsboy ad in *Newsweek,* 19 July 1943, p. 35; see Alfred E. Cornebise, *The Stars and Stripes: Doughboy Journalism in World War I* (Westport, Conn., 1984), 140.

44. Peter Aichinger, *The American Soldier in Fiction, 1880–1963: A History of Attitudes toward Warfare and the Military Establishment* (Ames, Iowa, 1975), 29, quoting from Robert E. Sherwood, *Roosevelt and Hopkins: An Intimate History,* rev. ed. (New York, 1950), 380–81; Harris and Mitchell, *Homefront,* 78.

45. Aichinger, *American Soldier,* 74.

46. For descriptions of insignia proudly worn as a designation of different Civil Defense functions and on the number of Civil Defense workers see Lingeman, *Don't You Know,* 51, 62. Advertisement for BVD in *Life,* 5 October 1942, p. 63; also see *Newsweek,* 14 December 1942, p. 48; and Lingeman, *Don't You Know,* 120, on shoe order.

47. "Fourth War Loan Campaign Book," RG208, entry 54, box 177, NA (emphasis in the original); on Textron see *Washington Times Herald,* 27 January and 1 February 1944, *Washington Daily News,* 31 January 1944, all in Treasury Department scrapbooks with clipping on War Loan drives, CRG 44 NN 375–181 in R56, NA. In World War I some war bond sales rallies offered participants who donated one dollar the opportunity of driving a nail in a coffin with the German kaiser's picture on it (see *The Great War—1918* in the PBS series "The American Experience").

48. Selden Menefee, *Assignment: U.S.A.* (New York, 1943), p. 29; Brinkley, *Washington,* 149.

49. *Life,* 4 May 1942, p. 32; Edward Lauber to Richard Russell, 16 August 1944, RG208, entry 2, box 12, NA; undated memo in file marked "Prison Industries," ibid., entry 285, box 1519. Although the government let it be known that even prisoners supported the war effort it did not publicize its vigorous campaign to recruit convicted felons into the military in exchange for parole; eventually more than one hundred thousand convicted felons served in the armed services, most of them honorably; see Kennett, *G.I.,* 19.

50. Fact sheet no. 12, no date, OWI Bureau of Motion Pictures, in Film Study Center, Museum of Modern Art, New York; author's interview with Cavalier Ketchum, June 1986. The war gave adults as well as children incentives for close observation. Some movie theaters provided free single-frame enlargements to customers who spotted family members in newsreel footage. See Fielding, *American Newsreel,* 294.

51. Archie Satterfield, *The Home Front: An Oral History of the War Years in America, 1941–1945* (Chicago, 1981), 176.

52. Kennett, *For the Duration,* 41, on the blind and deaf. Perrett, *Days of Sadness,* 336, notes that 10 percent of the Ford Motor Company's wartime work force was "blind, deaf, or crippled."

53. Letter from Roger Detert in *Milwaukee Journal,* January 1976.

54. William Manchester, *Goodbye Darkness: A Memoir of the Pacific War* (Boston, 1980); Irwin Shaw, *The Young Lions* (New York, 1948), 240; Fussell, *Great War,* 327.

55. *Washington Evening-Star,* 28 April 1943, copy in Treasury Department scrapbooks with clipping on War Loan drives, CRG 44 NN 375–181 in RG56, NA; "Speaking of Pictures," *Life,* 24 November 1941, pp. 10–13.

56. Quote on Rome from Dick, *Star-Spangled Screen,* 8.

57. John Donne, "The Crosse," in *The Complete Poetry and Selected Prose of John Donne* (New York, 1941), 243–44.

58. Handbook quoted in Richard H. Kohn, "The Social History of the American Soldier: A Review and Prospectus for Research," *American Historical Review* 86 (June 1981): 555.

59. Nichols, *Ernie's War,* 19; war diary in Wellington Wales Papers, box 2, State Historical Society of Wisconsin, Madison, Wisc. (SHSW).

60. Report of Guy Lemon, War Advertising Council, 10 March 1944, RG208, entry 54, box 177, NA; OFF Bureau of Intelligence Special Report #7, 12 May 1942, USIS, BSS, RG44, entry 149, box 1711, NA.

61. Shaw, *Young Lions,* 394.

62. Figures on government contracts in Blum, *V Was for Victory,* 123; woman quoted in Sherma Berger Gluck, *Rosie the Riveter Revisited: Women, the War, and Social Change* (New York, 1987), 141; on Nixon see Stephen E. Ambrose, *Nixon: The Education of a Politician, 1913–1962* (New York, 1987), 122. A document in OWI files, "A Chicago Study of Attitudes Pertaining to the War by Arthur W. Kornhauser," dated August 1942, reported that

when Chicagoans asked if some groups were especially well off as a result of the war, 56 percent responded yes, 24 percent no, and 20 percent did not know. The groups most often named as better off were "big businessmen, contractors, manufacturers, war profiteers, large income groups." In USIS, BSS, RG44, entry 149, box 1715, NA. On the more equitable distribution of family income by war's end see Perrett, *Days of Sadness,* 354.

63. Lucien Warner to Alan Barth, 9 October 1942, in file marked "Correspondence Panels Miscellaneous," in USIS, BSS, RGrr, entry 149, box 1711, NA (emphasis in original).

CHAPTER 3: *WAR AS A WAY OF SEEING*

1. Elshtain, *Women and War* (New York, 1987), 256; Lasswell, *Propaganda Techniques in the World War,* p. 47, quoted in Willard Waller, ed. *War in the Twentieth Century* (New York, 1940), 449.

2. Bound folder marked "Organization of Information Activities for Defense and War, 1940–42" by Harold F. Gosnell, in La Mar Seal Mackay Papers, box 1, Hoover; *Guide to Essential Wartime Printing and Lithography* (New York, n.d.).

3. MacLeish to J. R. Fleming and Alan Barth, 22 December 1941 in MacLeish Papers, box 52, LC; "OWI Domestic Branch List . . .," USIS, BSS, RG44, entry 149, box 1713, NA.

4. "Fourth War Loan Campaign Book," RG208, entry 54, box 177, NA.

5. "The Signal Corps Was Big Business" in James A. Code papers, box 2, Hoover; "OWI Domestic Branch List of Media Facilities and Services," 22 May 1943, USIS, BSS, RG44, entry 149, box 1713, NA; letter, Bureau of Graphics to American Red Cross, 29 March 1945, RG208, entry 237, box 1126C, NA; Gamble to House Ways and Means Committee, 3 December 1943, Gen Rec of the Treasury Dept, Office of the Sec, Gen Corr, RG56, box 199, NA.

6. La Mar Seal Mackay papers, box 1, Hoover; Byron Price papers, notebooks, p. 15, in box 3, SHSW; AG's office to Kodak, 2 September 1941, in file marked "AG 000.73–8–26–41," RG407, entry 360, box 4, NA.

7. Covert interview in Harris, *Home Front,* 72. Burns, *Roosevelt: The Soldier of Freedom,* 212. On overseas travel see Kennett, *G.I.,* 111, and Spector, *Eagle Against the Sun,* 382.

8. For the fullest and best account of changing official and popular attitudes toward aerial bombardment, as well as of actual changes in the capabilities in American air power, see Sherry, *Rise of American Air Power.*

9. Arnold memo, 10 June 1943, from Arnold Papers, Official Files, Jacket 36, Bombing; my thanks to Michael S. Sherry for this document. On the accuracy of the Norden bombsight, which made the idea of precision bombing seem plausible, see Spector, *Eagle Against the Sun,* 15. For some spectacular and often deadly examples of wartime blunders see Fussell, *Wartime,* 19–35.

10. Sherry, *Air Power,* 226–27; the air veteran Gibson Byrd described the indiscriminate disposal of bombs in an interview with the author, May 1974.

11. *New York Times,* 11 March 1945, p. 1; on "rising sons" see Paul Boyer, *By the Bomb's Early Light: American Thought and Culture at the Dawn of the Atomic Age* (New York, 1985), 13; for an example of a bombed city shown from great height see "Victory Loan Trailer," in LC; student quoted in Hess, *United States at War,* 133.

12. The exact death toll at Hiroshima will never be known, but all of the most recent and thorough estimates put the number at well over one hundred thousand people.

13. John Dower, *War Without Mercy: Race and Power in the Pacific War* (New York, 1986), 19, 86–93; Hess, *United States at War,* 74. For an example of a censored photo showing American soldiers helping a wounded Japanese soldier see 16 October 1942 photograph #80-G-12463 in SPB, NA. See also memo, General Hdq, Southwest Pacific Area to WD, 3 March 1945, which requests a waiver of an earlier policy restricting release of photographs in which the features of individual "Japs" were identifiable (the request was granted), 062.1–66, Public Information Div, RG165, entry 499, box 67, NA. This policy was partly due to the army's concern that photos of recognizable Jap-

anese soldiers might yield useful information to Japanese intelligence agencies; see Curtis Mitchell to Navy PR Office, 23 August 1943, 062.1–666, ibid., box 25.

14. *Variety* quoted in Dower, *War Without Mercy,* 322; Bureau quoted in Lingeman, *Don't You Know,* 186.

15. "Sixth War Loan Campaign Book," RG208, entry 54, box 177, NA. A print of *Action at Anguar,* produced by the War Department's Army Pictorial Service for the War Finance Division, is available at LC.

16. On war dead see Elliot Willensky, *When Brooklyn Was the World, 1920–1957* (New York, 1986), 260.

17. For an example of a racially based, potentially violent confrontation among American troops see David Brion Davis, "World War II and Memory," *JAH* 77 (September 1990), 584–85.

18. Manchester, *Goodbye Darkness,* 350; Kennett, *G.I.,* 174.

19. On the real Al Schmid see *Life,* 22 March 1943, p. 35.

20. Returning sailor photo #N31565 in RG208, SPB, NA.

21. *Time,* 22 December 1941, p. 3; newsreel from c. 8 November 1942 described in file "United News," RG208, entry 285, box 1520, NA.

22. On widespread public support for the relocation see Hadley Cantril, ed., *Public Opinion, 1935–1946,* prepared by Mildred Strunk (Princeton, 1951), 380.

23. Special Bulletin, 24 October 1942, OWI Bureau of Motion Pictures, in Film Study Center, Museum of Modern Art, New York (emphasis in original). The Office of Censorship reviewed in advance all stories and pictures of the camps where Japanese-Americans were confined. See letter from N. R. Howard, Press Div, to Gen. A. D. Surles, Director, BPR, in PR Div, RG165, entry 499, box 10, NA. On Little Tokyo and other ironies of wartime film imagery of Chinese and Japanese see Koppes and Black, *Hollywood Goes to War,* 72–74, and Lingeman, *Don't You Know,* 180–81.

24. Ralph H. Turner, "Photographers in Uniform," in F. L. Mott, ed., *Journalism in Wartime* (Washington, D.C., 1943), 77–82; transcript of Michael Lewis interview, p. 99,

Imperial War Museum, London (IWM); transcript of interview with Ernest Henry Walker, IWM; transcript of interview with L. Col. H. Steward MBE, p. 12, IWM; Zanuck recollections, typescript dated 18 December 1942, p. 63, file 004.52, RG165, entry 499, box 8, NA. Also see Fussell, *Wartime,* 190. For an excellent description of practical problems facing World War II combat photographers see Moeller, *Shooting War,* 194–96.

25. Landry to Wilson Hicks, *Life* Picture Editor, 5 November 1942, in file 000.77–111, Rec of the WD Gen and Special Staffs, Public Information Div, RG165; Thompson and Harris, *Signal Corps.*

26. George Biddle, *Artist at War* (New York, 1944), 124; author interviews with Gallagher, Morse, and Mydans, July 1988.

27. On changing attitudes toward death see Philippe Aries, *Western Attitudes toward Death from the Middle Ages to the Present* (Baltimore, 1974).

28. Bourke-White, *Purple Heart Valley,* 65; on fear of grass see Fussell, *Wartime,* 279; Ratcliffe quoted in Fussell, *Great War,* 55. Fussell notes that "dawn has never recovered from what the Great War did to it" (*Wartime,* 63).

29. RAF pilot quoted in Max Hastings, *Victory in Europe* (Boston, 1985), 54.

30. See Margaret Randolph Higonnet, Jane Jenson, Sonya Michel, and Margaret Collins Weitz, eds., *Behind the Lines: Gender and the Two World Wars* (New Haven, 1987), 28, on historical differences between men's and women's view of war.

31. Richard Whelan, *Capa: A Biography* (New York, 1983), 57; see also 56, 177, 187, 203, 211, 235–36.

32. Author's interviews with Mydans and Morse, July 1988.

33. Christopher Phillips, *Steichen at War* (New York, 1981). Steichen's presence led to an upgrading of the status of photographers, whom before his arrival the navy billeted with enlisted men rather than with officers. See Goldberg, *Margaret Bourke-White,* 269.

34. Paramount newsreel for 5 January 1944, NA; on the heavy-handedness of German use of humor see, for example, Leila J. Rupp, *Mobilizing Women for War: German and Amer-*

ican Propaganda, 1939–1945 (Princeton, N.J., 1978), 165.

35. Huston quoted in *Film: Book 2*, p. 29. For revealing documents related to the production of *San Pietro* see Culbert, *Film and Propaganda in America*, 3:227–319.

36. Brinkley, *Washington Goes to War*, 188; "large elements" in Davis to Mrs. Elizabeth Patton, 31 March 1947, Davis papers, box 2, LC. For more on Davis's career and integrity see Winkler, *Politics of Propaganda*, 31–32.

37. Roosevelt quoted in John F. Bratzel and Leslie B. Rout, Jr., "FDR and the 'Secret Map,' " *Wilson Quarterly* (New Year's 1985), 173; Blum, *V Was for Victory*, 12, 155; DeVoto letter to Davis in Davis papers, LC. On Roosevelt's efforts to avoid an open public debate on American foreign policy in the eighteen months before Pearl Harbor see Richard W. Steele, "The Great Debate: Roosevelt, the Media, and the Coming of the War, 1940–1941," *JAH* 71 (June 1984), 69–92.

38. Reply that "it is believed that the President would not desire to make reference to his own physical disability" in memo, General Staff to Asst Chief of Staff, 27 June 1944, 062.2 (case 19), Army Chief of Staff, RG165, entry 13, box 133, NA; on Roosevelt in amputee ward see Larrabee, *Commander-in-Chief*, 347. Roosevelt and those close to him established the practice of minimizing public exposure of the extent of his disability during the weeks after he contracted infantile paralysis in 1921. See Geoffrey C. Ward, *A First-Class Temperament: The Emergence of Franklin Roosevelt* (New York, 1989), 601, 634, 781–83. Ward includes rare photographs documenting Roosevelt's disability in illustrations following p. 590. During the final year of World War II a knee injury led Eisenhower to make frequent use of a cane or crutches, but like Roosevelt he avoided revealing his disability in public. See Ambrose, *Eisenhower*, 1:348.

39. Hutchinson quoted in Terkel, *Good War*, 133. On Roosevelt's physical appearance and the political dimensions of his depiction, see Brinkley, *Washington*, 105, 171, 182, 252, 260.

40. Larrabee, *Commander-in-Chief*, 145; transcript of 15 August 1945 talk in Byron

Price papers, box 3, SHSW; Patrick W. Washburn, *A Question of Sedition: The Federal Government's Investigation of the Black Press during World War II* (New York, 1986); Office of Censorship, "Code of Wartime Practices for the American Press," 1942, in file marked "AG000.73 1/24/42," RG407, box 4, NA.

41. For a thoughtful account of the origins and manifestations of Eisenhower's public-relations genius see Ambrose, *Eisenhower*, 1:172–76.

42. Thompson and Harris, *Signal Corps*, 112–13. On Eisenhower's commitment to giving historians full access to war records see Ambrose, *Eisenhower*, 1:456.

43. For a discussion of the response to ambiguities in Hitchcock's most controversial wartime film, *Lifeboat* (1944), see Koppes and Black, *Hollywood Goes to War*, 309–16.

44. Lucien Warner to Alan Barth, 9 October 1942, in file marked "Correspondence Panels Miscellaneous," USIS, BSS, RG44, entry 149, box 1711, NA; 13 November 1942 memo, "Developing Situation—Governments Information Policy Antagonizes Public and Press," ibid., box 1710; poll figures from "OWI Current Surveys," issue 27 (27 October, 1943), ibid., box 1715. See later poll from Cantril and Strunk, *Public Opinion*, 487.

45. On Los Angeles audience see note from Howard Langley, April 1943, in RG208, item 215, box 1063, NA; Roosevelt memo, 20 February 1941, in file marked "AG 000.7–1/22/41," RG407, entry 360, box 3, NA; concerns over *Battle of China* in memo, Maj. Gen. F. H. Osborn, Information and Education Div, to Gen. George C. Marshall, 1 November 1944, 062.2 (case 36), Army Chief of Staff, RG165, entry 13, box 133, NA. Kushlis quoted in Robert H. Abzug, *Inside the Vicious Heart: Americans and the Liberation of Nazi Concentration Camps* (New York, 1985), 138.

46. Manchester, *Goodbye Darkness*, 12; Manchester, *Glory and the Dream*, 285; cable from MacArthur to WD, 15 April 1945, 062.2 (case 44), Army Chief of Staff, RG165, entry 13, box 133, NA; Morella, Epstein, and Griggs, *Films of World War II*, 61; Biddle, *Artist at War*, 207. In *Up Front*, 131–32, 169–70, Bill Mauldin described the resentment of soldiers at phony wartime advertisements. For one exam-

ple of soldiers' criticism of a misleading photograph during World War I see Moeller, *Shooting War,* 149. Although most soldiers rejected glorified representations of combat, and only 13 percent could name as many as three of the "Four Freedoms" which Roosevelt identified as central to the war effort, they overwhelmingly supported that effort. In one large survey 65 percent expressed the belief that they were fighting to "guarantee democratic liberties to all peoples of the world." See Larrabee, *Commander-in-Chief,* 625–26.

47. Jones, *World War II,* 76; on Marine Fathers Group see Report from Director, Intelligence Div, Hdq Sixth Service Command, Chicago, 29 November 1942, 0000.73–43, Public Information Div, RG165, entry 499, box 6, NA; Snow to Lowell Mellett, 21 March 1942, in file marked "Newsreel Coverage," RG208, entry 285, box 1518, NA.

48. Memo, 12 July 1944, on newspaper items referring to minority groups in file marked "Nash Report—Minority Groups," USIS, BSS, RG44, entry 149, box 1714, NA.

49. "OWI Current Surveys," issue 24 (6 October 1943) in ibid., box 1715; "Government Posters in Wartime," October 1939, Mass-Observation Archives, IWM; Portland survey, done by Advertising Research Foundation, in folder marked "American Association of Advertising Agencies," RG208, entry 52, box 174, NA; Leo A. Handel, *Hollywood Looks at Its Audience* (Urbana, Ill., 1950), 122–23, 135.

50. Quoted in Gluck, *Rosie the Riveter Revisited,* 142.

51. Kennett, *G.I.,* 51–52.

CHAPTER 4: WAR COSTS

1. On the choice of San Francisco see Perrett, *Days of Sadness,* 413.

2. Davis from LC; memo from Philleo Nash to Corr. Panels Section, 29 June 1943, on "Negro-White Tensions in Baltimore," USIS, BSS, RG44, entry 149, box 1715, NA. In a letter to *Harper's* written shortly after the war one G.I. described bigotry as widespread among his fellow soldiers. He claimed that one from the South believed that to make their training more realistic white soldiers should be allowed

actually to kill black American troops. See letter from David Shair in *Harper's* 192 (April 1946), front section.

3. Menefee, *Assignment: U.S.A.* For two of many government reports on instances of alleged anti-Semitism, see Irving McClosky to OFF, 9 April 1942, in file marked "CPS. The early days in OFF," in USIS, BSS, RG44, entry 149, box 1711, NA, and, in the same file, Norman Burnside to OFF, 19 March 1942. On the Muskogee case see letter from J. J. Simons to Henry L. Stimson and related material in folder dated 8 March 1943, AG 291.21, RG407, entry 360, box 1103, NA. Polls taken before and during the war indicated that despite reports of Nazi persecution the majority of Americans opposed increasing Jewish immigration. See Perrett, *Days of Sadness,* 95–97. On anti-Semitism in Washington see Ward, *First-Class Temperament,* 254n. On Monterey County see report of Research Div, BSS, OWI, 2 March 1945, in USIS, Rec of the Chief of the Bureau, RG44, entry 138, box 1659, NA; on white people see National Opinion Research Center, September 1944, in Cantril and Strunk, *Public Opinion,* 381.

4. On early rumors of black aggressiveness see letter from Irving McClosky to OFF, 9 April 1942, in file marked "CPS. The early days in OFF," in USIS, BSS, RG44, entry 149, box 1711, NA; quote on bumping whites from 25 September 1944 memo "Current comments on attitudes toward minority groups" in file marked "Memoranda, 1944" in USIS, BSS, RG44, entry 149, box 1709, NA; Hitler quote in Larrabee, *Commander in Chief,* 640.

5. On Christian American Association see Menefee, *U.S.A.,* 61. Exchange with White House recorded in message 6 October 1943 from BPR to CINC SWPA, 062.1–811, Public Information Div, RG165, entry 499, box 26, NA, and memo 8 October 1943 from Director BPR to SigC in file 062.1 (1943), ibid., box 23. On Roosevelt's racial attitudes see Ward, *First-Class Temperament,* 766–67, and Blum, *V Was for Victory,* 12.

6. Terkel, *Good War,* 157; author interview with Dempsey Travis, 18 August 1988; John Hope Franklin, "Their War and Mine," *JAH* 77 (September 1990): 576–77.

7. Murrow to Davis, 15 December 1943,

in Elmer Davis Papers, LC. Novels by Norman Mailer, James Jones, and Irving Shaw, and Paul Fussell's *Wartime,* might be considered as some of the most striking fulfillments of Murrow's prophecy.

8. For one of many examples see the Treasury Department short *957th,* which juxtaposes ordinary U.S. news items, made trivial by the context, with footage of painfully wounded American soldiers being transported to a hospital ship for treatment.

9. *Life,* 10 November 1941, p. 38, and 5 July 1943, p. 2; *Newsweek,* 17 May 1943, p. 25, and 20 August 1945, p. 33; for billboard see item 44-PA-1361 in poster slide file, SPB, NA. For a drawing by David Fredenthal depicting a soldier crying after a battle see *Life,* 21 August 1944, p. 53.

10. For one example of the editing of an American soldier's "heavy breathing that just possibly might be a cover for sobbing" see successive versions of the script for the 1943 Warner Brothers film *Air Force* in United Artists Collection, mss., 99AN, series 1–2, box 9, SHSW. Perhaps the British were even more thoroughgoing than the Americans in suppressing suggestions of male tears; in 1944 they banned the U.S. hit song "I Heard You Cried Last Night" because "a man crying was not a good thought at the present time." See Susan Briggs, *The Home Front: War Years in Britain* (London, 1975), 201.

11. Satterfield, *Home Front,* 65; WD report, "Fear Symptoms Reported by Troops in Combat Divisions," cited in Joseph C. Goulden, *The Best Years, 1945–50* (New York, 1976), 20; Fussell, *Wartime,* 277. On the tendency of soldiers to put the best face on things in letters to home see Fussell, *Wartime,* 145. In *Great War,* 46, Fussell notes that constipation (also unmentioned in war movies) was actually a larger problem than soldiers' fouling themselves.

12. The considerations that determined who would and would not be depicted crying were complex. During the war, consistent with the policy of not showing Japanese wounded being treated, military censors withheld pictures of Japanese crying. John Garcia remembered that in training camp after he joined the U.S. Army "they would show us movies. Jap-

anese women didn't cry. They would accept the ashes stoically. I knew different. They went home and cried." Quoted in Terkel, *Good War,* 23.

13. See outtake footage and pictures listed in Army Signal Corps World War II still picture index under Malmedy, AV Div., NA.

14. Memo from John T. Gibbs to George H. Lyon, "Newsreels of Friday, February 4, 1944, " RG208, entry E-79, box 241, NA; stereographs filed under China in Keystone collection, California Museum of Photography, Riverside.

15. On the impact of late 1930s newsreels of Japanese atrocities in China see William Zinsser, "At Pearl Harbor There Are New Ways to Remember," *Smithsonian,* December 1991, p. 75.

16. G. S. Eyssell of Radio City quoted in Fielding, *American Newsreel,* 295. In a phone conversation, 24 April 1945, Harry Warner advised Col. Frank McCarthy, Sec., General Staff, that in his opinion newsreel companies were not using death camp footage because "they were afraid of making people sick in theaters and thus creating bad will for the theaters and newsreel companies." See memo on conversation in file 062.2, case 46, Army Chief of Staff, RG165, entry 13, box 133, NA. On the reluctance of OWI, Roosevelt, Hollywood, news magazines, and others to publicize available information on the Holocaust earlier in the war see David S. Wyman, *The Abandonment of the Jews: America and the Holocaust, 1941–1945* (New York, 1984), esp. 315, 322. For a description of those wartime Hollywood films that do allude to the camps without clearly documenting the extermination going on in some of them see Dick, *Star-Spangled Screen,* 207.

17. Alfred Chandler, Jr., ed., *The Papers of Dwight David Eisenhower,* vol. 4, *The War Years* (Baltimore, 1970), doc. 2418; Ambrose, *Supreme Commander,* 659.

18. Cantril, *Public Opinion,* 489; Susan Sontag, *On Photography* (New York, 1977), 19–20; *Newsweek,* 16 May 1988, p. 24. For a thoughtful discussion of American responses to the Holocaust see Abzug, *Inside the Vicious Heart,* esp. chap. 7, "Telling the Story." Abzug discusses "Lest We Forget" on p. 134. For an important assessment of the collection,

editing, and impact of visual evidence of the Holocaust, see David Culbert, "American Film Policy in the Re-Education of Germany after 1945," in Nichols Pronay and Keith Wilson, eds., *The Political Re-Education of Germany and Her Allies after World War II* (London, 1985), 173–202.

19. Gerhard E. Lenski, writing for the *Lutheran Standard* in August 1945, quoted in R. W. Ross, *So It Was True: The American Protestant Press and the Nazi Persecution of the Jews* (Minneapolis, 1980), 236. On Kushlis and other veterans, see Abzug, *Inside the Vicious Heart,* 137–38. For an argument that images of the Holocaust did have a widespread and profound impact on postwar American culture, see William S. Graebner, *The Age of Doubt: American Thought and Culture in the 1940s* (Boston, 1991), esp. 18, 37.

20. Abzug, *Inside the Vicious Heart,* 140; Gallup poll 8 February 1937 in Cantril, *Public Opinion,* 381; OWI survey described in Wyman, *Abandonment of the Jews,* 327. For a well-documented discussion of anti-Semitism in the United States during this period see Wyman, *Abandonment of the Jews,* 9–15.

21. *Life,* 29 March 1943, quoted in Polenberg, *War and Society,* 40; "Ivan Knows" on back cover of *Newsweek,* 6 December 1943; on "consumption communities" see Daniel Boorstin, *The Americans: The Democratic Experience* (New York, 1973), pp. 89–164. For the annotated screenplay of *Mission to Moscow* see David Culbert, ed., *Mission to Moscow* (Madison, Wisc., 1980). The effectiveness of the Soviets as wartime allies, combined with largely favorable coverage (visual and written) of Soviet life, had a marked impact on public opinion. In a survey done by the National Opinion Research Center in the summer the war ended nearly two out of three Americans replied "as good" to the question, "Do you think the kind of government Russia has is as good as she could have for her people at the present time, or do you think a different kind of government would be better for the Russians?" See memo, 8 July 1945, in file marked "Public Opinion Coverage," USIS, BSS, RG44, entry 149, box 1710, NA. Returning American soldiers had an even more favorable attitude toward the Soviets; remarkably, 99 percent be-

lieved that the Soviets had done their share or more in winning the war; only 2 percent had an unfavorable attitude toward the Russians as people (16 percent felt unfavorable toward the British). They were aware of the potential for future conflict, although they believed by nearly equal majorities that the U.S. would be able to avoid serious disagreements with the Soviets and the British in the future. Results from Army Information and Education Div poll given in memo to Gen George C. Marshall, 12 July 1945, in file 061.2 (12 July 45), Army Chief of Staff, RG165, entry 13, box 133, NA. Following normal wartime procedures with an ally, U.S. military authorities agreed to request Soviet approval before showing to the American public any footage shot by Russian cameramen. See WD to Commanding General, Mediterranean Allied Air Forces, in PR Div, file 062.1–50, RG165, entry 491, box 1, NA. One reader noted that in two *Time* covers featuring Stalin, one from the era of the Nazi-Soviet pact and one from 1943, his appearance shifted from "satanic" to "Christlike." By the postwar period his features were once again satanic. Reader comments quoted in the captions for an exhibition, "*Time* Covers the War," at the National Portrait Gallery, Washington, D.C., 7 December 1991 through 17 May 1992.

22. Articles on the Korean War in *Life* often displayed this tension between image and text. As Studs Terkel later noted, "*Life*'s editor Henry Luce was as cold a warrior as you could find, so he supported the fight. Still, some of the pictures he published captured the murkiness of this new conflict." Quoted in *Chicago Tribune* 18 January 1985, sec. 7, p. 45. The best account of visual reporting on the Korean War is Moeller, *Shooting War,* 251–322.

23. The *Postcard Journal* of the Lake County (Ill.) Museum, 4 (Fall 1987): 3, noted the abundance of World War II images and the paucity of references to Korea or Vietnam in the extensive Curt Teich Postcard Collection, which includes advertising material.

24. For a highly critical account of Johnson's politically motivated World War II involvement, and of his exaggerations of his wartime experiences, see Robert A. Caro, *The Years of Lyndon Johnson: Means of Ascent* (New York, 1990), 20–53. Other more bal-

anced accounts give greater weight to patriotic motives for Johnson's behavior but also document the immense proportions of Johnson's political opportunism and his exaggerations. See Paul Conkin, *Big Daddy from the Pedernales: Lyndon Baines Johnson* (Boston, 1986), 106–8, and Robert Dallek, *Lone Star Rising: Lyndon Johnson and His Times, 1908–1960* (New York, 1991), 230–41.

25. Rusk in interview that appeared in *Vietnam: A Television History,* program no. 4.

26. Discussion paper for meeting of OFF Committee on War Information, 12 May 1942, in Archibald MacLeish Papers, box 52, LC; Edward Klauber to Sec of Treasury, 5 April 1945, RG208, entry 54, box 176, NA; memo, 19 June 1942, Barry Bingham to MacLeish in file marked "War Crimes and Atrocities" in ibid., entry 1, box 12; "War Bond Sales Soar as D.C. Learns of Japanese Brutality," *Washington Herald Times,* 29 January 1944; Dower, *War Without Mercy,* 48–52. On public and press resentment over releasing atrocity pictures to coincide with war bond drives, see memo, 7 February 1944, Corr. Panels Section to Clyde W. Hart, USIS, BSS, RG44, entry 149, box 1716, NA. On box-office success of *Purple Heart* see Aubrey Soloman, *Twentieth-Century Fox: A Corporate and Financial History* (Metuchen, N.J., 1988), 64.

27. Phillip Knightley, *The First Casualty* (New York, 1975), 294; *Life,* 22 May 1944, pp. 34–45; Marshall cablegram and response to *Life* photo in file marked "AG 293.9 19 Aug 44," in RG407, entry 360, box 1513, NA; see also memo from Army Chief of Staff to Director, BPR, 28 July 1944, Public Information Div, DF, RG165, entry 499, box 36, NA. John Dower believes there would have been more outrage had the collected body parts been German or Italian instead of Japanese. See *War Without Mercy,* 65–66. In reviewing thousands of censored photographs in various depositories, I have never encountered any documenting that American soldiers took as trophies body parts of European soldiers. It no doubt sometimes happened, but if the visual evidence is indicative, soldiers far more often collected Asian body parts. See also Spector, *Eagle Against the Sun,* 411, and, for two differing reflections on such practices, Paul Fussell, "Postscript (1987)

on Japanese Skulls," in *Thank God for the Atom Bomb and Other Essays* (New York, 1988), 45–52, and interview with E. B. ("Sledgehammer") Sledge in Terkel, *Good War,* 62–63.

28. Nichols, *Ernie's War,* 35; Jones, *World War II,* 70; derogatory terms quoted in Aichinger, *Soldier,* 35. In addition to giving extensive examples of the creative genius shown in the use of the word *fuck* during World War II (*Wartime,* 95, 260), Fussell argues that because *fuck* was so overworked during that war, in Vietnam it appeared even more often in abbreviated form, as in the most common graffito of that war, FTA ("Fuck the Army").

29. Written accounts of village burnings and other disturbing actions by U.S. troops are far more numerous than visual accounts, in part owing to often successful attempts to discourage the latter. See, for example, Jonathan Schell, "The Village of Ben Suc," in *The Real War* (New York, 1987), 125–26. On this issue, on Cam Ne, and for an excellent general account of the visual and written coverage of the war in Vietnam see Daniel Hallin, *The Uncensored War: The Media and Vietnam* (New York, 1986). Quote from Hallin, *Uncensored War,* 133.

30. For a well-documented, critical account of coverage of Tet see Peter Braestrup, *Big Story* (New Haven, 1983). Quote from David Culbert, "Television's Vietnam and Historical Revisionism in the United States," *Historical Journal of Film, Radio and Television* 8, no. 3 (1988): 260. Polls from Clark Dougan, Stephen Weiss, and the editors of Poston Publishing Company, *The American Experience in Vietnam* (Boston, 1988), 204. In the preface to the paperback edition of his book Hallin summarizes the findings of the most thorough studies of Vietnam and the media: "Day-to-day coverage was closely tied to official information and dominant assumptions about the war, and critical coverage didn't become widespread until consensus broke down among political elites and the wider society. As for coverage of the 'other side,' . . . it never remotely approached what journalists recognize as balance in domestic political reporting." See Daniel Hallin, *The Uncensored War: The Media and Vietnam* (Berkeley, 1989), x. Hallin also notes

that there was not a single instance during the war of a security breach in which American journalists released militarily significant information unknown to the enemy. The Loan shooting first appeared as a film clip on NBC-TV on the evening of 2 February 1968, and was shown frequently after that on television and as a still photograph.. The general public was not alone in being protected from some of the war's most disturbing images. Nurses reported than when President Nixon's wife, Pat, visited a military hospital during the one presidential trip to Vietnam, the Red Cross kept her away from seriously wounded patients and showed her those who "could smile and wave." See Keith Walker, *A Piece of My Heart: The Stories of Twenty Six American Women Who Served in Vietnam* (New York, 1985), 195–96.

31. *Newsweek,* 5 September 1988, p. 28.

32. Hopkins to Eisenhower, 20 May 1944, in Chandler et al., *Papers of Dwight David Eisenhower,* vol. 3, doc. 1697. For a longer list of those who served in World War II see Manchester, *Glory and the Dream,* 283–84.

33. See Mura MacPherson, *Long Time Passing: Vietnam and the Haunted Generation* (New York, 1985), 165, on Clarence Long; on members of Congress who served in World War

II see Caro, *Lyndon Johnson,* 32. On Ali, see Thomas Hauser, *Muhammed Ali: His Life and Times* (New York: 1991), 142–202.

EPILOGUE

1. Annette Insdorf, *Indelible Shadows: Film and the Holocaust* (New York, 1983), 23–28.

2. Sacks letter, 14 July 1944, in Preston Sturges Papers, box 38, folder 19, University of California, Los Angeles. Sacks's sister, Israel Sacks, sent a typed copy of the letter to Sturges along with a letter of her own, dated 11 August 1944, praising Sturges's film *Hail the Conquering Hero.*

3. During the Persian Gulf War the *Chicago Tribune* ran an editorial cartoon in which rats represented the Iraqi Revolutionary Guard; but these rats had no identifiable racial features, and they might as easily have represented Wall Street felons or English soccer fans. Many crude caricatures of Arabs were generated by unofficial sources during the war, as seen for instance in T-shirts, available from vendors on Constitution Avenue in Washington, D.C., depicting Iraqi soldiers as "camel jockeys."

● ● ● ● ● ● ● ●

**SELECTED
BIBLIOGRAPHY**

BY FAR THE best source for official government imagery of war, including photographs, films, and posters by civilian and military agencies, is the National Archives (NA), which also has an extensive collection of commercially produced visual materials including many wartime newsreels. The vast and diverse visual holdings of the Library of Congress include a few official films not available at NA. Among the other useful sources are the poster collection at the Hoover Institution on War, Revolution and Peace in Stanford, California; the collection of oversized posters and of photographs from the morgue of the *Los Angeles Daily News* in the Special Collections Division of the UCLA Research Library; the stereographs of World War I and earlier wars in the California Museum of Photography at the University of California, Riverside; and the films and related promotional material in the Wisconsin Center for Film and Theater Research, an archive of the University of Wisconsin and the State Historical Society in Madison, Wisconsin.

The best source for studying pictures withheld from view is a collection of thousands of censored Army Signal Corps photographs from World War II and after grouped under the heading RG319 in the Still Picture Branch at the National Archives. Many other photographs in different record groups in the holdings of the Still Picture Branch also contain markings or

177

supplementary material indicating their publication history. For example, some photographs in the major Army Signal Corps grouping (RG111) display handwritten or stamped notations disclosing whether censors released or restricted them and, if they were restricted, when they eventually were declassified. The Still Picture Branch has the War Relocation Authority's internal shelf list of its negatives (RG210), which tells which photographs were "impounded." The Motion Picture, Sound and Video Branch of the Archives also houses an abundance of material not shown to the public during World War II, including unused Army Signal Corps footage and the *Staff Film Reports* series, which incorporates some footage released to the public and some shown only to high-ranking officers.

The National Archives holds most of the archival records essential for understanding official decisions regarding what to show to whom, and when. Especially useful are the Records of the War Department's Bureau of Public Relations included in the General Records of the Army Staff (RG165); the Records of the Office of War Information (RG208); the numerous surveys of public opinion found in the Records of the Office of Government Reports, United States Information Service, Bureau of Special Services (RG44); and pertinent materials in the Records of the Army Adjutant General (RG407) and the Records of the Treasury Department (RG56). Supplementing official records are such official publications as the series *United States Army in World War II,* including George Raynor Thompson et al., *The Signal Corps: The Test (Dec. 1941 to July 1943)* (Washington, D.C., 1957); George Raynor Thompson and Dixie R. Harris, *The Signal Corps: The Outcome (mid-1943 through 1945)* (Washington, D.C., 1966); and scholarly studies of government agencies such as Allan Winkler, *The Politics of Propaganda: The Office of War Information, 1942–1945* (New Haven, 1978). Many pertinent documents, as well as introductions, annotations, and other useful materials, are gathered in a four-volume series under the general editorship of David H. Culbert, *Film and Propaganda in America: A Documentary History* (New York, 1990–91), which has a microfiche supplement. The *Historical Journal of Film, Radio and Television* (Oxford, 1981–) also frequently prints documents, as well as scholarly articles, related to the visual presentation of the war.

Other especially useful archival collections include the Elmer Davis papers at the Library of Congress; the Byron Price and Wellington Wales papers at the State Historical Society of Wisconsin; the La Mar Seal Mackay papers at the Hoover Institution on War, Revolution and Peace; the Preston Sturges Papers in the Special Collections Division of the UCLA Research Library; the World War II files in the Film Study Center of the Museum of Modern Art, New York; and the transcripts of interviews with photographers and others involved in the visual presentation of World War II in the collections of the Imperial War Museum, London.

Books and articles that deal in whole or in part with various aspects of the visual imagery of war number in the tens of thousands. Among the most illuminating are John Dower, *War Without Mercy: Race and Power in the Pacific War* (New York, 1986), on American and Japanese perceptions and imagery of one another during and after World War II; Paul Fussell, *Wartime* (New York, 1989), a combat veteran's bitter critique of the gap between the war as presented and the war as experienced; Clayton R. Koppes and Gregory D. Black, *Hollywood Goes to War: How Politics, Profits and Propaganda Shaped World War II Movies* (New York, 1987), which makes extensive use of government records to study the topic described in the book's title; Karal Ann Marling and John Wetenhall, *Iwo Jima: Monuments, Memories, and the American Hero* (Cambridge, Mass., 1991), which tells wonderfully the story of the origins and exploitation of the war's most famous American image; and Susan Moeller, *Shooting War: Photography and the American Experience of Combat* (New York, 1988), a study by an experienced photojournalist and perceptive historian of the individuals and circumstances shaping American war photography from the Spanish-American War through Vietnam. Equally indispensable are two books from the war years, George Biddle, *Artist at War* (New York, 1944), and Bill Mauldin, *Up Front* (New York, 1945).

Useful surveys of the visual imagery of war include Jonathan Heller, ed., *War and Conflict: Selected Images from the National Archives, 1765–1990* (Washington, D.C., 1990); Jorge Lewinski, *The Camera at War: A History of War Photography from 1848 to the Present Day* (London, 1978); Ken McCormick and Hamilton Darby Perry, eds., *Images of War: The Artist's Vision of World War II* (New York, 1990); Anthony Rhodes, *Propaganda: The Art of Persuasion: World War II* (New York, 1976); Zbynek Zeman, *Selling the War: Art and Propaganda in World War II* (New York, 1978); and Frances Fralin, ed., *The Indelible Image: Photographs of War—1846 to the Present* (New York, 1985), the catalog of a show, organized by the Corcoran Gallery in Washington, D.C., in 1985, displaying remarkably powerful imagery of the human and material destructiveness of war. For a highly critical survey of some of the photographers here, see Rainer Fabian and Hans Christian Adam, *Images of War: 130 Years of War Photography* (London, 1985). Phillip Knightley, *The First Casualty* (New York, 1975) provides a general overview of war journalism.

Among the many studies of the home front, particularly attentive to visual issues are John Morton Blum, *V Was for Victory* (New York, 1976); Richard R. Lingeman, *Don't You Know There's a War On: The American Home Front, 1941–1945* (New York, 1976); and Selden Menefee, *Assignment: U.S.A.* (New York, 1943). Maureen Honey, *Creating Rosie the Riveter: Class, Gender, and Propaganda during World War II* (Amherst, 1984); Margaret Randolph Higonnet, Jane Jenson, Sonya Michel, and Margaret Collins Weitz, eds., *Behind the Lines: Gender and the Two World Wars* (New Haven, 1987); and Leila J. Rupp, *Mobilizing Women for War: German and American Propaganda, 1939–1945*

(Princeton, 1978) produce evidence of the impact of class, gender, and nationality on wartime visual experience. For a sampling of the other studies of institutional and other cultural forces that shaped wartime imagery, see M. Joyce Baker, *Images of Women in Film, 1941–1945* (Ann Arbor, Mich., 1980); Jeanine Basinger, *The World War II Combat Film: Anatomy of a Genre* (New York, 1986); Thomas Cripps, *Slow Fade to Black: The Negro in American Film, 1900–1942* (New York, 1977); David Culbert, ed., *Mission to Moscow* (Madison, Wisc., 1980); Bernard F. Dick, *The Star-Spangled Screen: The American World War II Film* (Lexington, Ky., 1985); Vicki Goldberg, *The Power of Photography: How Photographs Changed Our Lives* (New York, 1991); the chapter on Norman Mailer in Carol Shloss, *In Visible Light: Photography and the American Writer, 1840–1940* (New York, 1987); K. R. M. Short, ed., *Feature Films as History* (Knoxville, Tenn., 1981) and *Film and Radio Propaganda in World War II* (Knoxville, Tenn., 1983); Lawrence Suid, *Guts and Glory: Great American War Movies* (Reading, Mass., 1978), and Neil A. Wynn, *The Afro-American and the Second World War* (London, 1976).

Among the many other books that make some use of visual materials to explore the cultural antecedents and consequences of modern war, especially pertinent are Alfred Appel, *Signs of Life* (New York, 1983); Paul Boyer, *By the Bomb's Early Light: American Thought and Culture at the Dawn of the Atomic Age* (New York, 1985); Paul Fussell, *The Great War and Modern Memory* (New York, 1975); Michael Lesy, *Bearing Witness: A Photographic Chronicle of American Life, 1860–1945* (New York, 1982); and Michael S. Sherry, *The Rise of American Air Power: The Creation of Armageddon* (New Haven, 1987).

● ● ● ● ● ● ● ●

CREDITS

Figure 1.1. Courtesy National Archives, Still Picture Branch, 319-CE-19-SC-237442.

1.2. "Citizen volunteers assisting the wounded on the field of battle," Sharpsburg, Md., 17 September 1862. Pencil and Chinese white drawing by Alfred R. Waud. Courtesy Library of Congress, LC-USZ62: 1059.

1.3. *Harper's Weekly,* 11 October 1862, p. 649. Courtesy Library of Congress, LC-USZ62: 46782.

1.4. "The American wounded in France." *Independent,* 2 March 1918, p. 341.

1.5. "Marine receiving first aid before being sent to hospital in rear of trenches," Toulon Sector, France, 22 March 1918. Photograph by Sgt. Leon H. Caverly. *Colliers,* 27 July 1918. Courtesy National Archives, Still Picture Branch, 111-SC-12151 (*W&C,* no. 666).

1.6. *Life,* 15 March 1943, p. 97. Courtesy Magazine Publishers of America.

1.7. Courtesy George C. Marshall Research Foundation.

1.8. *Life,* 20 September 1943, p. 35. George Strock, LIFE MAGAZINE © 1943 Time Warner Inc.

1.9. "The five Sullivan brothers missing in action." Poster, 1943. Files of Office of Government Reports. Courtesy National Archives, Still Picture Branch, 044-PA-777 (*W&C,* no. 763).

1.10. Courtesy Library of Congress, Motion Picture Division, LC FAA 295.

1.11. Photograph by Ray R. Platnick. Courtesy National Archives, Still Picture Branch, 026-G-3345 (*W&C,* no. 926).

1.12. Courtesy National Archives, Still Picture Branch, 319-CE-3-SC-268444.

1.13. "An American soldier of the Antitank Co., 34th Regiment, who was killed by mortar fire," Leyte Island, Philippine Islands, 31 October 1944. Courtesy National Archives, Still Picture Branch, 319-CE-124-SC-261564.

1.14. "A soldier tries to ease the pain of this bleeding driver until medical aid arrives, after the jeep he was driving hit a German teller mine near Metz, Belgium," 8 September 1944. Courtesy National Archives, Still Picture Branch, 111-SC-193862.

1.15. "A medic gives first aid to a member of the 82nd Airborne Div. who was injured when a C-47 transport plane crashed during a mass training jump," Sissone, France, 14 March 1945. Photograph by Jack Clemmer(?). Courtesy National Archives, Still Picture Branch, 319-CE-19-SC-246918.

1.16. *Life,* 5 February 1945, p.27. Johnny Florea, LIFE MAGAZINE © Time Warner Inc.

1.17. Courtesy National Archives, Still Picture Branch, 319-CE-6-SC-236603.

1.18. "U.S. casualties on the U.S. 3rd Army front are loaded by men of the 3201 Quartermaster Service Company for burial at U.S. Military Cemetery, Fey, Belgium, 90th Infantry Division,

VIII Corps," 26 February 1945. Photograph by Billy Newhouse. Courtesy National Archives, Still Picture Branch, 319-CE-6-SC-201456.

1.19. "These wounded American soldiers in North Africa lay on their stretchers waiting to be loaded into a hospital train," 1943. Courtesy National Archives, Still Picture Branch, 319-CE—2-SC-236215.

1.20. Courtesy National Archives, Still Picture Branch, 319-CE-10-SC-277442.

2.1. *Life,* 11 May 1942, p. 5. Courtesy Association of American Railroads.

2.2. Courtesy National Archives, Still Picture Branch, 208-AA-34-P-1.

2.3. Courtesy National Archives, Still Picture Branch, 208-N-8973P.

2.4. Courtesy National Archives, Still Picture Branch, 053-WP-14 (*W&C,* no. 527).

2.5. Courtesy National Archives, Still Picture Branch, 44-PA-189.

2.6. Cartoon by Fore. *Newsweek,* 14 December 1942, p. 48. Courtesy NEWSWEEK.

2.7. *Newsweek,* 19 July 1943, p. 35.

2.8. Courtesy National Archives, Still Picture Branch, 208-N-32746-FF.

2.9. Courtesy National Archives, Still Picture Branch, 208 AA-354 C-1.

2.10. Courtesy National Archives, Still Picture Branch, 208-N-3314.

2.11. *Newsweek,* 10 May 1943, p.70.

2.12. Vivian King and Katherine Palinaire, Douglass Aircraft Company, Long Beach, Calif. Courtesy National Archives, Still Picture Branch, 208-NP-34–7.

2.13. Courtesy National Archives, Still Picture Branch, 319-CE-65-SC-237349.

2.14. Courtesy Poster Collection, Hoover Institute Archives, Stanford University, Stanford, Calif., US-6031.

2.15. Dempsey J. Travis, Aberdeen Proving Grounds, Md. From *An Autobiography of Black Chicago* (Chicago, 1981), p. 109. Courtesy Dempsey J. Travis.

2.16. Courtesy National Archives, Still Picture Branch, 44-PA-87.

2.17. Courtesy National Archives, Still Picture Branch, M9-WP-142.

2.18. Official OWI photograph by Roger Smith, 25 May 1943. Courtesy National Archives, Still Picture Branch, 208-NP-29180C.

2.19. Soldier wounded by Japanese grenades, 25th Combat Team, 93rd Division, 16 April 1944. Courtesy National Archives, Still Picture Branch, 319-CE-130-SC-246912.

2.20. Courtesy National Archives, Still Picture Branch, (*W&C,* no. 1221).

3.1. *Newsweek,* 13 December, 1943, p. 9.

3.2. Poster prepared for the Army Orientation Course by the Army Service Forces, Newsmap Series, 29 November 1943. Courtesy Department of Special Collections, University Research Library, University of California, Los Angeles.

3.3. Courtesy National Archives, Still Picture Branch, 44-PA-978.

3.4. Courtesy National Archives, Still Picture Branch, 407-CW-5.

3.5. "Liquid mustard gas stacked up at the 578th Ordnance Ammunition Co.," Brisbane, Australia, 17 June 1944. Courtesy National Archives, Still Picture Branch, 319-CE-3-SC-282832.

3.6. Courtesy National Archives, Still Picture Branch, 210G-3B-424 (*W&C,* no. 775).

3.7. Courtesy National Archives, Still Picture Branch, 111-SC-341418.

3.8. Camp Huckstep, Egypt, 30 May 1943. Courtesy National Archives, Still Picture Branch, 319-CE-2-SC-237834.

3.9. Courtesy National Archives, Still Picture Branch, 319-CE-121-SC-236850.

3.10. Poster, Salvage Division, War Production Board. Courtesy National Archives, Still Picture Branch, 44-PA-1679.

3.11. Courtesy National Archives, Still Picture Branch, 319-CE-3-SC-171054.

3.12. Courtesy National Archives, Still Picture Branch, 319-CE-56-SC-236987.

3.13. Courtesy National Archives, Still Picture Branch, 111-SC-150234.

3.14. Courtesy National Archives, Still Picture Branch, 319-CE-68-SC-248768.

3.15. Courtesy National Archives, Still Picture Branch, 319-CE-65-SC-236296.

3.16. Courtesy National Archives, Still Picture Branch, 319-CE-130-SC-235985.

3.17. Courtesy National Archives, Still Picture Branch, 319-CE-66-SC-246942.

3.18. Courtesy National Archives, Still Picture Branch, 319-CE-65-SC-236932.

3.19. Courtesy National Archives, Still Picture Branch, 319-CE-124-SC-237674.

3.20. Courtesy National Archives, Still Picture Branch, 111-SC-269134.

3.21. Courtesy National Archives, Still Picture Branch, 208-N-3581 (*W&C,* no. 901).

3.22. "Red-Handed." *Newsweek,* 12 April 1943, p. 46. Courtesy The Bettman Archive.

3.23. *Life,* 7 June 1943, p. 69. Courtesy Shell Oil Company.

3.24. *Life,* 20 July 1942, p. 20. Courtesy Parker Pen USA LTD.

3.25. Courtesy National Archives, Still Picture Branch, 80-G-468912.

3.26. "Fresh, spirited American troops." Cartoon by Bill Mauldin. From *Up Front* (New York, 1945), p. 21. Courtesy Bill Mauldin.

3.27. "Dust from nearby explosion causes this mother and son to scamper from cave." Photograph by W. Eugene Smith. *Life,* 28 August 1944, p. 79. W. Eugene Smith, LIFE MAGAZINE © 1944 Time Warner Inc.

4.1. Photograph by 1st Lt. Emmer. Courtesy National Archives, Still Picture Branch, 319-CE-2-SC-573664.

4.2. "Victory Speed 35 miles," between Lititz and Manheim, Penn., 1942. Photograph by Marjory Collin. Courtesy Library of Congress, LC-USW3TOI-11334-D.

4.3. Courtesy Chicago Historical Society and Perry Duis.

4.4. Courtesy National Archives, Still Picture Branch, 208-AA-346Q-7.

4.5. Courtesy National Archives, Still Picture Branch, 179-WP-1265.

4.6. Courtesy National Archives, Still Picture Branch, 319-CE-1-SC-305134.

4.7. Courtesy National Archives, Still Picture Branch, 208-AA-132N-4 (*W&C,* no. 1249).

4.8. Photograph by Joel Horowitz. Courtesy National Archives, Still Picture Branch, 319-CE-1-SC-236923.

4.9. Orr cartoon, "Let Us Hope," *Chicago Tribune,* December 5, 1941, showing Soviets and Germans as bucks with locked horns. Copyrighted 5 December 1941, Chicago Tribune Company, all rights reserved, used with permission.

4.10. *Newsweek,* 6 December, 1943, back cover. Reprinted by permission of the Monsanto Company.

4.11. Cartoon by Fitzpatrick, *St. Louis Post-Dispatch.* Reprinted by permission of the *St. Louis Post-Dispatch.*

4.12. Courtesy National Archives, Still Picture Branch, 319-CE-68-SC-291348.

4.13. Courtesy National Archives, Still Picture Branch, 319-CE-66-SC-241464.

4.14. Courtesy National Archives, Still Picture Branch, 111-SC-347803.

4.15. Courtesy National Archives, Still Picture Branch, 319-CE-107-SC-366324.

4.16. Courtesy National Archives, Still Picture Branch, 319-CE-10-SC-271823.

4.17. Courtesy National Archives, Still Picture Branch, 319-CE-130-SC-262353.

4.18. Courtesy Andrew T. Gerstmyer.

4.19. United States Information Service photograph. Courtesy National Archives, Still Picture Branch, 111-SC-611882.

4.20. Courtesy National Archives, Still Picture Branch, 208-N-43468 (*W&C,* no. 1360).

4.21. "Japanese school boys find amusement and interest in Sgt. Charles Roman's effort to photograph a group of them on a downtown street in Tokyo. Sgt. Roman of Bloomfield, N.J., and New London, Conn., was one of the first Americans to arrive in Tokyo." September 1945. Courtesy National Archives, Still Picture Branch, 111-SC-211749.

4.22. Courtesy National Archives, Still Picture Branch, 319-CE-124-SC-261634.

• • • • • • • •